CORPORATION GIVING

CORPORATION GIVING

F. Emerson Andrews

With a New Introduction by
Michael Useem

Transaction Publishers
New Brunswick (U.S.A.) and London (U.K.)

Library of Congress Catalog Number: 91-30050
ISBN: 1-56000-022-8
Printed in the United States of America

Library of Congress Cataloging-in-Publication Data

Andrews, Frank Emerson, 1902–
    Corporation giving/F. Emerson Andrews; with a new introduction by Michael Useem.
    p.   cm. – (Philanthropy and society)
    Reprint. Originally published: New York: Russell Sage Foundation, 1952.
    Includes index.
    ISBN 1-56000-022-8
    1. Corporations–United States–Charitable contributions–History–20th century. 2. Corporations–Charitable contributions–Law and legislation–United States–History–20th century. 3. Charities–United States–History–20th century. I. Title. II. Series.
HG4028.C6A53   1993
361.7'65'0973–dc20   91–30050
                                                                              CIP

Contents

Appendices

Tables

Figures and Map

Introduction to the Transaction Edition

THE CONCEPT of "corporation giving" is seemingly paradoxical. Business is in the business of making money, making the giving of money an inherently questionable act. To many, the contradiction was obvious. "[P]rofits belong to the stockholders," one company president complained to F. Emerson Andrews, "and it is the right of the individual stockholders to decide how much he wishes to give." Corporate philanthropy, an evident oxymoron to him, should be tossed into that scrapheap of misguided business policies.

Yet by midcentury this outlook was no longer universal in the executive suite, especially among the nation's expanding corporations. In what business historian Alfred D. Chandler termed the rise of the "visible hand," large-scale organizations were proving more adept at production than had the invisible hand of the market. And coming to preside over the great enterprises was a special breed of career executives. They professed allegiance to stockholder sovereignty, but they took their operational cues instead from the new profession of professional management.

Among the values of the emergent management culture was an emphasis on business largesse. Since it could not be readily reconciled with serving shareholder interests, corporate giving was recast as corporate calling, an act of professional responsibility. The emergent rationale was well articulated by an executive of General Motors Corporation in a 1936 commentary quoted by Andrews: "A corporation which derives generous benefits from community life must be willing to bear the corresponding burdens."

It is this paradoxical role of the corporation, and its attendant context and consequences, that form the focus of Andrews' *Corporation Giving*. Published in 1952, it constituted one entry in an extensive mapping Andrews was to complete of the U.S. philanthropic terrain. He had earlier charted the land of foundation giving in *American Foundations for Social Welfare*, published in 1946, and a later account, *Philanthropic Foundations*, was completed in 1956. A general typography was also drawn in *Philanthropic Giving*, a wide-ranging 1950 account of voluntary giving— individual, foundation, and corporate.

The several works were comprehensive in scope, capturing the historical and legal contexts in which the new institutions of philanthropy were taking shape. *Corporation Giving* was thus part of a broader portrayal of a burgeoning development in the early post-World War II years. F. Emerson Andrews acted as the study's chief draftsman, and the Russell Sage Foundation as its prime benefactor. Fueling the interest of both was an on-going transformation in the world of organized giving.

Backed by a 1907 endowment from a railroad fortune, the Russell Sage Foundation had already long been active in the areas of social science research, social welfare reform, and, increasingly, the study of private philanthropy. Andrews had initially been recruited to the Foundation in 1928 to head its publications department, and a fateful subsequent task was to assist the preparation of a 1938 edition of a directory of foundations. With this introduction to the world of philanthropic giving, Andrews saw opportunities for further initiative. The 1946 book on social welfare foundations, co-authored with Foundation director M. Shelby Harrison, was the opening product. The arrival of a new director in 1948, Donald Young, who had previously headed the Social Science Research Council, redoubled the Foundation's commitment to social science inquiry, social welfare, and organized philanthropy. Andrews was strategically positioned. With backing from the director and trustees readily extended, his general survey of philanthropy appeared two years later, and the special studies of corporate and foundation philanthropy were soon to follow. A career of distinguished service was to follow as well, as Andrews was later to serve for some years as president of a new organization created to foster knowledge of professional giving, the Foundation Center.

The Rise of Corporation Giving and the Publication of *Corporation Giving*

The appearance of *Corporation Giving* was both product and producer of a rationalization in the organization and purpose of corporate giving. The basic premises of contemporary practices were taking shape. It was this formative process, experimental and controversial, that attracted the attention of Andrews and the Russell Sage Foundation. When Andrews wrote the Foundation's director in 1950 to request support for a study of corporate giving, he quoted a call from a 1948 *Fortune* magazine article: "What is needed is basically a searching analysis of the criteria of all corporate contributions. . . . For no one has yet thoroughly measured the stake that American business has in philanthropy. It's big and getting bigger." The Foundation trustees quickly appropriated $15,000 for the project.

As chronicled in the book's early chapters, company giving could be traced to that nineteenth-century industry that dates so many elements in American business history, the railroads. Trainmen were often stranded in isolated locations, and YMCA programs offered the promise of social support that the railroads themselves were reluctant to provide. If suitably located, such programs could provide inexpensive accommodations and fraternal association. As a nonprofit organization whose services were not for sale, however, special inducements were required. Cornelius Vanderbilt of the New York Central Railroad came forward in 1888, underwriting a new YMCA facility in New York City. Other rail barons followed suit, and by 1910 more than 200 rail-related YMCA associations had been formed. In what must have been an early high watermark for voluntary support, some two-fifths of the YMCA budgets for rail-related locations that year derived from company subvention.

The special symbiosis that readily drove this early collaboration was gradually converted into support for more generic causes of less tangible benefit. By the early decades of this century, companies were directing significant grants to the American National Red Cross, war relief efforts, and federated drives for social services. Their support created a political base. When Congress later

considered a tax bill to impose for the first time a sharply graduated income tax on corporations, social service agencies lobbied
for a provision to permit deductible contributions. The Revenue
Act of 1935 enshrined the concept, permitting companies to donate up to 5 percent of their pretax net income to defined nonprofit
organizations.

Five percent set a kind of theoretical ceiling, but companies
otherwise found little guidance on how much to give, where to
give, or even why to give. It was into this uncharted territory of
private policy formation that Andrews brought his talents and
foundation resources. He dispatched questionnaires in 1951 to
1,200 companies sampled at random from the 19,000 firms in
Standard and Poor's *Register of Directors and Executives*. Re-
sponses came from 326 of the firms. He secured data from the Bureau of Internal Revenue, the forerunner of the Internal Revenue
Service, on levels of deductible contributions in company income
tax returns. And in the best tradition of synthetic analysis, he compiled information from an array of additional sources, ranging
from other surveys to contributions handbooks and legislative
records. The account was accessibly written "in English much
livelier," in the words of one reviewer (Bliven) "than is usually
found in books of this type." As a result, *Corporation Giving* stood
as a definitive stock-taking of corporate philanthropy at midcentury.

The importance of the moment can be seen in the figure on
page 5 that tracks the level of corporate contributions since 1936,
the year official statistics on business giving first became available
with the passage of the Revenue Act. Drawing on time series
reported by Andrews and later statistics, the figure displays two
ways of looking at the level of corporate giving. The percentage of
pretax net income is a good measure of giving commitment, at
least as seen by the donors. As seen by the recipients, however, the
dollar amount is what really counted. Seen through either lens, the
trend figures indicate that Andrews' assessment came at a
propitious moment.

After a momentary surge in the giving percentage of pre-tax
net income during the Second World War, the percentage slid
back toward its prewar average of about 0.5. In 1950, however, the

slope again reversed and the historic rate soon doubled, establishing a "one-percent rule" that was to dominate for three decades. Only in the 1980s did a new corporate norm come to prevail, again a doubling of the rate, to about two percent. There was less discontinuity in giving amounts, but here too Andrews stood at the edge of a growth era. In unadjusted dollars, corporate giving over the next four decades was to rise from $0.25 billion to $6.25 billion, more than doubling every ten years.

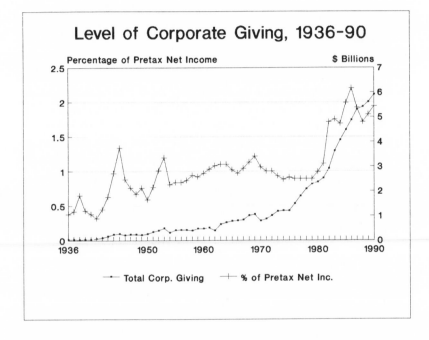

The Professionalization of Corporate Giving

With growth came a host of questions on how to orchestrate this new area of corporate activity. The questions were akin to those posed as companies innovated in any area, whether the adoption of new production technologies, information systems, or human resource programs. From his survey of and discussions with top management, Andrews set forth six "knotty" problems confronting companies:

o Should corporations give at all?
o How much should corporations give?
o What are the dangers to the beneficiaries?
o What should corporations support?
o What internal organization is needed?
o Can some corporation giving find new and creative patterns . . . not possible for other donors?

All six questions were on the mark. They pinpointed the key issues that managers then and now must address in operating any giving program. Testimony to their centrality, these questions were recurrently to appear in succeeding decades. As if variations on a theme, the same basic issues could be seen, for instance, in the 1975 report by the Commission on Private Philanthropy and Public Needs (chaired by John H. Filer); a 1979 guide to corporate giving by an experienced practitioner (Frank Koch); a 1982 project report on corporate philanthropy by the Council on Foundations; a 1991 handbook on corporate giving by another practitioner (James P. Shannon); and almost every survey of corporate contributions annually conducted by the Conference Board. Echoing Andrews' list, an article in the 1982 Council on Foundations project, authored by E. B. Knauft, opened thus: "How much do corporations give? What is the character or pattern of giving? How are decisions made? What influences giving?"

Corporation Giving offers answers to all the enduring questions, circa 1950. The fact that they were still being posed four decades later reflects the inherently evolving nature of corporate giving for which there were few enduring answers. Still, several practices emergent at the time of Andrews' investigation have come to prevail. Taken together, they signified the early professionalization of corporate giving, an approach used by larger firms to this day. Less accepted then than today, the book's description and prescription of the elements helped propagate their acceptance. To ensure the message was more widely heard, Andrews prepared articles appearing in the *New York Times Magazine, At-*

lantic Monthly, and *Readers Digest*; accepted numerous speaking engagements; consulted on a parallel study in Canada; and eventually even served as a trustee of a corporate foundation (Shell Companies Foundation). Five main elements of professionalization were identified by the book:

1. *Giving programs are shaped more by company objectives than by the personal interests of owners and managers.* "If big business was to bear what many considered a proper share of its responsibilities for community welfare," Andrews wrote, "a plan beyond the personal philanthropy of owners had to be devised" (23).
2. *Giving objectives are a mix of altruism and self-interest.* Extreme altruism–raised the specter of a questionable business act, while extreme self-interest raised the specter of a questionable charitable act. For Andrews, the necessary compromise was that of "enlightened selfishness" (113).
3. *Giving levels are driven by both business norms and individual company objectives.* Andrews observed that corporate "quotas" were developing around expected levels of giving. Sometimes such expectations were cast as the percentage of pretax net income, in other instances by local business community standards. Advised Andrews: "[I]t is easier to explain a gift to stockholders if it has been made in line with a communitywide plan including all other companies" (78).
4. *Giving allocations among major beneficiary groups are shaped as much by business convention as by recipient quality or need.* Established giving programs were already preferentially targeting organizations that were well managed and low risk. "Introduction of business methods and business judgement may result in wiser spread of contributors' dollars," Andrews approvingly observed. But he also lamented an evident preference for convention, observing that, "with a few honorable exceptions, corporate giving is still traditional and custom-bound" (125-26).
5. *Giving guidelines are formalized and administered by professional staffs, often through company foundations.* Contemporary practices were moving away from the "one-man decision"

and toward the processing of gifts through special committees, philanthropic specialists, and corporate foundations. Still, Andrews warned that such steps had far to go: "If corporate giving . . . is to bring maximum benefit both to the corporations themselves and to their communities, administrative procedures need to be adopted that look toward integrated, purposeful programs" (91).

As these and related principles took hold in the years that followed, corporate giving gradually professionalized. The contrasting signposts are many. Then, firms sometimes looked to one another for guidance on giving policies. Now it is commonplace to do so. In 1950, companies had typically operated their programs through the spare time of a single individual. Full-time professional staffs are usually in place now. Only one in twenty of the firms surveyed by Andrews had written policy statements. Now such statements are routinely circulated by most major companies.

It was a new profession nurtured within and among major companies sharing similar concerns and problems to be solved. Indicative of its momentum, the professionalization was also to spread outside the company world in two directions. One direction was into the world of trade and business associations, as many came to embrace and embellish the concept of corporate philanthropy. At the time of Andrews' study, corporate giving had attracted passing attention from only a few associations, including the National Industrial Conference Board, a business association for information sharing (later renamed the Conference Board); the National Planning Association, a forum for business and organized labor; and the American Society of Corporate Secretaries, an organization of those responsible for corporate governance. In the years that followed, almost all major business associations were to take an interest as well, ranging from the Business Roundtable, a select association of 200 chief executives of the nation's largest corporations, to local chambers of commerce. Separate national organizations were also founded or expanded to promote more giving and more effective giving, exemplified by the Business Committee for the Arts and the Council for Financial Aid to Education. Local organizations of private foundations and corporate givers, such as the Donors Forum of Chicago and the Associated Grantmakers of Massachusetts, further sought to professionalize the process.

The other direction in which the professionalization was to spread was into the recipient world. None of Andrews' surveyed firms had fallen prey to the Fund of the Widow of the Unknown Soldier, but he warned of widespread amateurism, occasional fraud, and even "subversiveness" on the solicitation side. He urged that companies use their position to enhance the quality of the recipients by insisting on sound fiscal and management practices. "In so doing," he concluded, "the corporation will not only make certain that its stockholders' money is more effectively spent; it will help raise the standards in the [non-profit] field" (148). It was a prescient call, for companies increasingly came to stress organizational capability in making grants. That trend could be seen, for example, in successive surveys of more than 400 large corporations by the American Council for the Arts in the late 1970s and 1980s. In evaluating applications for arts support, majorities placed management capability ahead of even artistic merit, and stress on this criterion grew faster than any other area.

The Transformation of Corporate Giving

If many questions Andrews raised about corporate philanthropy were enduring, so too were some of the answers. "Religion is mother of philanthropy," Andrews reminded us, as the bulk of voluntary support went (and still goes) to religious organizations. Yet virtually none came from business organizations then, and the same holds now. The 1950 survey revealed that only 4 percent of all company giving went to religious agencies, even counting such service organizations at the Salvation Army and YMCA. Andrews disapproved of the scant support, noting that "the church is one of the few institutions that have successfully resisted the trends toward state control" (226). Though in other areas his prescriptions were wise forecasts of what companies would come to do during the years ahead, here he was clearly off the mark. Contemporary surveys of corporate giving rarely find even more than 1 percent programmed for religious institutions. Company managers then and now fear that the diverse religious affiliations of their stock-holders, employees, and customers could make any gift a final gift. In certain areas, it seems, the historical patterns of corporate giving are immutable.

In other areas, however, the patterns have been less static. Such changes have made Andrews' account more of historic than factual interest to the contemporary reader, at least for the U.S. Readers outside the U.S. might still find much of direct relevance. American business has given money away on a scale and over a period unknown in any other advanced industrial democracy. This is partly a product of the unique cultural tradition of voluntarism that Alexis de Tocqueville had chronicled more than a century earlier in *Democracy in America*. Without international models from which to borrow, U.S. firms of necessity have had to invent their own. It is this homegrown organization and profession of corporate philanthropy that occupies much of *Corporation Giving*. Many international corporations are still in the early phases of cre-ating a tradition of company giving, several decades behind their American counterparts. If American business can fruitfully borrow from British banking, German manufacturing, and Japanese managing, companies in those settings could fruitfully learn from American giving, and few better starts on the formative phases are available than Andrews' treatment.

For contemporary American giving, however, the account did not and could not foresee several transformative forces that were to reshape its contours. Here the historical patterns of corporate giving are not immutable, and several would surely have figured prominently if an epilogue were to have been later completed. Among the recent forms of change are at least three: (1) the emer-gence of a diversity of giving forms; (2) the alignment of giving more closely to company strategy; and (3) the turbulence in giving resulting from acquisitions and related changes in corporate con-trol.

Diversity of Giving

In 1950, many companies discouraged the contribution of ad-vertising or other business services to charitable or cultural organizations; few corporations encouraged employees to become active in their communities; and most large firms conceived of giving in purely monetary terms. By 1990, however, giving had been richly redefined to include a diverse flow of assistance. Equipment, plant facilities, advertising, financial advice, and other business services had been added to the standard giving repertoire. The involvement of employees in voluntary community affairs and top management in the governance of nonprofit organizations had also become a managed process.

Alignment of Giving

In 1950, the leading advocates of expanded contributions were still making the case for more professionalized company giving. They sought two changes. One was to depersonalize the process, transforming control from the individual to the organization. The other was to enhance the "enlightened" component of the otherwise accepted formula of enlightened self-interest. Both objectives were subsequently achieved. By 1990, however, though the depersonalization remained, the second achievement was reversed. The objective now was instead to enhance the "self-interest" component of the key formula. The 1980s had witnessed widespread experimentation with such innovations as "cause-related marketing" and other ways of more closely aligning the giving function with the pursuit of competitive advantage. It was an era in which, in the words of two contemporary advocates, companies adopted a "more market-driven strategic management, bottom-line approach to philanthropy" in order "to obtain a tangible return for their contributions" (Mescon and Tilson, 49). For traditional critics of corporate giving, this practice could now be removed from the scrap heap of misguided practices. As an arm of product and image marketing, giving in their view had finally come full circle to properly serve shareholder interests.

Turbulence in Giving

In 1950, corporate giving was taking shape in a period of exceptional stability. American companies were competing well at home and abroad under the umbrella of the postwar international system. They created career systems fostering growth and security, and were rewarded with managerial commitment and loyalty. It was the heyday of what William H. Whyte aptly dubbed "the organization man." Giving programs were thus constructed under several favorable assumptions: earnings could be expected to steadily increase, senior management should be expected to stay, and company owners were expected to be patient. By the 1980s, however, none of the assumptions remained valid. Large firms, especially in manufacturing, entered a prolonged period of downsizing; managerial ranks experienced extensive turbulence as new teams were brought in to restore earnings; and shareholders, especially the large institutional investors, grew impatient with performance. The favorable assumptions of growth and stability of Andrews' era had given way to a less favorable foundation of turbulence and change.

Conclusion

Corporation Giving offers a still useful model for the creative combination of theoretical and practical knowledge. For the academic investigator, it meets the canons of scientific inquiry. Information is systematically integrated and judiciously interpreted. For the corporate actor, it meets the canons of applied analysis as well. Policy implications are systematically extracted and cautiously proposed. And for the prospective fund raiser, it meets the test of direct utility. The inner workings of corporate giving are well revealed to those who would turn them to their own advantage. As a result, for all three readers, then or now, the book well withstands the test of time. Whether it should withstand the test of utility offered by one reviewer soon after it was published is another matter. *Corporation Giving* said the reviewer (Corbin), "should be useful to every voluntary agency, big or small, that is considering asking business support for anything from a playground to a national disaster." But even this test may have been passed, since corporate givers have no doubt privately concluded on occasion that a disaster was among the projects they had underwritten.

The account can also usefully be read for another purpose. Corporate giving reflects corporate organization, and changes in the former have much to say about the latter. *Corporation Giving* thus offers an implicit commentary on the on-going transformation of big business. It was published in an era marked by the culminating success of the managerial revolution in which professional managers acquired final control over many of the nation's largest enterprises. The hard-driving and sometimes hard-bitten spirit of the founding entrepreneurs was giving way to an ethos of technocratic efficiency and social responsibility among the new mandarins. The expansion of corporate giving chronicled in the book was a reflection of, and window into, that transformation.

With four decades of development since the appearance of *Corporation Giving*, the scale of company contributions far exceeds anything visible in Andrews' day. Total corporate giving stood at $252 million in 1950; in 1990, the two largest business donors gave more than that alone. Yet even from the present-day vantage, the midcentury moment was opportune for F. Emerson Andrews' stocktaking. The basic templates for the corporate contributions function were under design. Sustaining values, professional norms, and organizational methods were in advanced stages of formulation, if not yet wide acceptance. With modest elaboration and fine tuning, they were to guide the giving function for the next quarter century. Andrews was present at the creation, and for understanding the present, his book stands as a timeless account of the past.

Michael Useem

References

American Council for the Arts. 1987. *Guide to Corporate Giving in the Arts*. New York: American Council for the Arts, 1987 and earlier years.

Andrews, F. Emerson. 1950. *Philanthropic Giving*. New York: Russell Sage Foundation.

Andrews, F. Emerson. 1956. *Philanthropic Foundations.* New York: Russell Sage Foundation.

Andrews, F. Emerson. 1973. *Foundation Watcher.* Lancaster, Pa.: Franklin and Marshall College.

Bliven, Bruce. Review of *Corporation Giving. New Republic* 127 (November 17, 1952): 30.

Chandler, Alfred D., Jr. 1977. *The Visible Hand: The Managerial Revolution in American Business.* Cambridge, Ma.: Harvard University Press.

Commission on Private Philanthropy and Public Needs. 1975, 1977. *Giving in America, and Research Papers,* 6 vols. Washington, D.C.: U.S. Department of the Treasury.

Conference Board. Various years. *Survey of Corporate Contributions,* annual editions.

Corbin, Hazel. Review of *Corporation Giving. American Journal of Public Health* 43 (March, 1953): 345-46.

Council on Foundations, editor. 1982. *Corporate Philanthropy.* Washington, D.C.: Council on Foundations.

Harrison, Shelby M. and F. Emerson Andrews. 1946. *American Foundations for Social Welfare.* New York: Russell Sage Foundation.

Koch, Frank. 1979. *The New Corporate Philanthropy: How Society and Business Can Profit.* New York: Plenum Press.

Knauft, E.B. 1982. "A Research Agenda for Corporate Philanthropy." In *Corporate Philanthropy,* edited by Council on Foundations. Washington, D.C.: Council on Foundations.

Mescon, Timothy S. and Donn J. Tilson. "Corporate Philanthropy: A Strategic Approach to the Bottom Line." *California Management Review* 29 (1987): 49-61.

Reed, Patricia. 1992, forthcoming. "Introduction" to F. Emerson Andrews, *Philanthropic Foundations,* Reissued Edition. New Brunswick, N.J.: Transaction Publishers.

Ruml, Beardsley and Theodore Geiger, editors. 1952. *Manual of Corporate Giving.* Washington, D.C.: National Planning Association.

Shannon, James P. editor. 1991. *The Corporate Contributions Handbook: Devoting Private Means to Public Needs.* San Francisco: Jossey-Bass.

Shea, Albert A., editor. 1953. *Corporate Giving in Canada.* Canada: Clarke, Irwin for the Committee on Corporate Giving in Canada.

Smith, Craig. "When Arts Marketers Call the Shots." *Corporate Philanthropy Report* 6 (April, 1991): 1, 7-10.

Whyte, William H. 1956. *The Organization Man.* New York: Simon and Schuster.

The archival assistance of the Russell Sage Foundation and the Rockefeller Archive Center is gratefully acknowledged.

PART I
CORPORATE GIVING

CHAPTER 1

The Corporation as a Giver

CORPORATIONS have risen to sudden prominence in the field of philanthropy. Their "gifts and contributions" as reported to the Bureau of Internal Revenue leaped from a level of $30 million in 1936 and $31 million in 1939 to a plateau of over $200 million in every year since 1944, with the probability that 1951 exceeded $300 million. The present importance of corporations as donors is indicated by the fact that since 1944 their recorded contributions in the United States have each year exceeded total collections of all community chests.

The full possibilities of this newly important resource in philanthropy are still unexplored, and the corporations themselves are often in doubt as to desirable procedures, reasonable amounts, and ultimate goals.

The Corporate Citizen

A business corporation has the primary responsibility of making a profit for its stockholders. Of course, not all incorporated enterprises are "business" corporations. A philanthropic foundation may properly declare that it exists to serve "the welfare of mankind," and industrialist Andrew Carnegie, after retiring from his steel interests, could testify to a governmental investigating committee: "My chief business is to do as much good as I can in the world; I have retired from all other business." But a business corporation that acted primarily on such principles might soon find itself in bankruptcy, with its machines rusting, its employees wageless, and community welfare far from improved.

An official of one of the largest corporations in America recently warned welfare agencies that cash gifts to them reduce the amount available for wages to employees and the sum that can be paid to the "savers" who have invested in business. Industry's first responsibility for the common welfare is to maintain a high level of efficient production with adequate wages and some surplus for plant improvement and profits.

The president of one company, replying to our questionnaire on corporation giving, expressed for himself and doubtless for many others a position that has a certain logic behind it:

> Contributions must come from either higher prices, lower wages and salaries, or profits. If you give to charity by raising prices or cutting wages, you create more problems than you solve. As for profits, they belong to the stockholders, and it is the right of the individual stockholder to decide how much he wishes to give, and to what agencies.

Lawyers have been fond of the phrase, "Charity has no business to sit at boards of directors *qua* charity," and it is clear that in a corporation, and especially in a publicly owned corporation, the Board has no right to make charitable gifts that have no relation to the company's business or to benefits to be derived by the company itself, unless expressly authorized by statute or charter.

Most corporations, however, do make contributions to a wide variety of welfare, health, and educational agencies. These contributions are justified sometimes as specific benefits, sometimes on quite general grounds. A statement of this position was made by Donaldson Brown, chairman of the finance committee of General Motors Corporation, in 1936:

> A corporation which derives generous benefits from community life must be willing to bear the corresponding burdens. . . . There is a justifiable corporate reason for its maintaining a lively interest

in social welfare. It cannot hope to thrive if it is surrounded by degeneracy and squalor.[1]

A recent statement appears in G. Clark Thompson's Foreword to the National Industrial Conference Board's 1950 report on company donations:

> Why must an increasing share of the charity burden fall upon industry's shoulders? The answer is simple. It needn't. Government is eager to assume these responsibilities. It is industry itself that is enlarging its philanthropic responsibilities, and it is doing so for three simple reasons.
>
> First, it fears the consequences of tax-supported and politically beholden charity with both the donor (the taxpayer) and the benefactor at the mercy of the bureaucracy.
>
> Second, income and inheritance taxes have reduced the philanthropic role of wealthy individuals, and corporations, as successors to the wealthy, are now the logical (and only) sources of large private gifts.
>
> Third, industry is becoming more socially conscious. In their desire to build their enterprises, industry leaders were often unconscious of the effects industrialization was having on the worker's personal security and the new social problems it was creating. Events of recent years have awakened management to these conditions and have stimulated a sincere desire on the part of industry to offer its workers and their families some of the things which they had lost or which they had been taught to want. Businessmen have also found that it pays to be charitable. In some cases, the advantages are direct, as in the case of research grants to universities. More often, the benefits take the form of better public acceptance of the company's products and a higher regard for it and its managers as citizens of the community.[2]

As later data will show, some corporations make no charitable gifts, taking the position that the whole of their funds, beyond plant needs, should go to employees, management, and stockholders, with the decision as to support of community and other philanthropic responsibilities devolving on these individuals.

[1] *Corporation Contributions to Community Chests.* Bulletin 89. Community Chests and Councils, Inc., New York, 1936, p. 1.

[2] *Company Policies on Donations: II.* Written Statements of Policy, by John H. Watson, III. Studies in Business Policy, No. 49, National Industrial Conference Board, New York, 1950, p. 4.

But in recent years the large majority of corporations are contributing to a wide variety of philanthropic causes. They believe these contributions pay in one way or another. Such gifts may increase business through improving customer relations. They may result in direct or indirect benefit to employees. They may aid research that will be of later benefit to the corporation. They may help in the education of future employees. By making further governmental expansion unnecessary, they may hold taxation down. By improving community facilities, they may help to provide better living conditions for workers and a more prosperous community as customers.

Opinion Research Corporation Findings

In 1948 the Opinion Research Corporation of Princeton, New Jersey, issued to its clients the results of a survey on attitudes of the general public, of community leaders, and of stockholders on corporation giving. The detailed findings[1] are confidential to clients, but permission has been granted to state these general conclusions:

> Of the general public, 80 per cent approve corporation giving to charitable causes; only 5 per cent definitely disapprove. When the same question was asked a group of community leaders—teachers, clergymen, lawyers, editors—a slightly smaller percentage favored: 78 per cent for, and 7 per cent against, with 5 per cent qualified support and 10 per cent no opinion. When the question was narrowed to those community leaders who hold stocks, substantially no difference was shown: 76 per cent for, and 8 per cent opposed. Under the still more searching question, "Should officers in the company in which you own stock give company money to charitable causes?" the favorable votes declined to 62 per cent, the negative rose to 13 per cent—still a strong approving sentiment.

On the subject of types of philanthropies, the community leaders placed welfare and health causes as first choices, giving qualified approval to support of education, but for the most part opposing gifts to religion. Recreation was approved if other and more important needs were already met. More opposition than

[1] *Meeting the Problem of Charitable Contributions.* The Public Opinion Index for Industry. Opinion Research Corporation, Princeton, 1948.

support was registered on company contributions to either foreign relief or veterans' organizations. On the question of local as against national causes, 40 per cent thought contributions should be mainly to local; 35 per cent, equally to both; 10 per cent qualified their statements; 14 per cent had no opinion; and only 1 per cent said mainly to national causes.

This survey indicates that the general public, including the stockholding group, approves corporation gifts and contributions, but expects them to be related to corporation or employee benefits.

Corporation Giving in the Total Picture

Although corporation giving has increased tremendously in the past decade, it is not a large proportion of the total annual receipts of private philanthropy in the United States. Such receipts, including income from capital, were estimated in the recent Russell Sage Foundation report[1] at $4,471 million.

TABLE 1. ESTIMATE OF RECENT ANNUAL RECEIPTS OF PRIVATE PHILANTHROPY IN THE UNITED STATES, BY SOURCE

Dollar figures in millions

Source	Amount	Per cent
Contributions from individuals	$3,304	74
Charitable bequests	182	4
Contributions from corporations	241	5
Foundations	133	3
Income from capital (except foundations)	611	14
Total	$4,471	100

SOURCE: Table 14 of *Philanthropic Giving*, which was derived from data of other tables of that study.

Corporate contributions of 5 per cent of total philanthropy may seem relatively small, but they are actually a very significant factor, and sometimes the chief reliance, in the areas in which corporations are accustomed to give. Religious agencies, supported almost wholly by individuals, alone account for about half of all philanthropic receipts. Certain other causes that have

[1] Andrews, F. Emerson, *Philanthropic Giving*. The Foundation, New York, 1950, p. 73.

"heart appeal" have developed mass collection methods capitalizing on the enormous giving potential of the millions of low-income givers; they need little corporation support. But many types of voluntary welfare agencies cannot undertake mass appeals and must rely on big gifts. For the very survival of such agencies, in this period when large private fortunes are diminished in number, corporation support may be essential; in some cases it represents the major portion of gift income.

Some Urgent Problems

Knotty problems remain.

Should corporations give at all? Indeed, have they the legal right, without specific stockholder consent, to donate corporation funds to causes that do not promise direct and commensurate benefits to the corporation itself?

How much should corporations give? If it is conceded that donations bestow benefits in terms of customer approval, employee relations, and perhaps the general prosperity and well-being of the community, at what point are these advantages overweighed by possible effects on prices, wages, or profits?

What are the dangers to beneficiaries? If it is known that a large corporation is a donor, will not gifts from individuals be discouraged? If an agency relies heavily on corporation gifts, what will happen in a depression year, when such gifts may be severely reduced and the needs of the agency are probably greater than usual? Will some corporations endeavor to control the policies of benefiting agencies, to the possible limitation or detriment of their services?

What should corporations support? The case is clear for some agencies, where benefit is direct and obvious. But what about higher education? Recreation? Religion? Veterans? The "American way"? Any of a thousand beckoning, but marginal, causes?

What internal organization is needed, so that a function that is financially insignificant in most corporations shall not consume inordinate executive time, and shall be performed effectively? A screening and evaluating procedure is necessary. Public relations and employee relations are considerations. What about in-plant solicitations? And shall executives be encouraged to give personal (and sometimes company) time to philanthropic campaigns?

Can some corporation giving find new and creative patterns, using the special knowledge and resources of particular industries for making contributions to the common welfare not possible for other donors?

These are a few of the questions troubling top management in corporations today. It is not supposed that this or any study can provide clear and final answers to many of them. But an objective statement of what many corporations are now doing in these fields and presentation of a variety of opinions and points of view may furnish useful guidance in a field now disorderly and chaotic.

CHAPTER 2

How Giving Grew

I T HAS BEEN indicated that corporation giving reached large proportions only in the past decade. A brief glance at how such giving began and slowly developed may be useful, however, in lending perspective and in showing origins of some present practices.

Conditions Under Earlier Industry

When business was small and usually owned by an individual or a few persons closely associated with the enterprise, little occasion existed for corporation philanthropy. If disaster struck a worker or his family, the employer often found some way to help out. When the minister's wife ordered and paid for a pound of meat, she often received a pound and a half; and her husband still fills in a special form at the railway station for his reduced fare ticket—and resents the need for accepting such handouts in place of an adequate salary. When a new hospital was to be built, substantial contributions were expected from the merchant, the manufacturer, the banker; but usually they contributed as individuals, not as companies.

In smaller, closely held corporations similar practices may still prevail. This was reflected in some of the answers to the questionnaire on which this study is largely based.[1] The president of one half-million-dollar corporation wrote, "Our gifts are all personal." Said another, "The specific dollar answers are not ex-

[1] See Appendix A, Method of the Study.

actly correct as three of the executives whose names are identical with the firm name make additional personal contributions in certain instances." A third refused to fill out our questionnaire, but wrote in explanation:

> As far as corporation gifts are concerned, it seems to me that it depends on the kind of corporation—whether a close corporation or one with many stockholders. Ours happens to be a close one. . . . Philanthropies are made by myself to the extent of about 25 per cent of my income.

As corporations grew in size, two things were happening that made the old patterns of individual, personal giving inadequate or inapplicable. In the first place, the corporation itself often became a commanding factor in the wealth, health, and social problems of the community in which it was located. If contaminated sources of water supply spread illness, the corporation work force was so severely cut that public health and adequate medical care for the whole community became a necessary corporation concern. Sometimes the nature or conditions of work within company walls created problems that had to be met by social agencies on the outside, and it seemed logical that a substantial share of the costs should be met by the corporation.

Second, in the larger corporations absentee ownership was usual. The great majority of the stockholders did not live in the communities in which the corporation had its plants, and were not intimately acquainted with the problems either of the employees or of the plant communities. If big business was to bear what many considered a proper share of its responsibilities for community welfare, a plan beyond the personal philanthropy of owners had to be devised.

The pattern for such a plan had been set up in the last quarter of the nineteenth century, under unique circumstances.

The Railroads and the "Y"

From their beginnings railroads have faced a peculiar personnel problem. Many of their employees need two homes. Even with runs regularized, it is often not possible to return trainmen the same day to their point of departure. The YMCA, offering supervised, economical accommodations and some of the advantages of a club, seemed a logical solution.

The YMCA movement, starting in London, was transplanted to North America in 1851 and found fertile soil. In 1868 its annual convention held in Detroit passed this resolution:

> *Resolved*, That the manufacturers of our country can make no investment that will bring them greater dividends than that of contributing largely to aid in the formation and sustaining [of] Young Men's Christian Associations within their various localities.[1]

As regards general business corporations, no evidence exists of substantial contributions to "Y" support at this early period, but the "Y" was already working specially with railroads. The same 1868 convention authorized employment of a man to undertake religious work among laborers on the Union Pacific Railroad, pushing westward from Omaha.

In 1872 the first organization of railway men into a YMCA was begun in Cleveland. Work was soon started in Chicago and Erie; in 1888 Cornelius Vanderbilt of the New York Central Railroad provided a building and facilities for the men at Madison Avenue and 45th Street in New York City at a cost of $225,000; and the important Pennsylvania system was entered by an Association in Altoona.

By 1890 Associations were reported at 82 divisional and terminal points and in every instance railroads helped financially. A usual practice at this stage was for railroad corporations to pay about 60 per cent of the operating budgets for railroad YMCA buildings, the employees making up the remainder. The Movement, highly evangelistic in its early period, accepted these funds at first with some questioning. Says the *History:*

> The conscience of the Movement was not clear at the beginning on the acceptance of corporation funds, but the practice was soon rationalized. "The shrewdest men, the most careful managers, are now ready to appropriate money for the purpose," declared a

[1] *Proceedings of the Thirteenth Annual Convention of the Young Men's Christian Associations* of the United States and British Provinces, 1868, p. 92.

speaker at the conference of 1882, "and the response they make to their stockholders is 'we are making money for you by it.'"[1]

By 1911 there were 518 local secretaries serving 230 railroad Associations, but by that time the support ratios were reversed, the membership providing 60 per cent, the companies 40. The varied forms of railway support were described:

> The Railroad Companies have appropriated for Railroad Young Men's Christian Association organizations, during the past thirty years, several million dollars. The secretaries have been generally placed on the pay-roll of the companies. The companies furnish coal, light and supplies, and contribute about one-third of the current expenses of the organization. One hundred and thirteen buildings have been erected costing $1,800,000. Of this sum the railroad companies have paid more than one-half. Most railroad systems are co-operating in the establishment of Associations at their principal division points, and consider them an indispensable part of railroad equipment for the economical and effective handling of passenger and freight business.[2]

Spurred on by success with the railroads, the YMCA expanded into other industries. An industrial department was organized as early as 1903, and by 1920 there were 154 industrial-type buildings worth $6.6 million, paid for by management and workers.

Meanwhile, where the "Y" was not able to rely so wholly on industry, it was developing the community drive for funds. It was the first national organization to employ skilled techniques in such fund-raising, with intensive and highly organized campaigns usually limited to a two-week period, and emphasizing solicitation of corporations.

The records are too fragmentary for estimates of the proportion of these funds contributed by corporations, but some individual items are available. In 1910, for example, new buildings estimated to cost $15 million were under construction. Among noted gifts toward them were $100,000 from a leading mail order house

[1] Hopkins, C. Howard, *History of the Y.M.C.A. in North America*. Association Press, New York, 1951, p. 234. Many of the facts in this section are taken from this source.

[2] "Christianity and Corporate Interests," *Association Men*, vol. 29, November, 1903, p. 49.

in Chicago; $50,000 from a public utility in Massachusetts; $10,000 from a steel company in Chicago.

In addition to corporation contributions to these intensive building-fund drives, the "Y" in many cities secured from business a substantial portion of the donations toward its operating budget. For example, in Cleveland during the thirteen years 1905 through 1917 corporations contributed 18 per cent of donations and contributions totaling $450,000. Similar percentages prevailed in Minneapolis and St. Paul for varying periods in which records are available.[1]

On April 6, 1917, the United States entered what was then too optimistically called "the" World War. It created welfare needs at home and abroad of such dimensions that philanthropic giving entered a new era in fund-raising. The YMCA was the only national organization with a well-trained fund-raising arm, and was first in the field. On April 27, 1917, it appealed for $3 million "to provide for the work of the YMCA among the men of the Army and Navy." By June 1 over $5 million had been subscribed. How much was contributed by corporations is not separately recorded, but newspapers reported at least one corporation gift of $50,000; and in St. Paul 41 known corporation contributions totaled $14,350, or 44 per cent of the total of $32,450 raised in that city.

Red Cross Dividends

The American National Red Cross decided, almost at the moment war was declared, that its tremendous program of relief work should be financed by voluntary subscription. Its War Finance Committee debated how much it could possibly raise to meet needs of a dimension never faced before by American philanthropy. Some members considered $25 million the extreme limit. The Committee finally settled on $100 million as the goal for its campaign of June, 1917. It enlisted many of the experienced YMCA leaders, national and local, who, in the new,

[1] Williams, Pierce, and Frederick E. Croxton, *Corporation Contributions to Organized Community Welfare Services*. National Bureau of Economic Research, New York, 1930, p. 56. This is the most authoritative general source on early corporation giving.

enormous drive, used the techniques for intensive solicitation of individuals and business that the "Y" had developed.

Many corporations, particularly the large national ones with their corps of legal advisers, felt that they could not safely make a contribution directly to the Red Cross without stockholder consent. To get around this difficulty the Red Cross suggested to the cautious corporations an extraordinary device—the Red Cross Dividend. How it worked is made clear from this recommended form, which the American National Red Cross sent out in the spring of 1917 to corporations that doubted their power to make direct contribution:

The Board of Directors of this Company, at its meeting held . . . passed the following resolution:

Whereas, the week from June 18th to June 25th, 1917, inclusive, has been set apart and declared by the President of the United States as Red Cross Week, during which a concerted countrywide effort is to be made to raise a large sum of money for war relief purposes for the American National Red Cross; and

Whereas, the Board of Directors of this Company believes that in this time of war generous contributions should be made to the Red Cross, by individuals, partnerships, corporations and other associations throughout the country, not only as obvious measures of humanity but also as great and most important parts in the preservation of the social and business structure of this country and other countries, and it is accordingly the belief of the Board of Directors of this Company that it should aid as substantially as possible in this effort by enabling stockholders to contribute a portion of their distributive interest in this corporation to those purposes:

Now, Therefore be it resolved [resolution in declaration of an extra dividend];

And Be It Further Resolved that the officers of the Company hereby are authorized and directed to notify stockholders of this action of the Board, and to request that every stockholder shall execute a form of dividend order to be enclosed with such notice, directing and authorizing the corporation to pay the amount of the dividend to which he would be entitled to the Red Cross War Fund, such orders to be returned to the corporation immediately.[1]

[1] Quoted in Williams and Croxton, *Corporation Contributions to Organized Community Welfare Services*, pp. 233–234.

It was further provided that stockholders releasing dividends amounting to $1.00 or more should be enrolled as annual members of the Red Cross.

At least 148 corporations declared Red Cross dividends, collecting $17,948,969.[1] Many such dividends were set at 1 per cent of the par value of stock; others at amounts per share ranging usually from 15 to 50 cents. But many corporations did not think this circumlocution necessary, and made their contributions direct. The Diversified Industries Division of the Red Cross fund-raising organization in Pittsburgh set as the corporation industrial goal, "One per cent of your estimated net earnings for 1917 for the Red Cross."

Nationally, the drive went over the top with $115 million, but the detailed records are gone and it is not possible to discover what portion of this total came from corporations. We have, however, the record of about $18 million through Red Cross dividends and slightly more than $11 million (partly duplicating the $18 million) in newspaper reports from 38 selected cities, recording contributions of 1,289 corporations. Certainly enough evidence exists to pin-point 1917 as the year in which corporation contributions first reached a substantial total in the history of American philanthropy.

Other Wartime Drives

As World War I intensified, welfare needs grew. In spite of oversubscription of both the "Y" and the Red Cross drives, both agencies had to campaign again, and other appeals multiplied. The chief national drives of World War I, and the amounts sought and contributed, are indicated in Table 2, which shows how rapidly the sights of philanthropy were raised under wartime pressures.

Corporation contributions are not available as a separate item for any of these drives, but various evidences indicate that they were substantial. For the November, 1917, YMCA drive Elbert H. Gary announced that subsidiaries of the United States Steel Corporation would subscribe $500,000; the Standard Oil Com-

[1] *The Red Cross Bulletin*, vol. 2, January 14, 1918, p. 1.

pany was reported in the press to have contributed $250,000. Data chiefly from contemporary newspaper accounts indicate that corporation contributions in various cities ranged from some 45 per cent of the total given (in Chicago) to 15 per cent in Louisville. It is quite possible that corporations contributed as much as $20 million to the second YMCA drive.

TABLE 2. CHIEF NATIONAL FUND-RAISING DRIVES OF WORLD WAR I

Dollar figures in millions

Date	Organization	Amount sought	Amount raised
1917			
April–May	YMCA	$ 3.5	$ 5.1
June	American National Red Cross	100.0	115.0
November	YMCA	35.0	54.5
1918			
May	American National Red Cross	100.0	168.6
November	United War Work Campaign	170.5	203.0

SOURCE: Williams and Croxton, *Corporation Contributions to Organized Community Welfare Services*, p. 49; and American National Red Cross, *The Greatest Freewill Offering in History*, p. 2.

The second American National Red Cross campaign, in May of 1918, was conducted in a changed atmosphere. The goal of $100 million was set with confidence, and nearly 70 per cent oversubscribed. The Red Cross Dividend device was abandoned. Returns from that source had been disappointing, many of the stockholders holding onto their money and failing to authorize its transfer to the Red Cross. Besides, the corporations that had contributed directly in the first drive had not been challenged, and additional legislation in a few jurisdictions gave new confidence to even the more cautious boards of directors.

For example, New York passed legislation before the time of the drive authorizing corporations to contribute, with the limitation that such contributions to war charities should not exceed in one year a total of 1 per cent on the capital stock outstanding. Further contributions could not be made except upon ten days' notice to the stockholders, and if objections were made by holders of 25 per cent of the stock the contribution had to be authorized at a stockholders' meeting. During the month of the campaign the Congress passed a bill permitting contributions to the American Red Cross by national banks out of money available for dividends. The committee soliciting corporate funds in Greater New York emphasized that corporations had not merely the right to make such contributions but it was their duty to do so for their own protection. It cited the opinion of former Supreme Court Justice Charles Evans Hughes on this subject:

> The question is not one of permitting the use of corporate moneys for what are or may be called "worthy objects" outside the corporate enterprise, but for the maintenance of the very foundation of the corporate enterprise itself.[1]

Corporation contributions were substantial, and this time they were all direct, without the complications of stockholder-released dividends. The total amount is not known, but some items are indicative. The New York Corporations Committee claimed $20 million, "of which only $13,000,000 was credited to the city campaign." The National Bureau of Economic Research, reviewing Red Cross files of contributors of $1,000 or more, discovered a total of 1,204 names of presumed corporations (some may have been partnerships or other unincorporated enterprises) in 210 communities in 27 states. Contributions of $5,000 or more from named corporations in New York City totaled nearly $9 million in the Bureau's list,[2] with these the largest:

United States Steel Corporation	$2,000,000
General Electric Company	500,000
Standard Oil Company (New Jersey)	500,000
American Telephone and Telegraph Company	250,000
Anaconda Copper Company	250,000
National City Bank	250,000
Phelps-Dodge Corporation	250,000
Union Carbide and Carbon Corporation	250,000
Utah Copper Company	250,000

Outside New York City no quarter-million corporation contributions appear to have been secured, the closest approach

[1] Letter of Charles E. Hughes to Charles D. Norton, dated May 9, 1918, from files of Red Cross Counselor, Washington, D. C.

[2] Williams and Croxton, *op. cit.*, pp. 236-237.

being International Harvester Company in Chicago, with $225,000.

From the known items and with the guidance of proportional data from certain cities—in Chicago corporations contributed 39.2 per cent of the total amount, in Grand Rapids only 7.8 per cent according to the Bureau tabulations—it might be guessed that corporate contributions to the second Red Cross drive approached $35 million; but accuracy is not possible.

The last of the great World War I drives was the United War Work Campaign in which seven important organizations joined, for the first time, in a fund-raising effort. These were the YMCA, YWCA, War Camp Community Service, Knights of Columbus, Jewish Welfare Board, American Library Association, and Salvation Army, all officially recognized by the government for welfare work among American soldiers. The YMCA, with the largest war program of the group, did the lion's share of the campaign work and was allotted 58.65 per cent of the proceeds. Although the Armistice was signed the very day the campaign officially opened —November 11, 1918—and the emphasis had to be shifted to demobilization needs, the goal of $170.5 million was oversubscribed by nearly $33 million.

Corporation contributions were heavily emphasized by the YMCA leaders in charge of the campaign. They tried to secure combined contributions from companies and employees, or in some cases to have the corporation match its employee contributions. Definite quotas for corporations began to be set; the amounts requested in Baltimore were 2½ per cent of estimated net earnings for 1918 for corporations engaged chiefly in war work and with earnings in excess of $500,000; 2 per cent of net earnings for corporations in the same income class but not engaged in war work; 1.5 per cent for enterprises with net earnings from $100,000 to $500,000; 1 per cent if net earnings were below $100,000.

The papers reported a resounding $5 million contributed by the United States Steel Corporation, with Mr. Gary commenting: "Since receiving the opinion of our counsel that such contributions are legal and proper, we do not hesitate to make them and charge the same to the expense account." The Standard Oil Company (New Jersey) was reported as subscribing $1 million. Few other reports of corporation contributions are available, for the Armistice crowded from the papers most other news during the campaign period, and the official records were never analyzed for this item.

The War Chests

In addition to these great national drives, communities everywhere were flooded with special appeals, chiefly for relief of sufferers in Europe. To meet this confusing situation some 400 communities organized war chests for united campaigns, and frequently these united campaigns included many or most of the local welfare agencies. This was the more likely in communities that already had federations of charity and philanthropy, organized to coordinate charitable relief work but in a few instances experimenting also with joint solicitation of funds.

The proportions the local agencies received of the totals raised varied greatly. According to the National Bureau of Economic Research[1] 63 local agencies in Cleveland received $296,000 out of a war chest total of $10,538,640 in 1918, or only 2.8 per cent. But in Grand Rapids 22 agencies received $194,142 out of $607,377, or 32 per cent. The same high percentage held for the 43 agencies in Minneapolis that participated in the war chest of that city. Generally speaking, the agencies found that their share in the united appeal, where both individual and corporate contributors were spurred on by wartime patriotism, was larger than they had been able to collect by themselves. Through these war chests many corporations learned a new pattern of giving for general community welfare which they continued through the device growing out of the war chests—the community chest.

Community Chests, 1920–1929

Shortly after hostilities ended most of the war chests disappeared, but a new organization had been formed in 1918, the American Association for Community Organization, now Com-

[1] Williams and Croxton, op. cit., p. 89.

munity Chests and Councils of America, Inc. The seeds of the chest movement had been planted, and with the help of this organization, they began to grow. In 1920 there were only 39 chests, raising from all sources about $20 million. But by 1925 there were 240 chests raising $58 million; and in 1929, 331 chests raising $73 million.

Corporations had a large share in this expansion. Chests were, in fact, excellently suited to many of the conditions of corporate giving. Responsibility toward needs of the community in which the corporation's employees make their home was, and is, a chief motivation in corporate philanthropy. The community chest, combining many types of agencies, provided a convenient channel through which much of that responsibility could be met with a single contribution.

The early record of corporation contributions to community chests is presented in considerable detail in the National Bureau of Economic Research study already referred to, and the situation in 1929, when the study was completed, is closely analyzed.[1]

Corporation contributions for the chests included in the study had been $2.5 million in 1920 and increased to almost $13 million in 1929. In the latter year the corporation contribution was 22 per cent of the total of $58.8 million raised by the 129 chests that furnished data to the Bureau. This increase, however, represented chiefly growth in numbers and coverage of chests rather than proportion of corporate contribution, for of the 129 chests studied, only 13 were in existence and could furnish records for 1920, and these 13 chests reported corporate contributions to be 23.8 per cent of the 1920 funds—a higher proportion than nine years later. But this proportion varied widely in different chest cities. Eleven of the 129 chests studied in 1929 received 40 per cent or more of their total funds from corporations. At the other end of the scale, 17 received less than 10 per cent.

A unique reversal of the community chest pattern was reported in Cambridge, Massachusetts. There, in order to initiate giving by corporations, a Manufacturers' Chest was organized as "a

[1] The several paragraphs that follow are derived from the Williams and Croxton study.

fund contributed annually by the industries of Cambridge for distribution to the welfare organizations of the city." It considered the programs and budgets of the welfare agencies of the city and made appropriations in accordance with its best judgment as to relative need, refusing contributions to agencies that failed to submit requested data. In 1928 this Manufacturers' Chest disbursed $31,195, representing about 22 per cent of total contributions reported by the benefiting Cambridge charities. With formation of the Cambridge Community Federation, this unique Chest ceased to exist in 1937.

Contributions to Nonchest Agencies

Corporations did not confine their contributions to community chests, even in chest cities; and in many cities chests did not exist. Data for other organizations are scattered, however, and difficult to assess. In these areas the National Bureau of Economic Research study, reflecting the period 1920 through 1929 in an admittedly "limited view," reports these conclusions:

> In most instances a smaller proportion of the total contributions to non-community chest charitable agencies is contributed by corporations than is the case when similar organizations participate in community chests. This is true whether the appeal by the non-participating organizations be for current expenses or for capital funds.
>
> Of all the welfare organizations raising funds independently of community chests, the Y.M.C.A. has been the most successful in getting corporation contributions. . . . National organizations other than the American Red Cross are shown to have raised an insignificant fraction of their funds from corporations.[1]

The Bureau attempted to analyze corporate contributions in the larger nonchest cities, including New York and Chicago. In New York 32 organizations, including 15 hospitals and the YM and YWCA, reported total contributions to current expense budgets of $3.7 million, of which corporations gave only $185,320, or 5 per cent. In Chicago 8 agencies reported $976,512 in contributions, with the corporate gifts $191,795, or 19.6 per cent. Both the United Charities and the Boy Scouts in that city reported corporate contributions of more than 23 per cent of total gifts.

[1] Williams and Croxton, op. cit., pp. 228–229.

Under conditions of stress corporation contributions might temporarily mount in totals and take fresh forms. A severe earthquake devastated much of Japan in 1923. A shoe manufacturing concern in New York State donated 16,000 pairs of shoes and $10,000 in cash. A food company released to the Japanese government $5,000 worth of edible oils stored in Japan or China. An oil company contributed $30,000 and sent two steamers from Shanghai loaded with food, water, clothing, and medical supplies. Railroads transported relief supplies free, and sometimes made cash contributions. The total raised was $10.4 million. In the 28 cities in which the National Bureau found it possible to identify corporation contributions, these amounted to $1.5 million out of a total of $4.5 million, or 34 per cent.

It is nevertheless apparent that in the prosperous, nonwar year of 1929 corporate giving was at a low level. Applying the 22 per cent found among 129 chests in the Bureau study to the total receipts of chests in that year, one arrives at $16 million for corporation contributions to all chests. Other agencies in chest cities and all agencies in the nonchest communities may have collected from corporations an additional $6 million toward current expenses and special building funds. The 1929 total probably did not exceed $22 million, as compared with $40 million or $50 million contributed by corporations in 1917 to the Red Cross and the "Y" alone, and still heavier wartime contributions in the year that followed.

The Great Depression

Only scattered records of corporation giving exist for the early depression years. From past experience it might be assumed that corporation contributions dropped sharply as dividends were omitted, employees laid off, and business failures increased. Certainly that had been the case with respect to chests in the minor depression of 1922. Corporation contributions to the 13 community chests continuously reporting from 1920 through 1929 declined from $2.5 million in 1920 to $2.0 million in 1922, not passing the earlier level until 1927 and closing the period at $2.8 million in 1929.

Unfortunately, the National Bureau corporation study ended with 1929, and government statistics on corporate philanthropy did not begin until 1936. The careful studies which Community Chests and Councils now conducts on this aspect of giving to its agencies began still later. Between 1929 and 1936 exists a gap with respect to knowledge of corporation giving that cannot be satisfactorily bridged.

It is possible that corporation giving did not show a severe drop in the early depression. The level in 1929 was not high, and heavy pressure was put on individuals and corporations in the first depression years for contributions to save the starving until we could turn that promised corner. Totals raised by community chests from all sources actually rose from $73 million in 1929 to $101 million in 1932.[1] Thereafter they dropped sharply, to $78 million in 1933, $70 million in 1935, and then began slowly to climb.

In the early depression years, before the vast federal-state relief programs swung into action, private agencies tried to carry the load with funds solicited in emergency drives. The task proved too great, but the sums collected were often substantial. For instance, in New York City, during the fall of 1931, the Emergency Unemployment Relief Committee ("Gibson Committee"), with 30,000 solicitors, collected $18 million, of which slightly more than $5 million came from 7,336 "corporations and business firms." But the next year's campaign fell off to $13.5 million with the contributions of 7,144 corporations and business firms at $4.2 million. By 1933 governmental relief programs were in operation and the Gibson Committee disbanded in September of that year. How much of the $9 million it collected from "corporations and business firms" came from true corporations as against the corner grocery, partnerships, and personally owned companies cannot now be determined, nor have such figures for the similar drives in many other cities been centrally collected.

Newspaper items offer sidelights on corporation giving in those difficult days, but no comprehensive picture. "Among the larger contributions were $13,483 from the employees and the American

---

[1] The year is the "chest year" in which the money is to be expended. In most instances the campaign occurred during the fall of the previous year.

Locomotive Company." "Until March 1 [1932] all Whelan drug stores throughout the country will fill without charge all prescriptions for sick and ailing unemployed, where the prescribing physician confirmed the destitution or straitened circumstances." "The Wanamaker store is contributing 1 per cent of its audited sales for the months of November and December [1931]." "The Motion Picture Industry's Organizations for Aid of Unemployed . . . announced that 300,000 of the 1,000,000 tickets allotted for these benefit performances had been sold." "Dealers contributed fresh vegetables, fruits and bread, valued at $74,500."

In 1936 Community Chests and Councils issued a small bulletin[1] including scattered information, but usually omitting the critical depression years 1931–1933. Two chests, it reported, had studied contributions of utilities in 28 cities; between 1929 and 1936 utility contributions averaged an increase of 40 per cent. Banks—those which had survived the disaster—were studied by another chest. In 30 cities "going" institutions had doubled their 1929 contributions in the emergency 1932 campaigns; in 1935 their contributions were about 50 per cent more than in 1929. In Pittsburgh total corporation contributions to the chest rose from $147,000 in 1929 to $600,000 in 1935, and in percentage of total receipts from 15 to 29 per cent. St. Louis showed a similar, though smaller, increase. Accumulated data from more than 100 chests showed increases in corporation contributions between 1929 and 1934 (and the two succeeding years) for six chain-store groups and ten large manufacturing companies, though not for each of the companies. Three of the chain-store groups and four of the large manufacturing companies gave less in 1934 than in 1929, but the others more than compensated for the difference. Totals were:

	1929	1934	1935	1936
	In thousands			
Six national chain-store groups	$149	$189	$199	$208
Ten large manufacturing companies	653	683	676	750

[1] *Corporation Contributions to Community Chests.* Bulletin 89, Community Chests and Councils, Inc., New York, 1936.

The Revenue Act of 1935

When the emergency relief administrations of the federal and state governments took over the tasks of supplying primary needs, they removed some of the pressures from private agencies; but the money the government used had to be collected, usually through taxes. By present standards such taxes had been low for many years. From 1909 through 1915 the maximum federal tax on corporations was 1 per cent of net income. World War I forced an increase and temporary imposition of excess-profits taxes, but until 1936 the maximum normal tax on net income was 13.75 per cent. In that year a new graduated corporation tax became effective, rising to a normal tax rate of 15 per cent on net income exceeding $40,000 and certain additional surtaxes on undistributed net income.

When it became obvious that this substantial increase in the corporation income tax was in prospect, alarm spread among welfare agencies, and particularly the community chests, which were receiving substantial corporation donations. One chest executive reported that "resentment has been growing over the discrimination against [corporations] in taxing their *pro bono publico* expenditure and it is becoming increasingly difficult to persuade them to make liberal contributions."[1] Tax exemption on charitable gifts had been granted individuals as early as 1917, to promote contributions for war purposes; now it was proposed for corporations.

This proposal was vigorously pressed, particularly by the social agencies. The president of Community Chests and Councils, Frederic R. Kellogg, pleaded the case before the House Ways and Means Committee in July, 1935.[2] Before the Senate Finance Committee Newton D. Baker was an influential witness. The Revenue Act, passed in August, 1935, included the desired provision, exempting from tax corporation contributions to defined

[1] Burns, Allen T., "Tax Exemption of Corporation Gifts," *Midmonthly Survey,* September, 1935, pp. 261–262.

[2] The next day, presumably as a result of these efforts, he suffered a paralytic stroke, and died a month later.

charitable agencies up to 5 per cent of net income, beginning with income year 1936.[1]

Growth in Recent Giving

As a result of this new provision, statistics on corporation giving, insofar as such gifts are reported for purposes of tax exemption, are available from 1936. In the absence of comparable preceding records, it is difficult to determine the effectiveness of the new exemption in promoting corporation giving. But the immediate effect was not great, for reported contributions averaged only $30 million annually for the years 1936 through 1939. Later, under the combined pressures of wartime needs and much higher corporation taxes, they rose sharply.

These newer developments are analyzed in the chapters that follow.

[1] The present version of this provision of the Internal Revenue Code, Section 23(q) is cited on p. 274.

CHAPTER 3

Who Gives,
and How Much

C OMPREHENSIVE data on corporation giving are available from 1936, the year corporations began reporting their gifts to the Bureau of Internal Revenue. Only the government, indeed, has the authority or the facilities needed for collecting data from so vast a field. Corporations in 1936 numbered 479,000, and by 1948 about 600,000. Unfortunately, these government figures, collected primarily for taxation purposes, do not include all the kinds of information that would be helpful to the student of corporate philanthropy, and have certain other limitations. They have therefore been supplemented by a special survey made on a sampling basis by Russell Sage Foundation in 1951, and reflecting 1950 data.

The Bureau of Internal Revenue Figures

The United States Treasury Department issues detailed reports on corporation tax returns for each tax year, published in *Statistics of Income*, Part 2, for the given year. These full reports are presently available from 1936 through 1945, with preliminary and less detailed figures furnished in press releases through tax year 1948.[1]

---

[1] Preliminary data for 1949 became available as this book went to press, and have been inserted in the frontispiece and in Table 3.

It is not blithely assumed that corporate income-tax returns represent, in all cases, a completely truthful picture. But most corporations undergo such careful audit that error from intentional falsification can scarcely be large, either in what the Treasury Department politely calls "understatement of income" or in overstatement of contributions, both of which would inflate the reported rates of corporate giving.

Many corporations include in one budget item philanthropies as these are commonly defined and costs of memberships, some of which are true philanthropies, some marginal, and some outright trade association and business expenses. Contrary to advance fears, our Survey indicated that for tax returns most corporations carefully distinguish among these types of expenditures, even though the same office procedure and internal budget are used, and do not report the purely business items as "gifts and contributions."

The government figures, indeed, often reflect an opposite inaccuracy. Section 23(q) of the Internal Revenue Code recognizes corporate gifts and contributions with respect to tax liability, but it does not confer on the corporation the power to make such gifts. State legislation on this subject[1] is varied and often unclear. When a gift is of such a nature that direct benefit to the corporation can be proved, many corporations prefer to deduct it as an ordinary business expense even though it also comes within all common definitions of philanthropy. This has an identical effect in reducing taxable net income, and in addition escapes the 5 per cent limitation. Further, certain corporations, such as mutual savings banks and insurance companies, do not report "compiled net profit" and in many instances employ quite different tax forms for their returns, so that their contributions are not tabulated in the usual manner.

Our Survey discovered that among the corporations sampled, sums "given to agencies for health, welfare, education, or religion as a business expense" amounted to 7.6 per cent of the amount separately reported under 23(q), or 0.036 per cent of net income. If this ratio holds for all corporations, welfare agencies were

[1] See pp. 235–239.

receiving from corporations in recent years from $10 million to $15 million more than the government figures reflect. No effort is made to correct for this item in the tables that follow, but it is large enough to merit this notice.

Annual Changes

Radical changes, for the most part upward, are reflected in the successive Bureau of Internal Revenue figures. As Table 3 indicates, contributions remained substantially stationary from 1936 through 1939, with some decrease in the 1937–1938 recession, though this decrease was less severe than the drop in profits for 1938. Contributions began to climb in 1940, along with business activity and profits from rearmament, soon to be all-out war. The contribution rate, however, remained substantially unchanged through 1942, gifts increasing only in proportion to profits.[1]

TABLE 3. CORPORATION CONTRIBUTIONS: AMOUNT AND PER CENT OF NET PROFIT, BY YEAR, 1936 TO 1949

Dollar figures in millions

Year	Net profit	Contributions	
		Amount	Per cent of net profit
1936	$7,771	$30	0.39
1937	7,830	33	0.42
1938	4,131	27	0.66
1939	7,178	31	0.43
1940	9,348	38	0.41
1941	16,675	58	0.35
1942	23,389	98	0.42
1943	28,126	159	0.57
1944	26,547	234	0.88
1945	21,345	266	1.24
1946	25,399	214	0.84
1947	31,615	241	0.76
1948	34,588	239	0.69
1949	28,387	223	0.78

SOURCE: *Statistics of Income*, U. S. Treasury Department, for the years indicated; *Press Release No. S-3079*.

[1] Here and elsewhere, net profit is profit after business deductions, but before taxes.

The war years 1942 through 1945 showed a great upsurge in corporation contributions, culminating in the record $266 million of 1945 at the unequaled rate of 1.24 cents on the dollar of net profit. This upsurge was extraordinary. As the frontispiece indicates, corporation contributions were in 1945 nearly nine times the 1936–1939 average, and they stood in 1948 at about eight times the index average. Profits also had grown considerably, but were in 1945 only three times the 1936–1939 average and about five times that average in 1948. Individual giving did not increase at this rate under the special impetus of war needs. According to our estimates detailed elsewhere,[1] gifts of living donors averaged $903 million from 1936 through 1939, and were three times as great in 1945. However, the individual index did not slump after 1945, but continued to climb.

It is surely more than coincidence that this great increase in corporation giving occurred in precisely the years when a severe excess-profits tax was in effect. In October, 1942, the Revenue Act was amended setting the new rate at 90 per cent on adjusted excess-profits net income, subject to a postwar refund of 10 per cent. Even at 80 per cent, corporations with profits in this bracket were able to contribute $1,000 to a chosen cause at a net cost to stockholders of $200. To what extent the high corporation giving of 1943 through 1945 was due to the increased and dramatic needs of wartime, and to what extent it was an acceptance of this great charitable "bargain," cannot be determined.

When the excess-profits tax was repealed for taxable years beginning January 1, 1946, welfare agencies that had been receiving heavy corporation support expected a disastrous drop. A drop occurred, but it was less than anticipated. Corporate contributions declined $52 million from the 1945 high, even though corporate profits were up $4 billion. At $214 million they were still the highest in corporate history except for 1944 and 1945.

In 1947 reported contributions climbed to $241 million, but corporate profits had climbed more steeply and the rate of giving was falling off. In 1948 the change was slight; the total declined

[1] *Philanthropic Giving*, p. 72.

two million although profits rose slightly, and the rate fell off further, but was still higher than in any year before 1944. The preliminary figures for 1949 showed no substantial change. Our sampling Survey, covering 1950, cannot safely be expanded to all corporations for reasons discussed.[1] The indicated rate of 0.5 per cent suggests a further decline in the rate of giving, partly offset in dollar totals by the large corporate profits of that year. In 1951 it is probable that the excess-profits tax again considerably increased both the rates and amounts of giving, and it is possible that a new record was set.

Asset Classifications

Do large or small corporations give more generously with relation to their incomes? From which groups does the most money come? Table 4 presents answers to these questions for 1948, the latest year for which detailed figures are available. This table merits study.

TABLE 4. CONTRIBUTIONS OF CORPORATIONS REPORTING BALANCE SHEETS: AMOUNT AND PER CENT OF NET PROFIT, BY AMOUNT OF CORPORATION ASSETS, 1948

Asset class (thousands)	Corporations (thousands)	Net profit (millions)	Contributions	
			Amount (millions)	Per cent of net profit
Under $50	235	$54	$4	7.48
50 under 100	97	471	6	1.38
100 under 250	100	1,388	17	1.24
250 under 500	43	1,577	19	1.18
500 under 1,000	25	1,861	22	1.16
Subtotal	500	5,351	68	1.27
1,000 under 5,000	27	4,978	54	1.08
5,000 under 10,000	5	2,545	22	0.85
10,000 under 50,000	4	5,653	38	0.68
50,000 under 100,000	.5	2,507	11	0.44
Subtotal	36	15,683	125	0.80
100,000 or over	.6	13,214	44	0.33
Total	537	$34,248	$237	0.69

SOURCE: *Press Release No. S-2808*, U. S. Treasury Department. Percentages computed from nonrounded figures.

[1] See pp. 268–271.

Some 537,000 corporations filed returns with balance sheets for 1948. But 500,000 of these—93 per cent—had assets of less than $1 million. These half million corporations made somewhat less than 16 per cent of the net profits but gave 29 per cent of the reported contributions, at a rate of 1.27 cents on the dollar of profit. (The smallest subgroup, corporations with assets of less than $50,000, would appear to have contributed at the extraordinary rate of 7.48 per cent, but this group percentage is inflated by both the deficits and the minor contributions of 109,000 small corporations which had net losses.)

Corporations of intermediate size, with assets between $1 million and $100 million, numbered some 36,000, or 7 per cent of the total. This 7 per cent had 46 per cent of the profits and made 53 per cent of the contributions at a rate of 0.8 per cent, slightly above the general average for that year.

The giant corporations, with assets of $100 million and over, numbered only 601 but realized 39 per cent of the corporate profits. Although this small group gave $44 million, or 18 per cent of the reported corporate contributions, it was at the exceedingly low rate of 0.33. Indeed, in all asset classes the rate of giving as compared with profits showed a marked descent as the size of corporation increased. The 601 giant corporations appear to have given in 1948 only one-quarter as much of their profits as the half million corporations with assets below $1 million.

These relationships were not peculiar to 1948; for example, in the last prewar year, 1941, the relationships were quite similar, though contributions for all asset groups were lower. In that year 407,000 corporations reported contributions of $57.6 million. Corporations with assets below $1 million were 94 per cent of the group, got 15 per cent of the profits, and gave 27 per cent of the contributions at a rate of 0.64 per cent of net profit. The intermediate corporations were 6 per cent in number, received 52 per cent of the profits, and gave 56 per cent of the gifts at a rate of 0.37. The very large corporations with $100 million or more in assets numbered 426, had 33 per cent of the profits, but gave only 17 per cent of the reported contributions at a rate of 0.18.

Appendix Table 42 presents similar data for 1945, the top year of corporate giving. But in that excess-profits-tax year, the large corporations came somewhat closer to the smaller ones in percentage rates.

These percentage rates, here and elsewhere, are presented with some hesitation. A railway porter was once asked by an inexperienced traveler what the average tip was. He declared it was two dollars. When he received this sum, he was profuse in his thanks, adding:

"You're the first that has come up to the average."

To establish the averages here presented for corporation giving, most corporations that give at all must give considerably more than the "average" to make up for a substantial number that give nothing, or that give, possibly generously, but fail to report those gifts so that they appear in the Bureau of Internal Revenue statistics. This happens when the gift is charged off as a business expense, in the case of "mutual" companies which have no profit item against which to charge contributions, and in life insurance companies, which fill out a different tax form where gifts are not separately reported.

On the other hand, the apparent rate of giving is increased by inclusion of both the gifts and the negative income of companies that sustained a loss in the period covered. It is for this reason that Appendix Table 42 has been presented in three sections—all returns, returns with net income, returns with no net income. In the group of smallest corporations about one-third of the 178,000 companies incurred deficits in 1945. They nevertheless reported contributing nearly half a million dollars. Both of these factors helped to increase the percentage credited to this class on the basis of all returns. The rate became 1.56 per cent, though it was only 0.93 for the profit-making corporations in this class. In other asset classes no-profit companies were much less prevalent, in prosperous 1945, and affected the averages only slightly.

Recent evidence on differences in rates of giving by size of corporation is available from our Survey covering 1950. As elsewhere explained, this sample heavily overrepresents the larger corporations (which are the smaller givers, in proportion to income) so that the year's over-all percentage is probably too low.

But the same relative decline in rate for larger corporations is indicated, and this tabulation includes not only contributions for which charitable exemption was taken, but also those made for similar purposes though charged as business expenses.

TABLE 5. CONTRIBUTIONS OF 326 SURVEYED CORPORATIONS TREATED AS CHARITABLE DEDUCTIONS OR BUSINESS EXPENSE, BY AMOUNT OF CORPORATION ASSETS, 1950[a]

Dollar figures in thousands

Asset class	Corporations returning questionnaire	Net income (thousands)	Contributions Amount (thousands)	Contributions Per cent of net income
Under $1,000	101	$5,728	$ 104	1.8
1,000 under 100,000	183	252,389	2,434	1.0
100,000 and over	42	1,066,607	4,251	0.4
Total	326	$1,324,724	$6,789	0.5

[a] Russell Sage Foundation Survey.

Number of Employees

The Russell Sage Foundation Survey also included number of employees as a criterion of size because some corporations, particularly those with branch offices, apportion their gifts by number of employees. Either criterion, assets or number of employees, may be misleading in certain cases. A corporation engaged in some kinds of finance might have very large assets and a mere handful of employees. But a messenger service run on a shoe-string might have many employees. Table 6 presents our findings on giving by corporations classed by number of employees.

Aside from irregularities in certain classes due to smallness of the sample,[1] trends in giving are in general the same as for corporations ranked by asset classes. The heaviest giving in proportion to net income is done by corporations with few employees, the least by the largest. But in number of dollars given, in this sample more than one-third of the total came from the nine corporations having 20,000 or more employees each; nearly one-half from the 17 largest corporations.

[1] And inclusion in the "under 50" class of one highly profitable financial corporation which gave nothing.

TABLE 6. CONTRIBUTIONS OF 326 SURVEYED CORPORATIONS: AMOUNT, PER CENT OF NET INCOME, AND AMOUNT PER EMPLOYEE, BY NUMBER OF EMPLOYEES, 1950[a]

| Employee class | Corporations returning questionnaire | Net income (thousands) | Contributions | | Number of employees | Contribution per employee |
			Amount (thousands)	Per cent of net income		
Under 50	35	$16,054	$41	0.3	1,145	$36
50 under 100	46	5,459	66	1.2	3,460	19
100 under 250	73	16,454	165	1.0	10,998	15
250 under 500	63	43,164	334	0.8	22,368	15
500 under 1,000	34	64,875	530	0.8	23,389	23
1,000 under 5,000	49	225,730	1,580	0.7	116,729	14
5,000 under 10,000	9	135,833	820	0.6	63,493	13
10,000 under 20,000	8	113,084	819	0.7	106,587	8
20,000 and over	9	704,071	2,434	0.3	314,165	8
Total	326	$1,324,724	$6,789	0.5	662,334	10

[a] Russell Sage Foundation Survey. Computations made from nonrounded figures.

The high contribution of $36 per employee for corporations with fewer than 50 employees is explained in part by the larger proportion of "approachable" executives in the smaller company and the probability that many closely held corporations are included. In these, personal charitable obligations or desires can sometimes be satisfied through a company contribution, which avoids also the corporation tax.

Type of Industry

Contributions vary also by type of industry, and by industrial subgroups. Part of this variation is due to conditions arising from the nature of the industry itself. Retail trade, obviously, is open to many solicitor contacts through customers, and one is not surprised to find its contribution rate high. Utilities regard as a special handicap the ruling that their contributions cannot be included as a cost in rate fixing. Some types of financial institutions, such as holding companies, have few contacts with the public and probably escape the devoted attention of most fund solicitors.

Our Survey discovered, moreover, that the amount of a contribution, and whether to contribute at all, is in many cases largely determined by the actions of other members of the same subgroup. Motor Company A calls up Motor Company B to discover what it is planning to do toward a given hospital campaign, and usually gives a proportional amount. But the contributions of Motor Companies A and B have little relation to the contributions of Chain Stores C and D, which check with each other but not with the motor companies. Conversely, the hospital solicitor is likely to report the contribution of Motor Company B (if it was generous) to Motor Company A and all other motor companies. In these ways closed cells of custom and habit grow up within each small industrial group, fixing a pattern of giving that may be quite different, in direction and amounts, from the giving of companies of similar size and profit position in other industries.

Appendix Table 41 presents full data on contributions by major industrial groups from 1936 through 1948. Lest that forest of figures conceal the major relationships and trends, Table 7 and Figure 1 present those data in condensed form for four years, showing percentage relationships.

Manufacturing. The manufacturing industries are overwhelmingly the most important, except in number. They constitute only about a fifth of the reporting companies, but include most of the very large corporations in America. In the thirteen years for which data are available, the compiled net profits of the manufacturing corporations have averaged more than 50 per cent of all corporation profit.

Contributions of manufacturing corporations have varied from a low of $10 million in depressed 1938 to $150 million in 1945. Percentagewise, these contributions were in only one year—1938 —below 40 per cent of the contributions of all corporations, and in 1944 they were 61 per cent of the total. The rate of giving has been close to the general average for all corporations—slightly less for all years through 1943, slightly above the average rate in 1944 and later years except 1948. But the outstanding fact is that manufacturing corporations account for about half of all corporation giving.

Table 8 further breaks down the major industrial classifications for the single year 1945. In that year, when the excess-profits tax was in effect, the rate of giving for manufacturing

TABLE 7. CORPORATION CONTRIBUTIONS: AMOUNT AND PER CENT OF NET PROFIT, BY MAJOR INDUSTRIAL GROUPS, 1936, 1940, 1944, AND 1948

Industrial group	Number of corporations (thousands)				Net profit (millions)			
	1936	1940	1944	1948	1936	1940	1944	1948
Mining and quarrying	14	10	8	9	$ 179	$ 207	$ 318	$ 1,153
Manufacturing	92	86	77	117	3,724	5,317	14,864	18,117
Public utilities	25	22	19	25	1,033	1,315	4,148	3,449
Trade	146	140	117	197	930	1,084	3,255	5,759
Service	60	41	35	50	10[a]	109	579	630
Finance, insurance, real estate, lessors of real property	116	143	134	161	1,848	1,280	3,115	4,683
Construction	17	16	12	23	38	68	139	577
Agriculture, forestry, and fishery	9	8	6	8	34	17	120	220
Not allocable	2	7	5	4	5[a]	49[a]	9	—[b]
Total	479	473	412	594	$7,771	$9,348	$26,547	$34,588

Contributions

Industrial group	Amount (millions)				Per cent of total				Per cent of net profit			
	1936	1940	1944	1948	1936	1940	1944	1948	1936	1940	1944	1948
Mining and quarrying	$ .7	$ .6	$ 3.4	$ 3.4	2.5	1.5	1.4	1.5	0.42	0.28	1.07	0.30
Manufacturing	12.9	18.5	142.1	119.5	43.0	48.6	60.7	49.9	0.35	0.35	0.96	0.66
Public utilities	2.9	3.7	18.2	16.0	9.7	9.7	7.8	6.7	0.28	0.28	0.44	0.46
Trade	6.4	8.5	44.9	66.1	21.4	22.4	19.2	27.6	0.69	0.78	1.37	1.15
Service	2.0	1.4	6.1	8.2	6.6	3.7	2.6	3.4	—	1.30	1.05	1.29
Finance, insurance, real estate, lessors of real property	4.3	4.9	16.3	20.2	14.3	12.8	6.9	8.4	0.23	0.38	0.52	0.43
Construction	.4	.4	2.2	4.8	1.3	1.0	0.9	2.0	0.98	0.58	1.55	0.84
Agriculture, forestry, and fishery	.4	.1	.9	1.0	1.2	0.2	0.4	0.5	1.05	0.50	0.75	0.47
Not allocable	—[c]	—[c]	.2	.1	0.0	0.1	0.1	0.0	—	—	2.16	—
Total	$30.0	$38.1	$234.2	$239.3	100.0	100.0	100.0	100.0	0.39	0.41	0.88	0.69

[a] Loss. [b] Loss; less than 1/2 million. [c] Less than $50,000.

SOURCE: *Statistics of Income*, U. S. Treasury Department, for the years indicated. Computations are made from nonrounded figures.

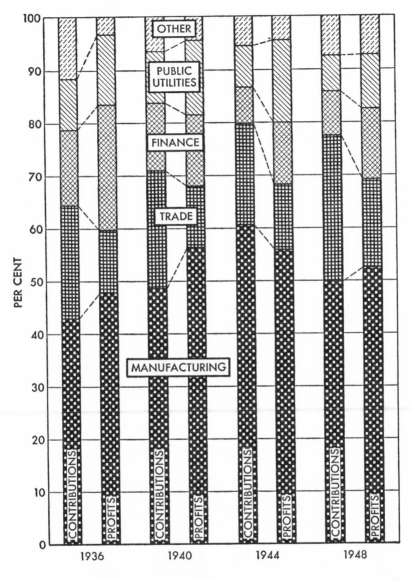

FIGURE 1. A COMPARISON OF CONTRIBUTIONS AND PROFITS OF
MAJOR INDUSTRIAL GROUPS

TABLE 8. CONTRIBUTIONS OF CORPORATIONS HAVING NET INCOME AND OF THOSE NOT HAVING NET INCOME, BY MAJOR INDUSTRIAL GROUPS AND SUBGROUPS, 1945

Dollar figures in thousands

Industrial group	All corporations filing income-tax returns				Corporations with net income				Corporations with no net income		
	Number of returns	Net profit	Contributions Amount	Per cent of net profit	Number of returns	Net profit	Contributions Amount	Per cent of net profit	Number of returns	Net loss	Contributions
TOTAL	421,125	$21,345,491	$265,679	1.24	303,019	$22,366,963	$263,390	1.18	118,106	$1,021,472	$2,289
MINING AND QUARRYING	*7,296*	*242,669*	*3,126*	*1.29*	*3,694*	*299,840*	*2,995*	*1.00*	*3,602*	*57,171*	*131*
Metal mining	848	69,050	983	1.42	205	79,325	956	1.20	643	10,276	28
Anthracite mining	148	8,301	143	1.72	85	10,267	141	1.37	63	1,966	2
Bituminous, lignite, peat	1,544	71,328	944	1.32	915	81,445	922	1.13	629	10,117	22
Crude petroleum, natural gas	3,309	59,250	672	1.13	1,722	85,943	600	0.70	1,587	26,693	71
Non-metallic	1,263	35,541	381	1.07	743	42,281	374	0.88	520	6,740	8
Mining and quarrying not allocable	184	801[a]	3	—	24	578	2	0.35	160	1,379	—[b]
MANUFACTURING	*79,112*	*10,256,776*	*149,728*	*1.46*	*61,680*	*10,582,966*	*148,802*	*1.40*	*17,432*	*326,189*	*926*
Food and kindred products	8,728	987,325	12,653	1.28	7,081	1,011,083	12,569	1.24	1,647	23,758	83
Beverages	2,591	409,087	5,676	1.38	2,082	418,403	5,642	1.35	509	9,315	34
Tobacco manufactures	210	140,722	1,401	1.00	178	140,928	1,401	0.99	32	206	—[b]
Cotton manufactures	824	277,861	6,605	2.37	766	282,318	6,604	2.33	58	4,457	1
Textile mill products, except cotton	3,579	451,121	9,624	2.13	3,141	454,280	9,608	2.11	438	3,159	16
Apparel and products made from fabrics	7,626	241,757	6,396	2.64	6,460	245,914	6,373	2.59	1,166	4,157	23
Leather and products	2,059	135,562	2,970	2.19	1,769	137,122	2,958	2.16	290	1,559	12
Rubber products	453	246,358	2,188	0.88	361	248,131	2,164	0.87	92	1,773	24
Lumber and timber basic products	2,335	115,545	1,223	1.06	1,607	123,863	1,192	0.96	728	8,318	31

	1	2	3	4	5	6	7	8	9	10	11
Furniture and finished lumber products	3,917	134,736	2,421	1.80	3,102	142,187	2,407	1.69	815	7,451	14
Paper and allied products	2,087	342,497	4,778	1.40	1,848	345,570	4,765	1.38	239	3,073	13
Printing and publishing industries	10,057	584,564	10,115	1.73	8,021	591,389	10,059	1.70	2,036	6,824	56
Chemical and allied products	6,186	1,031,585	11,387	1.10	4,414	1,060,309	11,345	1.07	1,772	28,725	43
Petroleum and coal products	442	351,935	3,622	1.03	311	371,124	3,535	0.95	131	19,190	88
Stone, clay, and glass products	2,770	211,201	3,250	1.54	1,952	224,135	3,212	1.43	818	12,934	39
Iron, steel, and products	6,526	1,242,152	18,832	1.52	5,068	1,291,163	18,730	1.45	1,458	49,011	102
Nonferrous metals and their products	2,440	268,210	4,906	1.83	1,853	276,400	4,873	1.76	587	8,190	34
Electrical machinery and equipment	1,871	594,708	7,427	1.25	1,345	619,645	7,263	1.17	526	24,938	164
Machinery, except transportation equipment and electrical	6,192	929,503	14,011	1.51	4,536	967,875	13,940	1.44	1,656	38,372	71
Automobiles and equipment, except electrical	620	170,183	1,208	0.71	501	184,628	1,204	0.65	119	14,445	4
Transportation equipment, except automobiles	1,102	1,016,643	13,399	1.32	739	1,051,409	13,373	1.27	363	34,766	26
Other manufacturing	3,951	252,539	4,078	1.61	2,853	261,180	4,047	1.55	1,098	8,641	31
Manufacturing not allocable	2,546	120,982	1,560	1.29	1,692	133,910	1,539	1.15	854	12,928	21
PUBLIC UTILITIES	*19,736*	*2,929,918*	*23,596*	*0.80*	*12,966*	*3,136,591*	*23,493*	*0.75*	*6,770*	*196,673*	*104*
Transportation	13,193	1,315,006	7,091	0.54	8,610	1,462,196	7,000	0.48	4,583	147,190	91
Communication	3,594	689,162	6,073	0.88	2,260	703,564	6,070	0.86	1,334	14,802	3
Other public utilities	2,949	935,750	10,433	1.11	2,096	970,431	10,423	1.07	853	34,681	10

TABLE 8. CONTRIBUTIONS OF CORPORATIONS HAVING NET INCOME AND OF THOSE NOT HAVING NET INCOME, BY MAJOR INDUSTRIAL GROUPS AND SUBGROUPS, 1945—(Continued)

Dollar figures in thousands

Industrial group	All corporations filing income-tax returns				Corporations with net income				Corporations with no net income		
	Number of returns	Net profit	Contributions Amount	Per cent of net profit	Number of returns	Net profit	Contributions Amount	Per cent of net profit	Number of returns	Net loss	Contributions
TRADE	120,948	3,364,059	55,634	1.65	97,550	3,440,250	55,319	1.61	23,398	76,192	315
Wholesale	35,681	1,216,288	18,543	1.52	28,898	1,249,546	18,441	1.48	6,843	33,258	103
Commission merchants	5,318	91,357	1,836	2.01	3,861	95,604	1,822	1.91	1,457	4,247	14
Other wholesale	30,363	1,124,931	16,707	1.48	24,977	1,153,942	16,618	1.44	5,386	29,012	89
Retail	71,209	1,880,527	33,601	1.78	57,682	1,922,863	33,428	1.74	13,527	33,336	173
General merchandise	5,327	956,040	17,713	1.85	4,686	958,598	17,705	1.85	641	2,558	8
Food stores, including market milk dealers	5,552	158,967	2,876	1.81	4,199	161,731	2,844	1.76	1,353	2,764	32
Package liquor stores	1,727	7,742	119	1.54	1,489	8,120	116	1.43	238	378	3
Drug stores	4,090	49,941	675	1.35	3,383	59,802	669	1.31	707	862	6
Apparel and accessories	10,220	271,509	5,333	1.96	9,072	274,103	5,321	1.94	1,148	2,594	12
Furniture and house furnishings	4,852	75,714	1,387	1.83	3,926	77,941	1,380	1.77	926	2,227	7
Eating and drinking places	9,750	67,050	957	1.43	6,719	74,166	919	1.24	3,031	7,116	38
Automotive dealers	7,847	67,505	1,004	1.48	6,205	71,784	977	1.36	1,642	4,279	27
Filling stations	1,721	13,624	75	0.55	1,182	14,395	72	0.50	539	771	4
Hardware	2,174	15,721	221	1.40	1,942	16,113	219	1.36	232	392	2
Building materials, fuel, and ice	6,955	78,793	1,291	1.64	5,723	84,082	1,275	1.51	1,232	5,289	16
Other retail trade	7,100	87,189	1,390	1.59	5,798	90,166	1,377	1.53	1,302	2,977	12
Retail trade, not allocable	3,894	39,733	560	1.41	3,358	40,863	554	1.36	536	1,130	6
Trade not allocable	14,058	258,244	3,489	1.35	11,030	267,841	3,450	1.27	3,028	9,597	39

54

	35,107	601,864	8,097	1.34	22,977	648,860	7,916	1.22	12,130	46,996	181
SERVICE											
Hotels and other lodging places	4,234	103,163	1,208	1.17	3,129	112,021	1,195	1.06	1,105	8,858	12
Personal service	7,953	54,141	1,102	2.03	5,679	59,573	1,069	1.79	2,274	5,432	33
Business service	6,628	77,597	1,131	1.46	4,080	83,423	1,086	1.30	2,548	5,827	45
Automotive repair services and garages	2,975	8,882	95	1.07	1,982	10,489	87	0.83	993	1,607	9
Miscellaneous repair services, hand trades	1,489	6,218	66	1.06	961	7,363	64	0.87	528	1,145	3
Motion pictures	3,934	265,843	2,611	0.98	3,167	273,455	2,595	0.95	767	7,612	16
Amusement, except motion pictures	3,725	69,182	1,525	2.20	1,881	74,960	1,509	2.01	1,844	5,779	16
Other service, including schools	3,981	15,796	335	2.12	2,003	25,959	287	1.10	1,978	10,163	48
Service not allocable	188	1,042	24	2.30	95	1,616	24	1.48	93	574	1
FINANCE, INSURANCE, REAL ESTATE, AND LESSORS OF REAL PROPERTY	135,573	3,688,869	22,046	0.60	90,568	3,946,823	21,522	0.55	45,005	257,954	524
Finance	32,944	1,831,276	16,706	0.91	25,600	1,896,324	16,552	0.87	7,344	65,047	154
Banks and trust companies	14,856	1,135,958	13,521	1.19	14,038	1,146,727	13,497	1.18	818	10,769	24
Long-term credit agencies, mortgage companies, except banks	2,928	279ᵃ	50	—	1,696	8,092	46	0.57	1,232	8,371	3
Short-term credit agencies, except banks	3,259	54,352	585	1.07	2,322	56,879	580	1.02	937	2,527	5
Investment trusts and investment companies	3,470	254,282	575	0.23	2,656	260,418	573	0.22	814	6,136	1
Other investment companies, including holding companies	1,839	306,877	1,176	0.38	1,388	321,244	1,172	0.36	451	14,368	4
Security and commodity exchange brokers and dealers	1,237	58,916	523	0.89	991	60,182	519	0.86	246	1,266	4

55

TABLE 8. CONTRIBUTIONS OF CORPORATIONS HAVING NET INCOME AND OF THOSE NOT HAVING NET INCOME, BY MAJOR INDUSTRIAL GROUPS AND SUBGROUPS, 1945—(Continued)

Dollar figures in thousands

Industrial group	All corporations filing income-tax returns				Corporations with net income				Corporations with no net income		
	Number of returns	Net profit	Contributions Amount	Per cent of net profit	Number of returns	Net profit	Contributions Amount	Per cent of net profit	Number of returns	Net loss	Contributions
Finance—continued											
Other finance companies	1,308	15,154	148	0.98	655	26,556	43	0.16	653	11,402	105
Finance not allocable	4,047	6,016	129	2.14	1,854	16,225	121	0.75	2,193	10,209	7
Insurance carriers, agents, etc.	7,594	1,495,555	2,023	0.14	5,529	1,523,376	1,949	0.13	2,065	27,822	74
Insurance carriers	2,002	1,467,966	1,433	0.10	1,626	1,493,534	1,379	0.09	376	25,568	55
Insurance agents, brokers, etc.	5,592	27,589	590	2.14	3,903	29,842	570	1.91	1,689	2,254	19
Real estate, including lessors of buildings	88,751	279,360	3,129	1.12	55,955	423,814	2,847	0.67	32,796	144,454	283
Lessors of real property, except buildings	6,284	82,678	188	0.23	3,484	103,309	174	0.17	2,800	20,631	13
CONSTRUCTION	11,834	112,913	1,899	1.68	7,811	146,224	1,827	1.25	4,023	33,310	72
AGRICULTURE, FORESTRY AND FISHERY	6,152	133,967	1,375	1.03	3,865	150,045	1,348	0.90	2,287	16,078	27
Agriculture and services	5,637	129,559	1,337	1.03	3,568	143,038	1,311	0.92	2,069	13,479	26
Forestry	261	506	6	1.18	145	2,564	6	0.23	116	2,058	—b
Fishery	254	3,902	32	0.82	152	4,443	32	0.72	102	541	—b
NATURE OF BUSINESS NOT ALLOCABLE	5,367	4,456	177	3.97	1,908	15,366	168	1.09	3,459	10,910	9

a Net loss. b Less than $500.
SOURCE: *Statistics of Income for 1945*, Part 2, U. S. Treasury Department. Percentages calculated.

stood at the high figure of 1.46 per cent. Among the subgroups, the highest contributions rate was recorded by "apparel and products made from fabrics" at 2.64 per cent, with several other subgroups in the clothing trades above 2 per cent. Many of these companies are small, and we have already seen that the rate of giving is higher in small corporations. In the apparel subgroup, the very liberal contributions of 1945 to the United Jewish Appeal are probably heavily represented.

The lowest contribution rates in the manufacturing category were made by "automobiles and equipment" (0.71 per cent) and "rubber products" (0.88 per cent).

Trade. Nearly a third of all reporting corporations are in the trade classification, but most of them—trade includes both wholesale and retail establishments—are quite small. Profits averaged under 15 per cent of all corporations. The contribution rate, however, is so exceptional that in all years except 1944 trade has accounted for at least a fifth of the contributions of all corporations, and in 1946 through 1948 it accounted for 27 per cent. Figure 1 shows clearly how far the contribution percentage for trade exceeds its share in corporate profits.

In all years the trade contribution rate has been substantially above the rate for all corporations. Reasons for this are not far to seek. Retail trade, in particular, has many direct contacts with its consumer-customers, who are often board members or solicitors for welfare agencies. The rewards for giving in terms of customer good will, and the penalties for not giving, are direct and important.

The detailed table shows that the rate for wholesale establishments is lower than for retail, though wholesale "commission merchants" have the highest rate in the trade category, slightly over 2 per cent. They probably are under exceptional personal pressures.

Among the retail groups, "apparel and accessories" are the highest, but all groups exceed the general average for corporations in 1945 except for "filling stations," which dropped to the extraordinary low of 0.55 per cent of profit. (Gas rationing was in effect during a large part of 1945.)

Finance. Financial institutions do not have the violent numerical fluctuations of trade corporations, but compare closely with them in number for the period 1936 to 1948 as a whole. The relative importance of financial institutions in terms of amount of profits declined during this period from approximately 25 per cent of all corporate net income to about 10 per cent in the war period and recovered slightly more recently. Contributions have not kept pace even with this profit position. In all recorded years except 1941, financial institutions as a group have contributed at a rate lower than that for all corporations. About 10 per cent— in recent years, less than 10 per cent—of all corporate contributions are reported from this group.

Table 8 indicates that in 1945, when the corporation giving rate was at the all-time high of 1.24 per cent, financial institutions averaged only 0.6 per cent. "Insurance agents and brokers" departed from the pattern with a rate of 2.14. (The few agencies listed under "finance not allocable" must be disregarded; their apparently high rate was inflated by inclusion of contributions from negative profits of more than a third of the group.) "Banks and trust companies" were close to the general corporation average, contributing $13.5 million at a rate of 1.19.

"Insurance carriers," with net profits exceeding those of the banks, report gifts of only $1.4 million at a rate of 0.1 per cent, the lowest for any group reporting. It is probable, however, that this figure is incomplete and inaccurate. The tax forms on which insurance companies report to the Bureau of Internal Revenue do not provide in the usual way for reporting contributions, and many of the larger insurance corporations are mutual companies, without "net profit," and therefore lack the usual tax advantage for itemizing contributions and gifts.

Utilities. Only about 5 per cent of the reporting corporations fall under the utilities classification, which includes transportation and communication as well as such other utilities as water, gas, and electric services. This small group of companies reports profits, however, that have in most years exceeded those of trade. Contributions by utilities have in all years been below the average for all corporations, and have been falling off considerably in relative importance. At the beginning of the period about 10 per cent of corporate contributions were made by utilities; at its close the proportion was down to 7 per cent. Utilities claim special difficulties in making charitable contributions in that such expenses are not generally allowed as a consideration in rate-making.

Although railroads were the first corporations to make substantial charitable gifts, chiefly to the YMCA, "transportation" had the lowest record among the utility subgroups in 1945— 0.54 per cent of profits.

Other Groups. The remaining industrial categories—mining and quarrying; service; construction; agriculture, forestry, and fishery; and those not allocable—receive no substantial portion of total corporate profits and the sum of their contributions has recently been only about 7 per cent of corporate gifts.

The service group accounts for about half the number of establishments in these five groups, and half the contributions. The rate has in all years been above the average for all corporations, as might be anticipated from the closeness of these companies to the consumer-customer. The 1945 detailed record shows some marked variations in service subgroups. "Amusement, except motion pictures" was highest with a rate of 2.2 per cent of net profits. "Motion pictures" were lowest, with a rate of 0.98.

Construction was above the corporate average in all years. Data from our Survey indicate that construction companies frequently contribute heavily to hospitals and other welfare agencies that have construction needs.

Mining and quarrying were close to the corporate average in rate of giving, but below it in more years than above. The same was true of agriculture, forestry, and fishery. The miscellaneous group, which could not be allocated, included in all years so many businesses showing loss that percentage figures are not pertinent.

The 1950 Survey. The sampling Survey (see Table 9) showed no marked changes among industrial categories. Because of the bias of this sample toward large companies, manufacturing is over-represented, and accounts for 47 per cent of the recorded con-

TABLE 9. CONTRIBUTIONS OF 326 SURVEYED CORPORATIONS: AMOUNT AND PER CENT OF NET INCOME, BY MAJOR INDUSTRIAL GROUPS, 1950[a]

Dollar figures in thousands

Industrial group	Corpora-tions	Net income	Contributions		
			Amount	Per cent of total	Per cent of net income
Manufacturing	182	$ 512,255	$3,159	47	0.6
Public utilities	46	242,485	979	14	0.4
Trade	33	45,863	787	11	1.7
Finance, insurance, real estate, lessors of real property	41	198,162	853	13	0.4
Other groups[b]	24	325,959	1,011	15	0.3
Total	326	$1,324,724	$6,789	100	0.5

[a] Russell Sage Foundation Survey.

[b] Mining and quarrying; service; construction; agriculture, forestry, and fishery.

tributions. But the rate of contribution was very slightly above the average for all companies. The 33 trade companies showed a remarkable contribution rate of 1.72 per cent. Utilities and finance, as in the government statistics, were below the average. The remaining categories are grouped together because of their small number; their rate is relatively low.

Geography as a Factor

A small group of industrial states in the Northeast, particularly New York, include the headquarters office of most of the large industries. Since the law requires that a corporation file its return in the collection district of its principal place of business or principal office, filings in New York State alone accounted for 27 per cent of all corporate net income in the United States in 1941 (see Table 10). Five industrial states in the Northeast— New York, New Jersey, Massachusetts, Pennsylvania, and Ohio —account for half the net income of all the states and territories. Add Illinois, Michigan, and California, and 70 per cent of the total is accounted for.

Unfortunately, the Bureau of Internal Revenue has not compiled statistics on corporate contributions and gifts by states and territories for years later than 1941, and even those data are

TABLE 10. CONTRIBUTIONS OF CORPORATIONS HAVING NET INCOME: AMOUNT AND PER CENT OF NET INCOME, BY STATE, 1936 AND 1941

State	Net income (millions)		Contributions			
			Amount (thousands)		Per cent of net income	
	1936	1941	1936	1941	1936	1941
UNITED STATES	$9,478	$18,111	$26,655	$57,227	0.28	0.32
Alabama	25	91	194	431	0.77	0.47
Alaska	1	2	2	6	0.22	0.27
Arizona	6	12	27	67	0.42	0.58
Arkansas	13	32	100	241	0.75	0.76
California	507	849	1,745	2,802	0.34	0.33
Colorado	61	74	259	295	0.43	0.40
Connecticut	144	492	468	1,508	0.33	0.31
Delaware	491	604	336	1,156	0.07	0.19
Dist. of Columbia	46	93	226	316	0.49	0.34
Florida	41	73	107	412	0.26	0.57
Georgia	64	130	168	453	0.26	0.35
Hawaii	47	55	366	606	0.77	1.11
Idaho	10	18	31	50	0.30	0.27
Illinois	793	1,479	2,239	4,987	0.28	0.34
Indiana	128	293	490	1,071	0.38	0.37
Iowa	50	83	308	495	0.61	0.59
Kansas	43	89	217	378	0.51	0.43
Kentucky	68	133	153	404	0.23	0.30
Louisiana	63	116	210	472	0.33	0.41
Maine	22	59	35	181	0.16	0.31
Maryland	125	209	431	861	0.35	0.41
Massachusetts	351	675	924	2,497	0.26	0.37
Michigan	721	1,326	2,351	3,539	0.33	0.27
Minnesota	124	205	860	1,120	0.70	0.55
Mississippi	12	25	40	137	0.33	0.56
Missouri	223	417	989	2,294	0.44	0.55
Montana	11	19	40	71	0.38	0.38
Nebraska	33	50	253	385	0.77	0.77
Nevada	12	13	75	24	0.64	0.19
New Hampshire	11	26	103	197	0.96	0.76
New Jersey	373	621	664	1,660	0.18	0.27
New Mexico	4	6	12	25	0.28	0.42
New York	2,691	4,909	4,440	11,838	0.17	0.24
North Carolina	104	221	115	423	0.11	0.19
North Dakota	3	5	26	34	0.97	0.63
Ohio	586	1,333	2,295	4,925	0.39	0.37
Oklahoma	81	117	200	293	0.25	0.25
Oregon	25	69	164	281	0.66	0.41
Pennsylvania	675	1,531	2,357	4,194	0.35	0.27
Rhode Island	40	125	295	420	0.73	0.34
South Carolina	23	86	58	147	0.25	0.17
South Dakota	3	6	25	46	0.73	0.74
Tennessee	53	109	297	590	0.56	0.54
Texas	213	369	556	1,668	0.26	0.45
Utah	17	31	59	113	0.36	0.37
Vermont	7	25	11	72	0.17	0.29
Virginia	95	217	230	622	0.24	0.29
Washington	64	183	290	521	0.45	0.28
West Virginia	53	89	250	329	0.47	0.37
Wisconsin	120	312	554	1,556	0.46	0.50
Wyoming	3	7	10	14	0.36	0.19

SOURCE: *Source Book*, U. S. Treasury Department (manuscript in files in Washington). Percentages calculated from nonrounded figures.

available only in the Bureau's manuscript *Source Book*. Table 10 compares giving with net income for corporations reporting in the various states and territories for 1936 and 1941, and the map offers the 1941 percentage comparisons graphically.

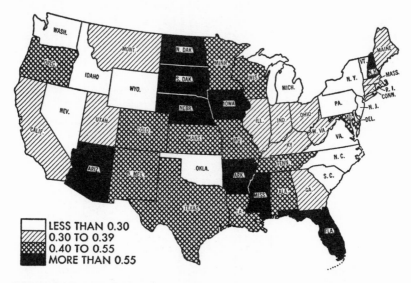

CORPORATION CONTRIBUTIONS AS PER CENT OF NET INCOME, BY STATE, 1941

It will be observed that "generosity" as measured by rate of giving is in almost inverse ratio to concentration of income. Of the eight states in which 70 per cent of the 1941 corporate income was concentrated, four are in the lowest giving group (less than 0.3 per cent) and the remaining four in the next to lowest (less than 0.4 per cent). No state in the highest group (more than 0.5) had corporate income in 1941 totaling as much as $100 million.

Regionally, the South and Middle West predominate in the two higher groups; the East and Mountain States are chiefly in the two lower groups. This is radically different from the ratios in personal giving, where high rates were "confined to the industrial East and a few southern states."[1] The geographical differences in corporate giving may be due less to regional influences

[1] *Philanthropic Giving*, p. 60.

than the already noted fact that big corporations give at lower rates than smaller ones, bringing down the rate for nearly all the highly industrialized states.

In terms of dollars, of course, corporate giving is still concentrated in the few highly industrialized states in spite of the lower rates. The eight states previously named—California, Illinois, Massachusetts, Michigan, New Jersey, New York, Ohio, and Pennsylvania—reported $36.4 million in corporate gifts in 1941, 64 per cent of the total for all the states. But it must not be assumed that the welfare agencies of these highly industrial states received all, or necessarily a large percentage, of the gifts of national corporations domiciled in them. Comprehensive data are not available, but the practices of two large corporations will be illustrative. Corporation A has its headquarters and principal manufacturing plant outside New York State; Corporation B is in New York City. Table 11 indicates the geographical distribution of their 1950 contributions.

TABLE 11. GEOGRAPHICAL DISTRIBUTION OF CONTRI-
BUTIONS OF CORPORATIONS A AND B IN 1950

State	Corporation A	Corporation B
Home state	$2,032,471	$101,875
State A	272,335	25,410
State B	174,100	6,585
State C	169,617	5,175
State D	17,750	3,535
State E	15,640	3,015
State F	15,135	2,930
State G	14,925	2,385
State H	11,825	2,035
Other states[a]	49,660	8,755
National organizations	200,696	—
Total	$2,974,154	$161,700

[a] For Corporation A, 19 other states; for Corporation B, 16.

The Nongivers

It is known that some, and possibly many, corporations make no gifts, either as a matter of policy or because of a particular financial situation. But the Bureau of Internal Revenue statistics give no hint as to how large this group is.

In our sampling Survey we made strong efforts to get reports from all corporations that fell within the sample. It became evident from the correspondence and follow-up interviews that the nongivers were resistant to our questionnaires. Even after persistent follow-up, with emphasis on the need for a full record of the nongivers as well as of the givers, we are certain nongivers are more numerous among the silent corporations than among those that finally reported. The sample is therefore biased toward givers, but the record is worth setting down.

Of 326 replying corporations, 12 reported no gifts at all—3.7 per cent. Of these, 4 reported a net deficit for the year, so that nongiving for them may have reflected no more than the financial position for one year.[1] On the other hand, two of the nongivers had net profits exceeding $6 million in 1950; another, half a million; and several others substantial income. A few added explanations: "We engage in scientific research on a nonprofit basis." "Our gifts are all personal." "We are a close corporation consisting of father and two sons, who made personal contributions in excess of $3,000 in 1950." One tried to list group insurance as a charitable contribution, but this was disallowed.

Corporation 1348 came close to the nongiver category, reporting $36 contributed out of a net income approximating $100,000; it added, "We're ashamed of this."

Generous Givers

Balancing the nongivers are a group of corporations which give far above the corporate average—some of them above the 5 per cent permitted as a tax benefit. Information on these givers is taken from our sampling Survey, since government statistics do not individualize returns.

Corporation 1899 reported contributing $252,949 with a net income of only $17,500, setting for that year an astronomical rate; this is a corporation capitalized in the "over $50 million" class, however, so that the situation is better described as a fairly normal contribution in a low-profit year.

[1] The corporation assigned Questionnaire 1313 was one of the four which came up with a net loss and no contributions.

Corporation 1707 gave $5,000 ($4,500 of it to the community chest) out of a net income of $30,000, at the rate of 17 per cent. Corporation 1797 reported $80,000 in contributions out of a net profit of $850,000—nearly 10 per cent. A construction company gave $66,000 out of profits of $1,300,000—slightly over 5 per cent.

In some of these cases it is possible that the gift was to meet an unusual need and does not represent a regular level of giving. But in the case of Corporation 1229, which gave $12,810 out of an income of $257,367, it is definitely reported that an effort is made to turn back to the community for welfare purposes 5 per cent of profits each year.

Several corporations pointed out the equivalent of liberal gifts for welfare purposes in various forms that cannot enter our statistics. Corporation 1235 considers it gave an additional $5,300 through a "33⅓ per cent charitable discount." Corporation 1028 sold $10,000 worth of merchandise "at cost to educational institutions." Several corporations reported furnishing slightly used or outmoded equipment to welfare or educational institutions without charge, and usually without entering it in the accounting.

Corporation 1246, a utility in Ohio, contributed $16,000 directly, but pointed out that "the State of Ohio has a special tax on the gross intrastate receipts of public utilities for poor relief. This tax amounted to more than $130,000 for our Company in 1950." Other corporations also indicated taxation as another form of their philanthropy. Said Corporation 1154, "Above does *not* include all kinds of taxes which are big and were sold us on the idea that it would take care of much of the private charity needs."

Among the generous must also be included the group of corporations which contributed although they suffered a net loss for the year; of course, their contribution rate cannot be expressed as a percentage of "profit." Seventeen of the 326 companies reporting in our Survey suffered a net loss on 1950 operations. Four of these, it has been noted above, gave nothing. The remaining 13 did make contributions, though usually they were not large. Corporation 1545 noted, "Operating at a loss as indicated above our contributions were naturally limited and confined to community chest and national health agencies." Corporation 1711 had a net loss of about $10,000, contributed $60, and noted that it also "carried sick benefit and hospitalization coverage on all of our employees at an expense of about $3,000 annually."

Four of the 13 corporations that contributed in spite of their deficit position did not bother to report these contributions as such in their corporate returns (where they would have had no tax advantage since there was no tax to pay); this is evidently a source of understatement of corporation contributions in the federal statistics, though the total so omitted is probably not large. Contributions of these four totaled $796. Contributions of all 13 corporations in the loss column totaled $10,305, an average of less than $800 each.

Gifts and Business Cycles

The increasing proportion of support that many social agencies now receive from corporations is viewed with concern by some agency executives. If a depression comes, will this corporate support drop severely or even vanish, just when the needs of such agencies become greatest?

We raised this question in many of our interviews with corporation executives. It was a problem nearly all of them had at least considered, and usually they were verbally reassuring.

"We do not tie our contributions to the profit position," said one. "We give in proportion to the need, as we see it. If we had to cut back, contributions would be one of the last items we would cut." Several companies have established corporation foundations primarily to level out their contributions over the good and bad years.

These are the answers, however, of only a few of the more thoughtful corporate givers. The dangers to philanthropic agencies of this close tie to the business cycle are probably real. No major depression has occurred since comprehensive data on corporate giving have become available, but the shreds of evidence are worth examining.

It has already been pointed out[1] that in the 1922 depression the record of a very few chests indicated a 20 per cent decline

[1] See p. 35.

in corporate contributions; that in the great depression in the 1930's, corporations apparently responded the first year or two to special drives, but may have fallen off later in contributions. Comprehensive statistics begin in 1936, when recovery was already well under way.

However, a minor recession occurred in 1937–1938. The compiled net profits of the reporting corporations dropped from $7.8 billion in 1937 to $4.1 billion in 1938, a decline of 47 per cent. Corporate contributions declined, not quite so sharply, from $32.7 million to $27.2 million—a drop of $5.5 million in one year, or 17 per cent. The following year both profits and contributions were back to substantially the 1937 levels.[1]

Another clue to what may happen may be derived from the data already referred to in Appendix Table 42, showing contributions in 1945 by asset classes, both for corporations with net profit and those without net profit. Table 12 averages the reported gifts of these two groups for each asset class.

TABLE 12. AVERAGE REPORTED CONTRIBUTIONS OF CORPORATIONS HAVING NET PROFIT AND OF THOSE NOT HAVING NET PROFIT, BY AMOUNT OF CORPORATION ASSETS, 1945[a]

Asset class (thousands)	Corporations having net profit	Corporations not having net profit
Under $50	$32	$7
50 under 100	106	14
100 under 250	258	28
250 under 500	642	77
500 under 1,000	1,257	73
1,000 under 5,000	2,634	169
5,000 under 10,000	6,743	201
10,000 under 50,000	15,972	1,138
50,000 under 100,000	41,700	833
100,000 and over	121,701	3,267

[a] Calculated from Appendix Table 42.

The most favorable record for companies with net loss was made by the smallest companies, those with assets under $50,000. In this class those that made a profit contributed an average of $32; those with a net loss gave $7, or more than one-fifth as much.

[1] See Table 3, p. 42.

But in the larger companies the contributions are smaller in comparison with assets and the falling off in a loss year is much more severe. In the $50 under $100 million class the companies showing a loss do not give a fifth as much as the profit companies —they give less than a fiftieth!

This table probably overstates the case. A corporation with a net loss is not entitled to any contribution deduction, since 5 per cent of a zero net profit is zero. Many of them, obviously, continue to list their contributions either through habit or in the mistaken hope of increasing a loss carryover. But probably others, particularly large corporations whose returns are prepared by skilled accountants and tax lawyers, do not enter contributions even though made. Therefore the drop in size of the average contribution in a nonprofit year is probably not so severe as this table suggests.

But this conditional and other direct evidence indicate a situation potentially dangerous. It merits further study on the part of both corporations and welfare agencies, and planned efforts to level off this threatening cyclical fluctuation.

Where the Gifts Go

Corporation income-tax returns itemize contributions and gifts, but the Bureau of Internal Revenue publishes no analysis of these items and the returns themselves cannot be examined. A few organizations such as the American National Red Cross and most community chests separately record corporate contributions, but many others do not.

Until the present Survey, general information on fields supported was available only in the annual survey of the National Industrial Conference Board, and this was confined to a varying number of large manufacturing corporations and was not conducted after 1948. Figure 2 presents the Conference Board data for 1948.

Our questionnaire[1] classified contributions under four main fields—welfare agencies, health agencies, education, and religious agencies—with subclassifications under the first three. In

[1] See pp. 265–266.

tabulating, a fourth category, miscellaneous, was added to care for the amounts corporations could not fit into the classifications provided and for corporations unable or unwilling to classify contributions. Fortunately, such cases were few; the small proportion finally showing up in miscellaneous is another testimony to the excellent cooperation we had from the responding corporations.

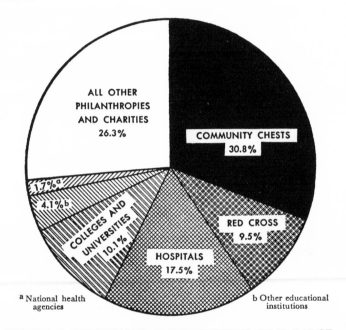

FIGURE 2. CHARITABLE CONTRIBUTIONS OF 79 LARGE
MANUFACTURING CORPORATIONS, 1948
SOURCE: *Business Record,* National Industrial Conference Board, January, 1950.

The resulting analysis of contributions in 1950 appears in Table 13 and Figure 3. As already pointed out, limitations in response and in the character of the random sample itself prevent using these 326 corporations as necessarily a true sample of all corporations. But this is probably the largest and the most nearly representative analysis of corporate contributions which has been made. A comparison of these data with the National Industrial

Conference Board survey indicates few marked differences, when changes in categories are taken into account.

The final two columns of the table analyze contributions of 73 large corporations, 59 of which appeared within the Survey sample, the remaining 14 being other large corporations from

TABLE 13. RECIPIENTS OF CONTRIBUTIONS OF 326 SURVEYED CORPORATIONS AND OF 73 LARGE CORPORATIONS, 1950

Recipient class	326 surveyed corporations[a]		73 large corporations[b]	
	Amount	Per cent of total	Amount	Per cent of total
Welfare agencies				
Community chests	$2,455,479	36.2	$3,428,434	22.3
Other welfare agencies	553,498	8.1	1,229,538	8.0
Total	3,008,977	44.3	4,657,972	30.3
Health agencies				
Hospitals	1,005,348	14.8	1,288,814	8.4
National health agencies	692,760	10.2	997,885	6.5
Other health agencies	106,110	1.6	513,117	3.3
Total	1,804,218	26.6	2,799,816	18.2
Education				
Scholarships and fellowships	187,546	2.8	319,625	2.1
Research in colleges	419,753	6.2	565,990	3.7
Institutional aid, schools and colleges	524,170	7.7	1,058,644	6.9
Agencies supporting "the American way"	305,965	4.5	477,976	3.1
Total	1,437,434	21.2	2,422,235	15.8
Religious agencies	278,037	4.1	510,046	3.3
Miscellaneous and unclassified	260,663	3.8	4,967,992	32.4
Total	$6,789,329	100.0	$15,358,061	100.0

[a] Russell Sage Foundation Survey.
[b] Each having assets of over $50 million.

which data were obtained in the course of interviews or correspondence. Differences in the giving pattern of "all corporations in the sample" and the 73 very large corporations are due chiefly to the increased miscellaneous item. Several of the largest corporations found it impossible or not desirable to itemize their contributions. If this $5 million undistributed item can be assumed to have fallen in the same proportions as the remainder,

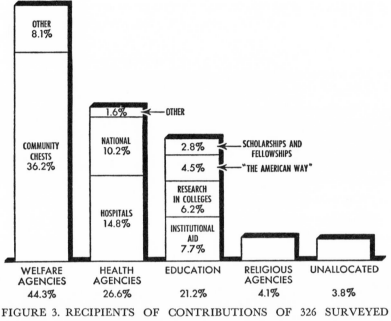

FIGURE 3. RECIPIENTS OF CONTRIBUTIONS OF 326 SURVEYED
        CORPORATIONS

then the big corporations show no marked divergences from the total group.

The distribution of corporate gifts is discussed and more closely analyzed in Part II, dealing with corporate beneficiaries.

CHAPTER 4

Budgets and Quotas

H OW MUCH should a corporation give? A few corporations would shorten that question to: Should a corporation give?—and answer it in the negative. But for the many companies that regard giving as a community responsibility (or even a public relations and business opportunity) and desire to discover their share, difficult questions remain.

Should giving be proportioned to profits? Is the number of employees a measure of community responsibility? What about the company with branch plants or sales offices? Should giving be guided by need, and if so, who determines that need among the various petitioning agencies? How reasonable are the company quotas set by community chests and by some of the larger national agency drives?

The Record on Budgets

Many companies have not considered their contributions program with the care it has begun to deserve. The president of a nationally known corporation laid before us a list of his 1950 contributions and then, at our suggestion, called for his 1940 record.

"Why," he exclaimed, "I had no idea how our contributions have grown, or the new directions they've taken!"

Except possibly in its candor, his statement would not be unique. The giving program of many corporations has grown by bits and pieces, each new year largely duplicating the past year, but with additions due to new pressures. The program has seldom been considered as a whole.

Relatively few companies set up a contributions budget. Item 17 in our questionnaire read:

We $\frac{do}{do\ not}$ include an item for contributions at the beginning of our budget year.

Thirty-three companies did not report on this item. Of the remaining 293 only 98, about one-third, reported budgeting for contributions. It might be anticipated that the larger companies would be more likely to set up a contributions budget than smaller firms. This was true up to the $50 million class; few large companies reported budgeting for contributions; none, actually, in the $100 million group. The record in this respect is shown in Table 14.

TABLE 14. CONTRIBUTIONS AS A BUDGET ITEM IN SURVEYED CORPORATIONS, BY AMOUNT OF CORPORATION ASSETS, 1950[a]

| Asset class (thousands) | Number of corporations | | | | Per cent reporting contribution budget |
	Reporting contribution budget	Reporting no contribution budget	Not replying to this question	Total returning questionnaire	
Under $500	8	52	2	62	13
500 under 1,000	10	27	2	39	26
1,000 under 5,000	31	48	6	85	36
5,000 under 50,000	41	34	6	81	51
50,000 and over	8	34	17	59	14
Total	98	195	33	326	30

[a] Russell Sage Foundation Survey.

Some of the companies having no budget item for contributions use as their guide the practice of preceding years. Says Corporation 1570:

We do not budget our corporate gifts in advance but a careful record of all contributions during the year is made and through the experience of prior years we are able to anticipate fairly accurately the demands which will be made upon us in any year. Of course, special situations arise each year which are not recurrent but in most cases, especially those of a local nature, we know of these long in advance and through our record of previous years we are able to control the over-all amount of contributions.

On the other hand, mere existence of a budget item for contributions does not ensure fresh consideration each year, or even that the company will adhere to the budget. But at least one responsible officer, and more probably a committee, has had the matter specifically called to mind.

Corporations with Branches

Giving is additionally complicated for corporations that have branch offices, production plants, or sales offices in a number of cities. In many cases, for public relations and other reasons, it is important that the actual contribution be given from the branch office to the local solicitor, though the amount may have been determined and possibly the check written in the main office. A troublesome question is the proportion that should be given from the national office, and from local offices or plants.

In an effort to discover current practice our questionnaire included this special section:

For corporations with local branches

21. We distribute our contributions approximately ....% from the national office, ...% from local offices or plants.
22. Within the local budgets, decision of the local management is final for
    ☐ all amounts; ☐ amounts not exceeding $..............
23. The size of the local contribution budget is determined primarily by
    ☐ relative business; ☐ number of employees; ☐ ....
    (specify)

Sixty-eight corporations completed the branch-office section of the questionnaire. Table 15 presents their answers to the three questions.

All but three of the reporting corporations with branches take pains to distribute at least a portion of their philanthropies through local plants and branch offices. Indeed, five companies report all payments through local branches with none made from the national office. But in dollar amounts nearly half the companies—27—report 20 per cent or less distributed from the branch office, and most of the remainder, not more than 50 per cent. It is clear from the table that the central office pays out most of the charitable funds.

The local plant or sales manager has considerable autonomy in deciding where the gifts should go. In 26 companies his decision is final for all amounts, though he may be limited by an over-all annual total. In 13 additional companies he need not refer proposed contributions unless they exceed at least $100, and in one case, $2,500. Fifteen other companies require referral of quite small contributions, and ten give him no discretion without

TABLE 15. CONTRIBUTION POLICIES OF 68 SURVEYED CORPORA-
TIONS HAVING LOCAL BRANCHES, 1950[a]

Number of corporations making specified replies to three questions concerning policies

1. PROPORTION OF TOTAL CONTRIBUTIONS DISTRIBUTED FROM BRANCH OFFICES							
None	Per cent					Proportion varies	Question not answered
	1 to 20	21 to 49	50	51 to 99	100		
3	24	12	10	11	5	1	2

2. SIZE OF CONTRIBUTION FOR WHICH LOCAL MANAGEMENT DECISION IS FINAL								
None	Amounts not exceeding					All amounts	Other replies	Question not answered
	$5 to 50	$100	$200 to 250	$500	$2,500			
10	15	7	4	1	1	26[b]	2[c]	2

3. FACTORS CHIEFLY DETERMINING PROPORTION OF LOCAL CONTRIBUTIONS[d]		
Proportion of total business	Proportion of total employees	Other factors
41	24	27

[a] Russell Sage Foundation Survey.
[b] Four of these specified "not exceeding budget."
[c] One replied "most"; one, "no policy."
[d] Some corporations specified several factors.

referral to the central office. One company, conceding unusual authority to the local sales manager over both the direction and the total amount of charitable gifts, points out that undue generosity will probably be prevented by the fact that the manager's own annual bonus is dependent on the net profit of his branch, and contributions are a charge against that net profit.

The size of the contribution of the local office is determined chiefly by its relative business position in the company, 25 companies considering only this factor. The remaining 16 of the 41 companies checking this factor consider also other elements in the situation, including number of employees. Twenty-four companies are influenced by the number of their employees in given localities, though this is seldom the sole factor.

The "other factors" are too diverse for tabulation, but they can be illustrated. Eight companies mentioned as important factors the local conditions, needs, and campaign quotas. Four companies were influenced by "amounts given by other firms" and "contributions of other utilities in the same territory." Four companies looked largely to benefits for their operations, specifying "public relations," "extent to which Company is benefited by charities included in the local budget," and "growers' and trade relations." Three companies were guided by their own prior year's contribution. One company gave locally "only as a matter of pressure." In another, each subsidiary was allotted the same amount; in still another, length of time the branch was in operation was a decisive factor.

Corporation 3020 takes the following factors into consideration in determining its share in the budgets of local organizations:

a. Position of the Company in the community

b. Record of previous payments

c. Payments to similar organizations in other communities

d. Assessed value of the Company's real estate in relation to total assessed valuation in the community

e. Amounts subscribed by the Company's employees, as an indication of their interest in the project

f. The extent of participation by other industrial companies, large and small

g. Total budget or amount being raised in the community

h. The generally large expenditures by the Company in the community for employee benefits, life and other insurance, plant hospital facilities, etc., which tend to relieve the burden on welfare organizations

Corporation 3015 finds its local contributions affected by another powerful factor:

Our contributions are large because of the heavy competition in contributions with local merchants who are able to make personal contributions through their stores and thereby deduct corporation tax. The chain stores are very conscious of the need for good local relations in view of the many bills, federal, state, and local, constantly being directed against chain store enterprises. Our state trade associations, designed to look after general store interests for all companies, spend much of their time keeping chain stores in line as heavy contributors.

Quotas Set by Outside Agencies

Frequently the corporate giver discovers that the soliciting agency has very definite ideas as to the amount of the gift. These ideas may be no more than hopes, or they may be based on intricate quota calculations, weighted for the general state of industry, importance of the particular industry in the community, and the relative position of the given company in that industry. In many cities such quotas are set by community chests, sometimes with the cooperation of industrial leaders; and less frequently by large independent drives.

A strong case can be made either for or against such quota systems, even when the solicitor adopts the softer, less compulsive term, "yardstick for corporation gifts." In the past, many corporations have resisted. Quotas in definite mathematical terms smack of taxation and lend themselves to pressure tactics. Facts gathered to support them invade what some companies still regard as private information on their operations, profits, and relative standing. If quotas are high, resentment is aroused and few corporations take them seriously. If they are minimal with a view to gaining acceptance from most corporations, the large, pace-setting gift is discouraged and probably lost. Because of the many complicating factors, no quota system has yet been devised which will be agreed upon as fair to all companies. Finally, the "lift" which should spring from voluntary giving is lost in mathematical formulas and questions of duty.

The International Harvester Company, in instructions to managers, puts it this way:

> As a matter of policy, we will not accept suggested formulas prepared by some organizations as a means of determining how much we should give. We do not believe any such formulas can work

equitably for all types of businesses in the community. We will listen to suggested formulas, but all contribution solicitors should be frankly told the Company cannot follow them.[1]

Nevertheless, quota systems are spreading, often with the encouragement of corporation executives. If the cause is a genuine community responsibility, most companies desire to do their share and they welcome assistance in finding out what that share is. In the absence of an accepted yardstick, they are subjected to all sorts of pressures and squeeze plays from important customers or others whom they must not offend. And it is easier to explain a gift to stockholders if it has been made in line with a communitywide plan including all other companies. But the yardstick must be a reasonable one, and the building of such yardsticks for corporation giving is still only in the experimental stage.

Chapter 2 reported for the drives of World War I a few attempts at quotas, based usually on a percentage of net earnings. But profits as a sole criterion are dangerous; they tie giving to the business cycle and fail to recognize other important factors. Many later attempts at refinement have been made. Chain stores have sometimes budgeted 0.1 per cent of gross sales to be contributed through division or unit managers. Attempts have been made at setting standards for chest contributions for individual industries, such as $2.50 per room for hotels, $1.00 for each $2,500 of sales in department stores, $25 per million in deposits for savings banks, or from $5.00 to $30 per employee in various industries. Two recent efforts at finding an acceptable yardstick may be worth detailed examination.

The Los Angeles "Fair Share" Quota Plan

The Los Angeles Community Chest, preparing for its 1950–1951 campaign among corporations, has done one of the most thorough research jobs[2] in this field in the country. First, the

---

[1] *International Harvester Contributions, Policies, Procedures.* Issued by International Harvester Contributions Committee. Reprinted in full in Appendix F, pp. 330–336.

[2] Prepared by Robert R. Dockson, economist, the Prudential Insurance Company of America, and submitted to the writer, with helpful comments, by Guy Thompson, campaign director for the Chest.

Chest determined the campaign goal for the whole community. Then, on the basis of comparative statistics for chests in other large cities and in consultation with some corporation leaders, it settled upon 35 per cent of this total goal as the corporation quota—a compromise between the 42.4 per cent raised from corporations in big chests and the 31.7 per cent of recent Los Angeles experience. This resulted in a dollar total to be raised from corporations of $2,750,000.

The 121 separate "industry sections" represented in Los Angeles were then examined with respect to ability to contribute (measured by their profit) and responsibility to the community (measured chiefly by number of employees). Community profit data, not generally available, were computed from the United States Department of Commerce national figures for each industry; the number of local employees was obtained from a community survey. The "ideal" distribution of corporation contributions for Los Angeles resulting from the profit and employee factors, given equal weight, appears in Figure 4 by major industry divisions.

But, as data elsewhere in this study indicate and as the Los Angeles executives knew from their records, different kinds of industry have not been contributing in "ideal" proportions, and it was not to be expected that the wide differences could be ironed out in a single year. So, in addition to *ability* and *responsibility, inclination* to contribute was made a factor; indeed, the main factor. The actual contribution in dollars of each industry section in the 1949 campaign was taken, and slightly adjusted up or down in accordance with the current level of activity in that industry.

In dollar figures the yardstick worked out this way in Los Angeles. The 1949 contributions of all corporations to the Community Chest were $2,058,102. Adjusted for current economic conditions, which for most industries showed a slight improvement, this "intermediate quota" rose to $2,120,274. But the 1950–1951 quota had been set at $2,750,000. The difference of about $630,000 was apportioned among the various industries on the basis of the "ideal" distribution—profits and number of employees. This meant that no industry group was asked to

FIGURE 4.

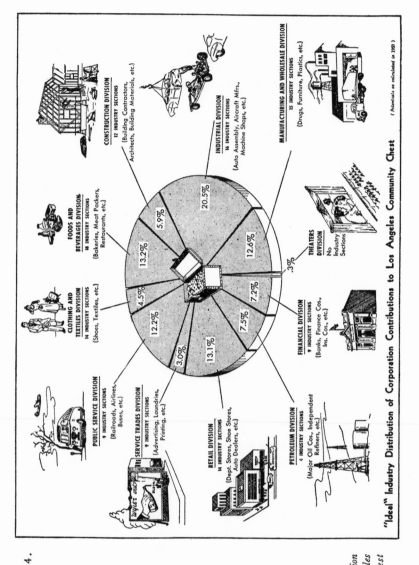

CONSTRUCTION DIVISION
12 INDUSTRY SECTIONS
(Building Contractors, Architects, Building Materials, etc.)

INDUSTRIAL DIVISION
16 INDUSTRY SECTIONS
(Auto Assembly, Aircraft Mfrs., Machine Shops, etc.)

MANUFACTURING AND WHOLESALE DIVISION
15 INDUSTRY SECTIONS
(Drugs, Furniture, Plastics, etc.)

FOODS AND BEVERAGES DIVISION
18 INDUSTRY SECTIONS
(Bakeries, Meat Packers, Restaurants, etc.)

CLOTHING AND TEXTILES DIVISION
14 INDUSTRY SECTIONS
(Shoes, Textiles, etc.)

THEATERS DIVISION
No Industry Sections

PUBLIC SERVICE DIVISION
9 INDUSTRY SECTIONS
(Railroads, Airlines, Buses, etc.)

SERVICE TRADES DIVISION
9 INDUSTRY SECTIONS
(Advertising, Laundries, Printing, etc.)

FINANCIAL DIVISION
9 INDUSTRY SECTIONS
(Banks, Finance Cos., Ins. Cos., etc.)

RETAIL DIVISION
14 INDUSTRY SECTIONS
(Dept. Stores, Shoe Stores, Auto Dealers, etc.)

PETROLEUM DIVISION
7 INDUSTRY SECTIONS
(Major Oil Cos., Independent Refiners, etc.)

20.5%
5.9%
13.2%
12.6%
4.5%
12.2%
.3%
3.0%
13.1%
7.5%
7.2%

(Potentials as calculated in 1951)

"Ideal" Industry Distribution of Corporation Contributions to Los Angeles Community Chest

change drastically its previous-year contribution, but the changes, up or down, were largest, percentagewise, for the industry groups farthest from the "ideal" yardstick. The final total was called the "fair share" quota, and within each industrial division it was divided among individual companies in accordance with formulas developed within those trade sections, usually by the industrial leaders themselves.

An element of this plan's design is that, if adhered to, it will gradually bring the contributions of the industrial sections closer and closer to the "ideal" proportions. The campaign in the fall of 1950 raised among corporations $2,257,787, which was 82 per cent of the goal of $2,750,000 and a 9.7 per cent increase over 1949.

The Greater New York Fund Yardstick

The "chest" situation in New York City presents difficulties. New York is headquarters for many large corporations having branches in other cities, which greatly complicates the question of responsibility of these national organizations for local welfare services. (One large corporation with assets in the many millions and employees in the tens of thousands has its head office but only four employees in New York City; what are its responsibilities toward local welfare?) Also, New York does not have a true community chest. The Greater New York Fund solicits from corporations and employee groups, not from individuals in their homes. However, the Fund can be said to function as a true chest for the publicly owned corporation, with which we are here chiefly concerned.

The Fund estimated the "need" of its 423 agencies (budgeted expenditures less income from sources such as client payments and endowment) at $45 million for 1951. Corporate income being just less than a quarter of national income, the share of publicly owned corporations was tentatively set at $10 million. But since corporations had contributed slightly less than $3.7 million the previous year, to triple the goal was obviously unrealistic for a single year, and it was decided that the 1951 goal should be $7 million. How should this goal be apportioned?

The Fund's booklet, *Yardstick for Giving*, explains the complicated formula adopted for New York's unusual situation, where national companies might have few production employees but a heavy managerial overhead. Briefly, an attempt was made to estimate productivity value per production employee for each industrial group, and this value was multiplied by the total number of employees, production or managerial, in these groups in New York City. These totals for all industrial groups were then related to the total corporation goal. In certain fields such as mutual insurance companies and banks other formulas had to be improvised.

By this process the corporation goal of $7 million was apportioned to each industry division in the form of a dollar total. Previous giving, the factor assigned most weight in the Los Angeles formula, was given no weight at all in the New York formula, though the facts were set off in an accompanying table. Discrepancies were wide. The publicly owned electrical corporations, which gave only $36,000 in 1950, were asked to give $195,000 in 1951—more than five times as much. Casualty and surety companies, with quotas set by number of employees, were asked to increase their gifts more than 13 times the 1950 amount. On the other hand, both the rubber and the telephone and telegraph industries found their 1951 quotas working out to less than they had given in 1950.

Once dollar totals had been assigned for each industry division, the breaking down of that total for individual companies was left to the industry itself, with advice from the Fund statisticians. A usual formula (identical with the Los Angeles "ideal" formula for industry division proportions) was to weight equally the profits of the company and its number of employees. In other words, if Company A in the chemical group had 5 per cent of the profits of that group but only 1 per cent of the employees, its quota was 3 per cent of the total assigned to the chemical group. Of course, extreme cases developed where the formula could not be applied; it was not used at all for companies with fewer than 25 employees in New York City.

The amount raised from corporations in New York City did not come close to the yardstick goal of $7 million; it was $4.1 million. But this represented a substantial increase over the $3.7 million of 1950.

Self-established Quotas

In practice, most companies set giving quotas of some sort, sometimes quite formally based upon area sales and total sales, number of employees, net profit, or still other factors and combinations of factors; sometimes by sheer force of precedent.

As we have seen in the preceding chapter, actual practice has varied widely. Over the years for which records are available, a steep rise in the average for all companies has occurred. For all years, fairly consistent variations among the different types of business appear. Within a particular trade or industry, variations among companies are even more wide. Clearly, practice is not yet stabilized and corporations are still feeling their way.

The general trend since 1936 has been sharply upward in dollar amounts and substantially upward in proportion of net profit.[1] From 1936 through the first war year, 1942, the reported amount of contributions rose from $30 million to $98 million, but the percentage of net profit was 0.41 for the seven years as a whole and very close to that figure for each of those years except 1938, a year of depressed income. From 1943 through 1945, the height of the war effort, most corporations greatly increased their gifts under the combined stimulus of wartime appeals, high profits, and heavy taxes. The amount rose to a peak of $266 million in 1945 and the rate to 1.24 per cent of compiled net profit. With the repeal of the excess-profits tax both amounts and rates descended again, but by no means to the levels of the 1930's. Government figures extend only to 1949, with a rate of 0.78; our sampling Survey suggests that the rate was probably somewhat lower by 1950. But in 1951 an excess-profits tax was again in force and it is probable that both amount and rate have again risen. This increase in giving in the past fifteen years undoubtedly

[1] See Table 3, p. 42.

corresponds in general with the experience of most individual companies.

Substantial variations have also been pointed out among asset classes and different types of corporations. In general, large corporations give a lower proportion of income than small companies. Business enterprises close to their customers, such as trade and service companies, give more liberally than the others. These differences are probably largely due to appraisal in the various segments of industry of the practical value of such gifts in the corporations' own interests. In part, they may reflect habit and precedent, with little recent rethinking of the whole problem.

The greatest differences, of course, are in the practices of individual companies. These are obscured in statistical summaries, and can be discovered only by interview and individual case studies. Our Survey disclosed a number of companies, in a variety of businesses and asset classes, that gave nothing at all as a matter of considered policy. On the other hand, a few gave the full 5 per cent for which tax deductibility is allowed, and a very few gave more than this. But not many corporations have thought the question through and set a quota for themselves. Even where philanthropy is a budget item, the amount appears to be set usually by experience of the year just past and the anticipated "demands"—rather than any self-sought opportunities—of the year ahead.

New ferments, however, are working. Our Survey came upon several other efforts at finding the facts in this area, some of them conducted by single companies for the confidential information of their officers in arriving at a more informed policy on giving. The American Society of Corporate Secretaries issued a *Corporate Contributions Report* in 1950. The National Industrial Conference Board holds three conferences a year on donations and its report, already noticed, listed these "ten factors which managements usually consider when authorizing charitable donations":

Business Conditions. Profits; business outlook; dividend record.

Precedent. Size of past donations; past relations with solicitor.

Legal Restrictions. Federal tax regulations; state laws; corporate by-laws.

Gifts of Other Companies. Competitors; leading companies; companies of similar size; number of companies in community.

Employees. Number of employees in community. Benefit to employees; interest of employees; employee gifts.

Sales Volume in Community.

Assessed Value of Property in Community.

Soliciting Organization. Importance of its work; extent to which it operates locally; character of its appeal; aims; quality of administration.

Budget of Organization. Character of other contributors; Better Business Bureau evaluation; amount to be raised; likelihood of meeting its goal.

External Pressure or Commercial Advantage. Interest of large customers in solicitation; "social blackmail."[1]

In August, 1951, the Business Committee of the National Planning Association issued a report urging business to consider the full 5 per cent of net income allowed as a tax deduction as a desirable quota for gifts and contributions, at least under present tax rates. Said the Committee in a resolution accepting the report:

> The substantial increases in net corporate earnings and in tax rates are making it desirable for American business to reappraise its policy with respect to tax exempt expenditures for educational, scientific and welfare purposes. Hitherto, these expenditures have been a great deal smaller than the potential total of five percent of net corporate income before taxes which is exempted for these purposes under the existing revenue laws. But, in the new situation, business management will recognize increasingly the direct and indirect benefits which it can obtain through well organized and soundly conceived expenditures of this type on a broader scale.[2]

The authors of this report, Beardsley Ruml and Theodore Geiger, suggest that "A dollar wisely and soundly invested in worthwhile educational, scientific and welfare activities comes back manyfold over the longer term. . . . Like investment in

[1] *Company Policies on Donations: II.* Written Statements of Policy. National Industrial Conference Board, New York, 1950, p. 11.

[2] Ruml, Beardsley, and Theodore Geiger, *The Five Percent.* Planning Pamphlet No. 73. National Planning Association, Washington, 1951, p. viii.

new plant and equipment, they more than repay their cost in the future and can be among the most productive and remunerative forms of business expenditure."[1]

Contributions are a minor part of corporate expenditures, but their growing importance in public relations and in the promotion of many direct corporate objectives has induced many corporations to consider afresh their proper place in the total budget.

[1] As we go to press the National Planning Association is making an impressive contribution to literature in the field in its *Manual of Corporate Giving*, edited by Beardsley Ruml in collaboration with Theodore Geiger, The Association, Washington, 1952.

CHAPTER 5

Administration

$\mathbb{A}$LTHOUGH gifts and contributions are not, dollarwise, a major item in the budgets of most corporations, their potentialities for creating good will or ill will and the difficult problems they sometimes raise make careful administration important. Present practice varies from the one-man decision, characteristic of most small companies and some large ones, to the special committee, the philanthropic specialist, and the separate corporate foundation. No one pattern will be satisfactory for all companies, but exploring recent experience may prove useful.

Who Considers Appeals?

We asked the responding companies these questions about authority to act on appeals:

12. Requests for contributions are referred to (title or titles)......
    ....
13. Contributions of $........ or more require special action by
    ....

Answers to Question 12 appear in Table 16. Seventeen of the 326 corporations did not reply to this item.

In the corporations studied requests for contributions go to one person in nearly 90 per cent of the companies. This person is the president himself in one-third of the cases, and in another third the president or, if he is occupied, another top officer. The concentration of this duty in the hands of the president alone is, as might be expected, more pronounced in the small than in the larger companies—46 per cent of companies with assets below $1 million, against 20 per cent of the group with assets of $50 million or more.

TABLE 16. OFFICERS OR COMMITTEES TO WHICH CONTRIBUTION REQUESTS ARE REFERRED IN 309 SURVEYED CORPORATIONS[a]

| Officer or committee | Number of corporations | | | | Per cent of all corporations replying to questionnaire |
	Assets under $1 million	Assets 1 under 50 million	Assets 50 million or over	Total	
Officer					
President	42	52	12	106	34
President or other top officer	25	49	26	100	32
Treasurer	12	22	3	37	12
Secretary	7	12	0	19	6
Other top officer	1	9	4	14	5
Subtotal	87	144	45	276	89
Committee					
Contributions committee	1	1	8	10	3
Finance committee	0	4	2	6	2
Board of directors	1	4	2	7	2
Subtotal	2	9	12	23	7
Local or district manager	3	4	1	8	3
Other	0	1	1	2	1
Total	92	158	59	309	100

[a] Russell Sage Foundation Survey.

Other top officers given sole responsibility for this function are 37 treasurers and 19 secretaries. Less frequent choices (included in "other top officer" in Table 16) are six vice-presidents, of whom one is in charge of public relations; in two cases, the chairman of the Board; a personnel manager; an assistant to the president; an assistant to the vice-president; a director of public relations; a director of customer relations; and a head bookkeeper—who "follows a procedure established by formula."

The committee procedure is followed by only 7 per cent of the companies, most of these in the largest category. The advantages of contributions committees have been so widely discussed in corporation circles that it has been assumed they are a usual pattern in most larger companies; but in this study only 10 such committees were found altogether, and even in the largest companies, only 8 among 59 companies. In addition, occasionally the finance committee, or even the Board of Directors itself, undertakes these duties.

Eight companies delegated their giving to local or district managers. Another, a holding company, reported giving nothing from its own profits, but passed on all requests to its subsidiaries, which were in direct contact with customers. Still another forwards all requests for contributions to its corporation foundation. This and other uses for business foundations are discussed in the next chapter.

Although the shaping of the giving program is in the hands of one individual in the overwhelming majority of the companies, this decision is often not final, at least for larger amounts. One hundred and seventy-one companies reported that confirming action is sometimes required.

Table 17 indicates that many corporations require confirming action on contributions, at least on those of larger amounts. Most of the big corporations that specified amount were satisfied to apply such checks only on three-figure contributions—seven of them merely on contributions of $5,000 or more. Smaller corporations make few or no contributions of this size, and may require special action on much smaller amounts. Most of those that did not specify amount probably require a routine check on all contributions. The extreme in this respect was reported by Corporation 1999, whose president was required to review all contributions of $1.00 or more; his review must have been severe, for out of a net income of nearly $500,000 in 1950, no contributions whatever were made.

In nearly half the cases, the Board of Directors was the referral body, acting in all seven cases where the amounts referred were $5,000 or more. The president functioned in a little more than a fifth of the companies, the executive committee in another fifth.

TABLE 17. SIZE OF CONTRIBUTIONS REQUIRING SPECIAL ACTION IN 171 CORPORATIONS AND OFFICER OR COMMITTEE ACTING ON LARGE GIFTS IN 174 SURVEYED CORPORATIONS[a]

	Number of corporations				Per cent of total
	Assets under $1 million	Assets 1 under 50 million	Assets 50 million or over	Total	
Amount requiring special action					
$50 or more	6	10	2	18	11
100 or more	8	21	8	37	22
250 or more	4	6	1	11	6
500 or more	2	15	7	24	14
1,000 or more	1	7	6	14	8
5,000 or more	–	–	7	7	4
Not specified	12	36	12	60	35
Total	33	95	43	171	100
Officer or committee acting on large gifts					
Board of Directors	12	42	22	76	44
Chairman of Board	1	4	0	5	3
President	12	20	6	38	22
Executive Committee	5	17	13	35	20
Finance Committee	1	3	2	6	3
Treasurer[b]	1	2	1	4	2
Stockholders	1	1	0	2	1
No provision	2	6	0	8	5
Total	35	95	44	174	100

[a] Russell Sage Foundation Survey. Three corporations furnished information only for the second portion of this table.

[b] In one case, vice president if budget is exceeded.

An Integrated Program

It is evident from this showing, and from our interviews and correspondence, that corporate giving is not at present a carefully considered, integrated program in most companies. Only 30 per cent of the companies set up a contributions budget at the beginning of the year. The "program," if it may be called that, is usually last year's contributions plus a few new items based on spot decisions of the president or another chief officer made in time he is able to borrow from his ordinary and urgent duties. Further referral of the larger contributions is not uncommon, but the referral body or person appears usually to act as a watchdog of the treasury rather than a board of strategy for creative and effective giving.

Some companies feel that their improvised methods for handling contributions are not adequate, and are considering changes. Our Survey asked for this information:

19. We $\frac{are}{are\ not}$ considering changes in our present policies and procedures on philanthropic contributions.

Eighteen companies replied that they were currently considering changes. Of the remaining 308, negative replies came from 292 and 16 did not answer, but may be presumed to be among the negatives. All 18 companies considering changes were in asset groups of $500,000 or more—all but 4 of them in the $1 million or more categories.

If corporate giving, whatever its amount, is to bring maximum benefit both to the corporations themselves and to their communities, administrative procedures need to be adopted that look toward integrated, purposeful programs. What that procedure should be depends in part upon the character of the corporation and its particular personnel, but some of the practices in this field are worth setting down. Questions of ultimate policy are discussed later; we are concerned now with mechanics.

Processing Charitable Appeals

Requests for funds come by mail, by telephone, through personal visits to chief executives in their offices or homes, and across the counter from customers in some retail and service establishments. In all but the smallest communities these solicitations are so numerous and varied that no one person, and certainly not the busy president, can be well informed on all the community agencies and needs involved, not to mention the many national and special appeals. A procedure for processing them is needed.

Many companies require that all appeals be put in writing—both as a matter of record and in order to reduce the danger of rackets—and route these to one individual, who becomes a part-time, or in a few cases a full-time, expert in philanthropy. He maintains records from year to year, accumulates knowledge and files on particular charities and types of appeals, and becomes familiar with various information agencies.[1]

In a large company this may be a full-time job, meriting the employment of an expert in the field. The Standard Oil Company (New Jersey) was one of the earliest to develop such specialized service, but a number of others have followed. One large New York corporation hired a man with previous experience in social work who pointed out that duplicating payments were being made to several agencies that were soliciting both independently and through a federated fund. Another corporation, upon centering this function in one person, discovered that as many as six different appeals from the same agency were received, often being handled in different offices. Better acquaintance with the soliciting agencies may also result in positive benefits to the company:

> To obtain the maximum value from organizations we support, I recall that when we made our initial contribution to the New York Public Library Reference Department, I worked with the Library personnel gathering material which would describe the facilities they have available for use. This was put in the form of a circular letter and distributed to all of our department heads, as well as our domestic affiliates. This is done wherever possible on organizations which can provide services that are deemed useful to our Company.[2]

When this function is part-time, the person handling it may be one of a considerable variety of company officials. The corporation secretary inherits this duty so frequently that the American Society of Corporate Secretaries published in 1950 a *Corporate Contributions Report*, outlining the policies of its members. The treasurer or assistant treasurer is sometimes chosen; his experience in interpreting financial statements can be useful, but only if he regards his duty as much more than that of watchdog. Several corporations have placed this function squarely in their public relations department. The person chosen usually handles both contributions and memberships; the procedures are similar,

[1] On information agencies and racket avoidance see Chapter 8.

[2] Address by Claude L. Alexander, of the Standard Oil Company (New Jersey), on "Problems and Practices of Corporate Giving," sponsored by the Public Relations Society of America, November, 1950.

and many memberships are at least borderline contributions, though others are outright business expenses.

The larger corporations, which may need to act upon several hundred appeals a year, usually develop a record card for each such appeal. Figure 5 is a composite of a number of such cards, suggesting data that may be desired.

The Contributions Committee

Although only 3 per cent of the corporations in our Survey sample had special contributions committees, such a device has much to commend it and is being increasingly adopted in the larger companies. Possibly the first such committee was the General Electric Company's Committee on Payments to Organizations, set up about 1925. Now called the Subscriptions Committee, it consists of the secretary of the Company, the vice-president in charge of employee and community relations, the vice-president in charge of public relations, and the vice-president in charge of customer relations.

Such a committee consists usually of from three to six members. In the larger companies it may employ an executive secretary or "leg-man" who initially receives all appeals, gathers pertinent facts, conducts routine correspondence, keeps the records, and makes recommendations. The committee itself sits weekly, biweekly, or monthly to take action on the appeals presented and to consider general policy. Its decision is usually final except for very large amounts, or those which would exceed the budget. In smaller companies one of the members of the committee takes care of the preliminary processing.

Composition of the committee is important. Its decisions affect customer relations and company standing in the community quite out of proportion to the relatively small sums it administers. The General Electric committee, described above, suggests most of the types of interest that are represented—the company viewpoint, employee relations, customer relations, the general public, and the local community. Many companies also include the treasurer or budget director, for office convenience, and sometimes the president or his direct representative.

[FACE]

Name of organization....................................

Address...

Date organized................Gifts deductible?...........

In community chest or other united fund?..................

President........................Paid staff head..........

Solicitor(s)...

Purpose of organization................................

....

....

Gift for current expenses?..........Capital funds?...........

Reason for Company interest?...........................

Other companies contributing...........................

Report on organization................................

    by..

[BACK]

FINANCIAL DATA

Year	Previous year			Current year				Our gift		
	Total expenditures	Spent on administration	Present endowment	Total budget	From fees, interest, etc.	From chest	To be raised from gifts	Amount asked	Amount approved	Date paid

FIGURE 5. SUGGESTED RECORD CARD FOR CONTRIBUTION
APPEALS

The Standard Oil Company (New Jersey) has a six-man committee employing a full-time executive secretary; the committee consists of the executive assistant to the president, the assistant to the chairman of the Board, the secretary of the Company, the head of the public relations department, the director of budgets, and the head of the employee relations department.

In one large corporation the chairman of the Board reported spending as much as 40 per cent of his own time on contribution matters. This is unusual; but a contributions committee should be so constituted as to ensure breadth of vision and authority to formulate new policies.

Legal and Tax Aspects

It will often be profitable and sometimes is essential to have gifts reviewed by someone familiar with legal and tax aspects. If the gift directly benefits the corporation, it may sometimes be taken under Section 23(a) of the Internal Revenue Code as a business expense instead of under Section 23(q). Gifts in products, or gifts in the form of appreciated assets, have special advantages under some circumstances. Chapters 13 and 14 discuss these problems in greater detail; the point here emphasized is that the administrative setup should provide for careful review of these factors.

The Question of Public Relations

The private donor has been enjoined to "let not thy left hand know what thy right hand doeth, that thine alms may be in secret." His giving is to proceed out of pure altruism, with no thought of credit or direct advantage to himself. But if we accept the premise that the giving of corporate funds is not even permissible legally unless the corporation benefits, a very different policy results. Of course, the gift should be soundly made so that it will genuinely help the person or institution who receives it, with an ultimate benefit to the corporation, but the favorable public opinion created by knowledge of the gift may be the most important benefit. Corporations seldom hide their philanthropic light under a bushel, and it is no accident that their contributions committees usually include the director of public relations.

Said one company operating a chain of food stores:

> We get more advantage out of giving a $20 basket of groceries to the Ladies' Aid of a local church than from $1,000 to the X—— Agency. More of our customers know about it.

Publicity has also its dangers, as Corporation 1297 found out:

> When we first began business, we made contributions to various organizations, but soon found that it was very difficult and detrimental to our public relations to try to choose and pick organizations to receive donations. On one occasion a rumor was out that we donated to a high school band, whereupon many other of the 24 high schools in the area sent delegates to collect money for their band as they explained that if we gave to one they realized that we would have to give to all.

If favorable publicity is to result from the giving program, good administrative practices are important. Requests for contributions should be received courteously and handled promptly. Someone should have time and facilities for investigating each proposal so that the company's money may be spent effectively and its name may not be associated with dubious enterprises. If a gift is made, it should be given graciously and in as personal a manner as possible. When a refusal is in order, grounds of the refusal should be stated if the request was made personally. Consistency in company policy should be maintained so that refusals will not appear arbitrary or capricious.

Where branch offices or plants are involved, even if the central office determines and appropriates the whole amount, many companies divide the national contribution into local checks, to be distributed by the branch manager directly to his community agencies or local branches of national agencies. When this is done, purely mathematical divisions of the total based on branch business or number of employees must sometimes be modified. Corporation 3015 considers that "the extent to which the drive is organized and supported locally should determine whether the store should contribute, and the amount of contribution." Another corporation, which had decided upon 40 cents per employee as the local contribution in a certain national drive, discovered that "this raised a howl from certain small stores where obviously they could not contribute 80 cents for two employees; a minimum of $25 was set."

Plant Solicitation of Employees

In World War I it was not unusual for job workers, salaried employees, and the company treasury to make a joint contribution to some chosen charity, all in the name of the company. This practice roused heated objection from labor, and it exists today only in rare exceptions. But labor is a large contributor to philanthropic causes, and philanthropic agencies in increasing numbers try to solicit these contributions in the work place.

Employee giving is not properly a part of corporation giving, and appears nowhere in our financial summaries. It nevertheless has become a major problem in many plants in terms of permission for such solicitations within the plant, requests for payroll deductions, and time consumed. We therefore included two items on employee solicitation in our questionnaire so as to explore present practices:

25. We $\frac{do}{do\ not}$ permit plant solicitation of employes. If YES, we limit such drives to .... per year.

26. We $\frac{do}{do\ not}$ make payroll deductions for charitable contributions. If YES, we limit them to ....
    smallest amount
    per..
    week, month, etc.

All but 13 of the companies in our main sample responded to this question, so that the record shown in Table 18 may be regarded as substantially complete.

Nearly two-thirds of the companies—65 per cent—permit charitable solicitations within the plant. But this is less frequently true in small companies than in large, with size measured by number of employees. More than half the companies with fewer than 100 employees forbid plant solicitation. No company in this sample with 20,000 or more employees forbade such solicitation, and only 17 of the 106 companies with 500 or more employees—16 per cent—put up that barrier.

TABLE 18. POLICIES ON EMPLOYEE SOLICITATION AND PAYROLL DEDUCTION FOR CHARITABLE CAUSES IN 313 SURVEYED CORPORATIONS[a]

Policy	Number of corporations by number of employees								Per cent of total
	Under 100	100 under 250	250 under 500	500 under 1,000	1,000 under 5,000	5,000 under 20,000	20,000 or more	Total	
EMPLOYEE SOLICITATION:									
Permitted									
One drive only	4	11	7	3	5	6	1	37	12
Two drives only	12	16	17	15	17	3	5	85	27
Three drives	2	3	3	3	5	–	–	16	5
Four or more drives	2	2	1	2	1	2	–	10	3
No limit, or not qualified	12	6	9	5	5	2	–	39	12
Own solicitation committee	3	5	1	3	3	1	2	18	6
Total permitted	35	43	38	31	36	14	8	205	65
Not permitted	41	28	22	2	12	3	–	108	35
Total	76	71	60	33	48	17	8	313	100
PAYROLL DEDUCTION:									
Permitted									
Minimum $1.00	5	8	10	5	9	1	–	38	12
Minimum 50¢	1	2	2	1	5	1	–	12	4
Minimum 25¢	–	3	–	1	5	–	–	9	3
Minimum 10¢ or 5¢	2	1	–	2	1	2	1	9	3
No minimum or not qualified	13	24	21	9	11	6	2	86	27
Other[b]	4	3	2	–	4	–	–	13	4
Total permitted	25	41	35	18	35	10	3	167	53
Not permitted	52	29	26	15	12	7	5	146	47
Total	77	70	61	33	47	17	8	313	100

[a] Russell Sage Foundation Survey. Although answers concerning each of these policies were received from 313 corporations, only 309 supplied information on both.
[b] Explained in text.

But the picture changes radically when one looks at the conditions under which drives are permitted. All of the larger companies put strict limitations on in-plant drives. Two of them specified that only their own solicitation committee was permitted to act. All the rest limited drives in any year to not more than two. Where two drives were permitted, they were usually in behalf of the community chest and the Red Cross. Many of the smaller companies did not limit the number of drives, or had no settled policy.

Companies are somewhat less generous in permitting payroll deductions for contributions; 53 per cent of the sample were willing to make such deductions, many of them under special conditions only. Size of company was here not so clear a pattern. The largest and the smallest companies were the two groups in which less than 40 per cent permitted deductions. The record was better than 50 per cent for all other groups, rising to 74 per cent for companies with between 1,000 and 5,000 employees.

Many companies put a lower limit on the sums they will deduct, 38 of them refusing to deduct less than a dollar at any pay period. Fifty cents, 25 cents, and 10 cents were breaking points for additional companies. A few set up other types of restrictions on deductions. Three will deduct only for a drive conducted by the plant's own solicitation committee. Corporation 1236 will make a deduction only once during a year; Corporation 2110 limits them to two payments; Corporation 1434, to one-twelfth of the annual pledge.

Deductions are usually made in behalf of a specific organization, most frequently the community chest. But in a few companies the accumulation goes toward a common fund ("a company sponsored community chest" Corporation 1519 calls it) administered by a committee of employees, or employees and management. Corporation 1027 describes such a plan:

> Employee contributions are made to the ————— Company Employee's Community Services Fund. All employees give to it. Disbursements to various local fund appeals are made by a committee of employees. We find that this procedure has been most satisfactory.

Corporation 1410 has a similar plan administered "by a committee representing the employees and Company," set up in 1950 by a joint committee of the labor union and management. "The purpose of the plan," writes the committee of this Community

Service Fund, "is to enable each employee to contribute on a payroll deduction basis a small amount each week for local charities and emergency relief and do away with all requests for donations within the plant."

Uniformity does not exist with respect to either employee solicitation within the plant or payroll deductions. Some companies believe that all such plans are too much like taxation, taking personal choice and the voluntary spirit out of giving. They may also lend themselves to abuse in actual, or suspected, pressure by management, overenthusiastic foremen, or labor itself. Says Corporation 1035:

> We do not permit plant solicitation of employees even though we are frequently subjected to pressures from soliciting organizations. The fact that some companies do so makes our position more difficult. However, it is the policy of our Company that no management representative make individual solicitation of employees for gifts to any cause. This policy is based on the sincere belief that any solicitation by management may result in action by an employee that he would not voluntarily wish to take, but which he would feel forced to take rather than risk the displeasure of the management solicitor. Our Company feels that we have served the cause well if we give every opportunity for bulletin board display and the display of circular material for any drive which we have chosen to assist.

At the other extreme is a company which sets up a definite "general schedule for payroll deductions" worked out to the penny for each job classification, and with "$\frac{1}{3}$ of 1% of salary" for salaried employees and "1% of monthly salary" for officers and other key employees.[1]

Another company has a unique plan for contributions to the community chest which is not quite payroll deduction. Employees are permitted to work on a Saturday, when time-and-a-half is in effect, with the regular time (eight hours' pay) going to the community chest, and the overtime (four hours' pay) going to the employee. "This has worked out very well and the employees look upon it with great favor," reports this company.[2]

[1] Cited in *Corporate Contributions Report.* American Society of Corporate Secretaries, New York, 1950, p. 26.

[2] *Ibid.*, p. 31.

CHAPTER 6

Corporation Foundations

SOME CORPORATION foundations are simply a device for the more orderly handling of the multiplying charitable requests; others are philanthropic banks, making it possible to level off contributions between good and bad years; still others are beginning to reach out into imaginative, experimental programs related to the company's special interests and resources. They are becoming numerous; we found nine in our Survey sample, all in corporations with assets of one million or more. If this average of 4 per cent prevails among the 37,000 corporations in these asset classes, there may be as many as 1,500 business-related foundations in the United States at the present time.

The Foundation Idea

A philanthropic foundation may be defined as a nongovernmental, nonprofit organization having a principal fund of its own and established to maintain or aid social, educational, charitable, or other activities serving the common welfare. Its predecessors, which were usually endowments for limited purposes, existed from earliest history, at some periods in considerable numbers.[1] The special ingredient which distinguishes the foundation in the American understanding of the name is wide freedom of action. With a very few exceptions, such organizations have arisen only in the United States and nearly all of them within a half century.

[1] For a more extensive discussion of foundations, their history, organization, and methods of operation see Harrison, Shelby M. and F. Emerson Andrews, *American Foundations for Social Welfare*, Russell Sage Foundation, New York, 1946.

All the large, earlier foundations were established by individuals out of their own personal wealth. That wealth came from profits of industry (the various Carnegie benefactions from steel, the Rockefeller Foundation and General Education Board from oil, for example), but the industry did not itself contribute any funds and the foundation had no connection with the industry except, sometimes, as a large stockholder.

Such foundations were and are effective instruments for the giving of personal fortunes. They could be set up so that only the income would be spent; or both income and principal, at the discretion of the trustees; or the spending of the whole corpus could be made obligatory within a stated period, as was the case with the Rosenwald Fund. The donor could narrowly limit the field of operation, but most of them wisely made only general provisions, leaving broad powers to the trustees for adjustment to changing conditions and needs. These foundations have an enviable record of accomplishment and leadership in their first half-century, though their funds have actually not been large. We estimated in 1950 that 1,007 known private foundations had only about $133 million to spend,[1] as compared with the $239 million in corporate gifts in the latest year of record. But such foundations represent the venture capital of philanthropy, and with their accumulating knowledge of how to give and by applying their funds at strategic places, particularly in research, they have made outstanding contributions in such fields as medicine, public health, education, social welfare, and economic research.

Enter Business

Even in the earliest days of foundations some individuals, setting up a foundation, desired it to benefit especially their business, or employees in that business. The John Edgar Thomson Foundation, established in 1882, is a special trust to be applied to the education and maintenance of the daughters of deceased railroad employees, with preference in the following order: first, daughters of men killed in performance of their duties while working for the Pennsylvania Railroad; next, the Georgia Rail-

[1] *Philanthropic Giving,* p. 93.

road; then, affiliated lines of the Pennsylvania system; finally, any railroad within the United States. The Altman Foundation was established in 1913 by Benjamin Altman to promote the social, physical, or economic welfare and efficiency of the employees of B. Altman and Company (New York department store), but also "to aid charitable, benevolent or educational institutions within the State of New York."

Sometimes the purpose was even more directly related to business. The James F. Lincoln Arc Welding Foundation conducts research in arc welding. The Statler Foundation was established by Ellsworth M. Statler for research for the benefit of the hotel industry in construction and operation of hotels and in training hotel workers.

In recent years of heavy corporate, personal, and estate taxes the tax-exempt position of foundations lured many businessmen into uses of this device with tax savings rather than philanthropy as the primary objective. Some of these uses grew into severe abuse, and resulted in passage of the Revenue Act of 1950 which taxes against foundations their unrelated business income, regulates leasebacks, and denies tax exemption if income is unreasonably accumulated or certain "prohibited transactions" are undertaken.[1]

This chapter does not deal with the many types of foundations that were created in the war and postwar period with tax avoidance primarily in mind; most of them have been shorn of their special advantages, and many have been abandoned. We are concerned here with the organization and operation of corporation foundations set up primarily as an aid to orderly and effective giving.

Advantages of Corporation Foundations

A corporation foundation is a legal entity separate from its parent company, though it often has a board of trustees chosen from the officers and directorate of the company. To set up and administer such a separate organization involves some expense and trouble; what compensating advantages does it offer?

[1] See Chapter 14 and Appendix B.

Flexibility in timing gifts is one major advantage. Many corporations do not know until nearly the close of their fiscal year what their profit position will be, or—in these years of retroactive tax legislation—what tax rates will apply. For the many companies whose giving is affected by their profit position, amounts cannot be finally determined until profits are known near the end of the year, and then there may not be time for wise philanthropic choices and needed investigation. But if a company foundation exists, the total amount can be turned over to it in one lump sum for more leisurely final disbursement.

This flexibility may be of financial advantage to the corporation:

> Corporation A desires to make annually a contribution of $10,000 to its local community chest without regard to its profit position. In 1952 it has normal profits, and contributes $10,000 at a tax saving of the 52 per cent corporate income tax, or a net cost of $4,800. In 1953 it experiences a bad year, with no net profits. It contributes $10,000, but with no tax advantages.
>
> Corporation B desires to make identical contributions and has identical profit experience. But it has a company foundation to which it contributes $20,000 in profit-year 1952. The foundation pays the community chest $10,000 in 1952 and in 1953, but the company has been able to deduct the whole amount in its taxable year and has saved its stockholders $5,200 over Corporation A.

Flexibility may be of even more importance to social agencies. They are aware that in a severe recession many corporations would not follow the plan of Corporation A and give in spite of losses; contributions would be severely cut or completely eliminated, at the very time when demands on the agency were highest. Any device that prevents this dangerous tie between corporate giving and the business cycle by leveling off income from this source is welcomed. Some quite informal arrangements have been made. One community chest in Ohio reports it holds $714,000 "in trust and escrow," built up chiefly by corporations in good years when they had the ability to give and could take maximum tax advantage, with a "gentleman's agreement" that it would be held for a lean year when the chest was in need and corporations less able, or unable, to contribute.

The corporation foundation is a more logical and convenient device for achieving this desirable end. The International Harvester Company established the International Harvester Foundation primarily as a "peaks and valleys" foundation, in order that funds could be accumulated in years of good business results to take care of giving in periods of poor business, when appropriations from the Company would necessarily be reduced.

National companies incorporated in states with state corporation taxes have sometimes found that their contributions were deductible under the state tax only if made to a charitable agency within that state. A company foundation incorporated in that state fulfills the necessary condition, and the contribution it receives may later be more widely distributed. Gifts to individuals become deductible when made through a foundation.

Corporation foundations offer also administrative advantages. Requests for contributions are channeled to the foundation, relieving business executives of the chores of acknowledging and handling, and reducing the "heat" put upon them by personal solicitors. Such requests can be effectively checked in an office set up for that purpose, under an executive who devotes much or all of his time to such tasks. Budgeting is a simpler matter when all recurring drives and most emergency causes can be provided for with one annual appropriation and it is not necessary that this appropriation be wholly used within a single calendar year.

If the corporation wishes to embark upon a program of original and creative giving, advantages of which are discussed in the next chapter, a corporation foundation offers a favorable climate. The foundation can include among its trustees one or more outside experts from the chosen field, affording wider knowledge and inspiring public confidence. The foundation can hire paid staff suited to its special undertakings. It can accumulate contributed funds where this is necessary either for a large initial expenditure or to ensure continuance.

Setting Up a Foundation

A variety of legal procedures are available for setting up a corporation foundation. By far the commonest form of organization, however, is incorporation under the laws of a particular state.

The laws of incorporation for charitable organizations differ widely in the various jurisdictions. The incorporators are usually the original members of the board of trustees (or a part of that board, to be filled out later). In a corporation foundation most or all of these trustees are selected from among the officers and directors of the company. If a substantial part of the foundation's activity is to be in the field of employee welfare, an employee representative may be desirable; and one or more public representatives, who may be specialists in some field of particular interest to the foundation, will add breadth of knowledge and increase public confidence. A board of from 5 to 12 members, depending upon the size of the foundation and the complication of its program, will provide variety in points of view without being too large for efficiency. The original board has usually power to fill vacancies and possibly to expand the board membership. Election may be for life, or depend upon holding a specific office in the company, or be for a stated term, often of three years with times of election arranged to overlap.

In a very few general foundations trustees are paid, but such practice is frowned upon as not necessary and not in the public interest. Payment is even less desirable in a corporation foundation, where most of the trustees are already receiving salary or other substantial income from the company. The foundation is the corporation's good citizenship program, and it is essential that no suspicion exist that any individual is personally profiting from this function. Expenses in attending meetings may properly be paid, and the trustees have power to employ whatever professional or secretarial help is needed for the proper functioning of the organization.

The statement of purpose should be broad, to permit the wide changes in scope and activities which experience and new conditions may make desirable. If a statement of specific immediate purposes is important, it may be presented in nonbinding language in a letter of gift, or even an instrument of trust, thereby avoiding the dangerous rigidity and binding restrictions that might follow inclusion of such a statement in an instrument of incorporation.

Corporate charters, to avoid possible question as to their tax-exempt status, often follow closely the wording of Section 101(6) of the Internal Revenue Code[1] or similar sections in the laws of their state defining a charitable corporation. Appendix E[2] presents a sample charter. The charters and other basic documents of 18 general foundations are reprinted in *Charters of Philanthropies.*[3]

To establish tax exemption for a foundation, its officers file with the Collector of Internal Revenue for its district an affidavit or questionnaire, together with a copy of the articles of incorporation, declaration of trust, or other similar instrument, a copy of the bylaws or other code of regulations, and the latest financial statements. The Treasury Department, if satisfied, will confirm by letter the tax-exempt status. Usually such a ruling is obtainable after twelve full months of actual operation.

Many general foundations have been set up in perpetuity, or at least with heavy restrictions on the expenditure of the original corpus. This does not seem appropriate for corporation foundations, which are primarily instruments for current giving. The sample charter has therefore provided power to disburse income or principal.

The Charitable Trust

Some companies have achieved most of the purposes of a foundation through the device of a charitable trust. If funds contributed to such a trust are to be tax-deductible, they must be committed irrevocably to charitable purposes. Such a trust need not claim exemption under Section 101(6) but can file under Section 162(a).

Under some circumstances the income of such a trust will, however, be taxed to its creator. This may occur if the corpora-

[1] Presented in Appendix B, p. 276.

[2] See pp. 328–329.

[3] Chambers, M. M., *Charters of Philanthropies*. Carnegie Foundation for the Advancement of Teaching, New York, 1948.

tion keeps substantial administrative control, such as voting stocks held by the trust or closely controlling its investment, or if power to revest principal or income to the grantor remains in the hands of the grantor or of any person not having a "substantial adverse interest." Legal advice should be sought on these complicated questions.

Some corporations have set up such trusts within the local community trust or in a bank. In the community trust, actual final authority for disbursement resides in the trust's distribution committee, though the donor's wishes are almost invariably followed. A tax-free irrevocable charitable trust established in a bank can be disbursed as to either principal or income at such times and for such charitable purposes as the corporation, or a committee it selects, may elect, but the funds need not be paid out in the year of receipt. Such a trust is established by a simple form of trust agreement, and the bank collects a fee for acting as trustee and preparing necessary reports. Several large banks recently broadcast to corporations an invitation for the establishment of trusts of this kind.

Such trust agreements can be set up speedily and they free the corporation officers from details of investment, accounting, and reporting to the government. These are substantial advantages where the program is not broad enough to warrant the wider freedoms available under the incorporated foundation.

Administration of Foundations

If the incorporated foundation is the form chosen, some thought must be given to administration. The problem will vary with the size of the foundation and with the type of program it desires to conduct.

A program confined to making grants is relatively simple, and requires a minimum of staff. The small corporation foundation will conduct such a program without any paid staff. The trustees decide on the sums to be disbursed, and probably the company contributes the needed secretarial help. But for effective distribution of larger sums at least one paid staff member is desirable, to conduct necessary investigations into the merits of appeals, handle correspondence, appraise accomplishment, and be the eyes of the foundation, seeking out new opportunities for useful social "investment" of its gifts.

A few corporation foundations conduct special programs of their own, in such fields as research, service, scholarships, or employee welfare. A small permanent staff may then be desirable, and for particular projects, outside organizations or individuals may be retained. Where choices among recipients are involved, it is important from the public relations point of view that they be made objectively, with no suspicion of personal influence. For example, the Ford Motor Company Fund grants scholarships to some of its employees' children; but the winners are determined on the basis of the scholastic aptitude test with final selection by the Ford Scholarship Board, composed of outstanding educators.

Examples of Corporation Foundations

It is already obvious that corporation foundations are widely varied in legal form, purpose, organization, and methods of operation. Some are not foundations at all, but pure trade associations or other business combinations assuming the name for the dignity it carries. Probably most company foundations lack any large corpus, serving chiefly as channels for current giving with only enough accumulation to even out the lean years; in this they differ radically from the traditional foundation, which was usually established with a large original gift, making grants from the income of this endowment.

Even the donor may vary. Many corporation foundations receive income not only from the corporation, but from officers and chief stockholders; this is frequently true in closely held corporations, where the foundation serves as both a family and a corporation foundation. In the case of the Henry L. Doherty Educational Foundation, the employees of the Cities Service organization are contributors, with Cities Service Company approximately matching their contributions; 105 scholarships were awarded for 1950–1951.

Corporation 2034 is wholly owned by one family. It contributes to a combined family and corporation foundation:

> The Fund was set up in 1941 by members of the family and the bulk of its funds have come from that source, but over the years we have also made some rather substantial corporate contributions. One of the objectives in doing this was to set up a Fund which would be ready to maintain corporate giving responsibility in bad years. The existence of the Fund also permits some indirect corporate giving which would not otherwise meet corporate policy.

The Rich Foundation of Atlanta received a small endowment from members of the Rich family but its operating income is mainly from profits of the department store of that name. However, not all giving is done through the Foundation:

> The Foundation was organized mainly to differentiate between the constant, recurring calls upon the store and long-range development programs. The store, in the main, still carries these recurring calls from the community and the Foundation gifts thus far have been mainly in the direction of education and health programs.
>
> Among the large gifts from the Foundation have been a building to house the Emory University School of Business Administration here in Atlanta; a radio station for the city, county and surrounding communities owned and operated by joint boards of education; and an out-patient clinic for the Georgia Baptist Hospital. These grants have totaled around a half million dollars in the past few years. The Foundation is at present restricting its grants to programs in the Atlanta area.[1]

Says Corporation 2031:

> The principal purpose of the Foundation is to permit the A—— Corporation to participate in various charitable activities on a uniform basis irrespective as to whether the profits of the corporation would warrant such activity. In addition we have found that referring all the requests for contributions to the directors has developed in a more equitable distribution of available funds.

The Nutrition Foundation presents still another variation, with support coming from a large number of corporations. At the beginning of 1952, 77 food manufacturers, related companies, and some individuals had contributed a total of $4.2 million to

[1] Letter from Raymond R. Paty, director of the Rich Foundation, to the author.

the Nutrition Foundation for basic research and education in the science of nutrition. Its board includes both food industry executives and representatives of the public; leading nutrition authorities and other scientists serve on its advisory committees.

One corporation took a substantial block of its excess profits in 1945 and set up a "foundation"—actually a trust fund—within the community trust of its city. In this instance final rights over distribution rest with the community trust distribution committee, but in practice the expressed desires of the corporation have always been followed and its officers have no doubt that this will remain the case. No additions have been made to this fund, which is dwindling every year.

A few corporations have used their foundations to initiate and carry on imaginative programs especially related to their own interests, or to improve living standards in special ways. One of the projects of the Sears-Roebuck Foundation, supported entirely by Sears, Roebuck and Company, is the "Cow-Hog-Hen" program which gives purebred livestock to clubs of farm youngsters to improve and diversify livestock in their communities.

The Bulova Watch Company, one of the few corporations which does give substantially 5 per cent of its net income before taxes, has set up the Bulova Foundation from contributions of the Company and some of its chief officers. The Foundation has established the Joseph Bulova School of Watchmaking in Woodside, Long Island. This handsomely appointed school accepts only disabled veterans, whom it trains free as watch repairers. A large proportion of them are paraplegics (wheel-chair cases) and the School has its own wheel-chair basketball team. At the close of its first five years, in the summer of 1951, it had graduated 346 men, 95 per cent of whom were gainfully employed, chiefly in retail jewelry stores. The Bulova Watch Company does not itself employ these graduates. This is an example of corporation giving that is contributing to the national economy by returning to self-support and taxpaying status some hundreds of men who might otherwise have remained a public charge, and is paying vastly greater dividends socially, in giving this courageous group a new stake in living.

Additional examples could be cited, but most corporation foundations are still in the stage of functioning as a mere administrative convenience in channeling gift requests, or as philanthropic banks, leveling through good and bad years the ordinary contribution program. If they are given imaginative direction and some freedom to experiment, corporation foundations may become pioneers and pathfinders in corporate giving, finding ways of applying corporate gifts that will bring increased credit to business and larger benefits to communities.

CHAPTER 7

Policies in Giving

WHAT ARE the motives underlying corporate giving? What policies have developed with respect to local giving as opposed to national, for buildings and endowment as against current expenses, in special fields such as education, religion, veterans?

Motives and Purposes

The motives of a donor are seldom completely known, even to himself. In the field of personal giving, the conventional and admired pattern is the gift wholly for others, with no tincture of personal advantage. Observers may suspect more than coincidence when a man makes a substantial gift to a college and the same year receives an honorary degree, but the man speaks only of his love for learning and his special affection for this college. Corporation giving, however, is not based on pure altruism. The chief consideration, at least in the eyes of the law, must be a hard-headed weighing of the advantages of the gift to the corporation, its employees, its stockholders and customers. Enlightened selfishness is a legal requirement.

Much corporation giving undoubtedly proceeds from mixed motives. It is done in behalf of a soulless entity with selfish advantage obligatory, but by persons whose hearts sometimes outvote their heads. Even when motivated by wholly selfish reasons, it is done before a public that has not learned to discriminate between corporate and personal giving. Therefore statements concerning gifts usually emphasize the corporation as a good citizen contributing to worthy causes out of a sense of public responsibility, with little or no hint of the enlightened selfishness that is properly a factor in most such gifts. One corporation keeps two sets of files, a public file on the needs and accomplishments of various agencies and the contributions made, and a private file on the special concern of the corporation with these agencies, such as interlocking board memberships, customers prominent in the charity, and the need to placate or please special groups.

We desired to dig beneath the public statements into the real motives and purposes of corporate giving. Our question, with space for multiple answers, was phrased in this way:

> 24. Please name the factors you give most weight in deciding on a contribution. (A confidential down-to-earth statement would be most helpful—benefit to the company, stockholder pressure, keeping government out of the area, public reaction if we do not contribute, or other.)

Of the 326 cooperating corporations, 78 declined to answer this question. The remaining 248 named from one to four or five factors influencing them, to a total of 436 answers—an average of nearly two apiece. Since these answers were in their own words, division into the nine categories of Table 19 and Figure 6 has had to be somewhat arbitrary.

As the table indicates, 30 per cent of the replying corporations frankly acknowledged benefit to the company as a chief factor in their giving; this proportion rose to more than half (25 out of 49) of the largest corporations, but it was less than a fifth of the "under $1 million" asset group. Benefit to employees was a factor with fewer than one in ten. Public relations considerations and customer pressures were instanced by almost the same proportions of companies as direct company benefit. The first three factors, all of which involve direct or indirect business benefits, are collectively quite influential in guiding and motivating contributions, by this showing.

Factors 4 through 6 are the group in which self-interest is not explicit. These were reported by an even larger proportion of the companies, rising to 42 per cent for "duty to the community."

TABLE 19. FACTORS INFLUENCING GIFTS IN 248 SURVEYED COR-
PORATIONS[a]

Factor	Number of corporations				Per cent of corporations answering question
	Assets under $1 million	Assets 1 under 50 million	Assets 50 million or over	Total	
Benefit to company	14	35	25	74	30
Benefit to employees	3	13	6	22	9
Public relations or customer pressure	12	39	18	69	28
Duty to community	31	53	20	104	42
Moral obligation or corporate citizenship	13	18	8	39	16
Worthiness of cause	32	34	11	77	31
Example of other companies	3	5	5	13	5
Limiting governmental expansion	6	10	5	21	8
Profit position or tax savings	8	8	1	17	7
Total answers	122	215	99	436	–
Corporations answering question	74	125	49	248	–

[a] Russell Sage Foundation Survey.

Undoubtedly such factors have a strong personal appeal to most of the individuals controlling corporate gifts and are influential in nearly all corporation giving; but the reader must judge,

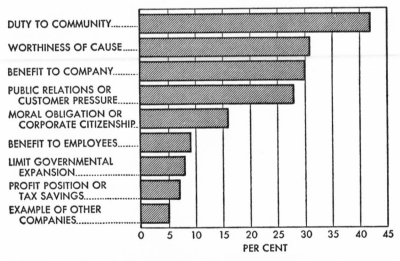

FIGURE 6. PER CENT OF CORPORATIONS REPORTING CERTAIN
FACTORS INFLUENCING THEIR GIFTS

partly in the light of the other choices, whether these motives had quite the predominating influence the bare statistics would suggest.

Only a few corporations, chiefly large ones, specified the example of other companies as an important factor in their programs. A slightly bigger group was influenced by the desire to limit the expansion of government in welfare fields. Said Corporation 2160, contributing in spite of a net loss for the year:

> We believe that if we do not all contribute, the burden will be placed on government, which in turn will only increase taxes to take care of it, and this would be worse.

Seventeen corporations were influenced by their profit position or the possibility of tax savings. The Survey was undertaken in the spring of 1951, when corporate tax rates were high but the more severe Revenue Act of 1951 had not yet been passed.

Further light on underlying motives may be shed by a few direct quotations that could not be wholly reflected in the tabulations; they are identified only by corporation number.

> 1593. We do not believe that we should donate our stockholders' money to any cause, however good. They may contribute themselves if they so desire.

> 2006. It has been a traditional policy of X—— since its founding to contribute to worthwhile community enterprises. . . . In the aggregate this usually has exceeded 5 per cent of its profits.

> 1664. Stockholder desires.

> 1379. Union pressure.

> 1283. As a mutual life insurance company . . . we should consider where the Company will benefit directly or indirectly, such as by health agencies.

> 1809. We contribute more liberally to the agency that may be our customer; pressure of the trade as used by a community fund in appointing someone known to us personally in our trade to call and solicit our donation in person.

> 1797 (which gave 9 per cent of 1950 net income). Pressure from bankers, etc.

> 1842. As trustees of policyholders' funds from all over the country, contributions have not been made to local charities.

1865. We probably give more weight to the need of the organization for financial help than any other factor. We give no weight to publicity value as such.

1087. We decide pledges by worthiness of project—whether or not it is collected directly by organization or by a professional firm. We frown on professionals that put on drives as we think a worthwhile project should succeed in collecting without the work of professionals.

Contributions to Capital Funds

Practice varies widely with respect to contributions to capital funds, whether for buildings or endowment. Many corporations definitely exclude building funds from their programs, or try to. Says Corporation 1123:

> We do not contribute to building funds or funds for capital expenditures. Many of these projects are worthy, but since the amount of money we believe it desirable to contribute should bear a reasonable relationship to our operations, it would be difficult to support all these without reducing our contributions to other groups like the Community Chest.

Others subscribe only under special conditions, where benefit to employees or the company is reasonably direct. Says Corporation 3020 in its printed policy manual:

> In general, the Company will not make subscriptions in connection with endowments or the construction or alteration of buildings and other permanent facilities of outside organizations. It will, however, consider giving its support for the construction of hospitals, YMCA's, YWCA's, etc., or additions to such facilities, in localities where it has a substantial number of employees or their families who use the facilities. In many cases, the Company expects to give its support on the basis of wide local community participation, especially by its own employees.

Other companies feel quite differently:

> There should be no distinction between contributing to a building fund or an operating fund; contributions to building funds that qualify should be limited to not more than one-half of one per cent of the amount to be raised.[1]

[1] *Corporate Contributions Report.* American Society of Corporate Secretaries, New York, 1950, p. 58.

Indeed, some companies give a major portion of their contributions for buildings. Corporation 1623 reported "about 90 per cent"; it was a construction company. A manufacturer of cutting tools gave 87 per cent, chiefly to hospitals.

In order to discover actual recent practice our Survey included this item:

15. We $\frac{do}{do\ not}$ contribute to capital-fund drives (buildings or endowment). If YES, such contributions in 1950 represented about ....% of our total gifts.

TABLE 20. POLICY ON CONTRIBUTIONS TO CAPITAL FUNDS AND PROPORTION OF SUCH GIFTS IN 305 SURVEYED CORPORATIONS[a]

Policy and percentage in 1950	Number of corporations				Per cent of corporations answering question
	Assets under $1 million	Assets 1 under 50 million	Assets 50 million or over	Total	
Permitted:					
None in 1950	12	19	10	41	13
Under 10 per cent	2	8	7	17	6
10 under 15	3	9	5	17	6
15 under 25	2	6	5	13	4
25 under 50	5	7	6	18	6
50 under 75	2	6	3	11	4
75 or more	3	3	1	7	2
Proportion not stated	4	20	2	26	8
Total permitted	33	78	39	150	49
Not permitted	59	77	19	155	51
Total	92	155	58	305	100

[a] Russell Sage Foundation Survey.

Table 20 shows clearly the small extent to which corporations contribute to capital funds. All but 21 of the companies in the sample answered this question. Of the 305 answering, 51 per cent do not permit capital contributions at all as a matter of policy, and an additional 13 per cent, while occasionally making such gifts, made none in 1950. Almost two-thirds of the sampled corporations, therefore, made no capital contributions in 1950.

Of the remaining 36 per cent of corporations that did contribute, most reported that only very small proportions of their gifts were for capital funds. Only 18 corporations, 6 per cent of the group, reported that 50 per cent or more of their contributions were in this category. Large corporations were somewhat more apt to contribute for capital funds than smaller ones.

TABLE 21. CONTRIBUTIONS OF 256 SURVEYED CORPORATIONS TO ANNUAL DRIVES, BY AMOUNT OF CORPORATION ASSETS, 1950[a]

Per cent of total contributions	Number of corporations				Per cent of corporations answering question
	Assets under $1 million	Assets 1 under 50 million	Assets 50 million or over	Total	
Under 10	–	–	2	2	1
10 under 25	4	3	–	7	3
25 under 50	2	8	4	14	5
50 under 75	12	23	13	48	19
75 under 80	9	10	6	25	10
80 under 90	9	14	5	28	11
90 under 100	27	42	16	85	33
100	16	23	8	47	18
Total	79	123	54	256	100

[a] Russell Sage Foundation Survey.

Annually Recurring Drives

On the other hand, most corporations do make a large percentage of their gifts to annually recurring drives, such as community chests and the Red Cross. Table 21 shows the percentage

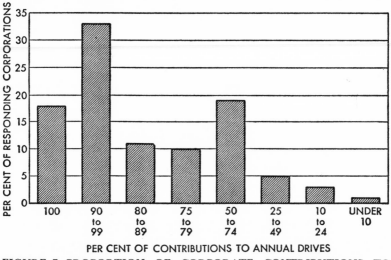

FIGURE 7. PROPORTION OF CORPORATE CONTRIBUTIONS TO ANNUAL DRIVES

distribution of such contributions among the 256 corporations which answered this question, and made contributions in 1950.

Ninety-one per cent of the reporting corporations contributed at least half of their 1950 gifts to recurring drives. Indeed, if this sample is representative, more than half of all companies gave at least 90 per cent of their contributions to such drives; in this sample, nearly a fifth of them gave 100 per cent in this way.

In this respect the practices of very large corporations do not differ markedly from the other groups. The total picture is one of heavy concentration on giving to established causes that campaign from year to year, with little latitude for fresh decisions except as to changing amounts.

Written Statements of Policy

Larger corporations have sometimes found it useful to issue a multigraphed or printed statement of policy on contributions for circulation to principal executives and branch managers. Though such a practice has much to commend it, our Survey indicated that it is not yet general. Of the 326 cooperating corporations, only 18—less than 6 per cent—reported written policies. All but two of these 18 were relatively large, with assets exceeding $1 million.

Such documents usually include a preamble setting out the company's general attitude toward contributions; a statement concerning the types of organizations and causes to which contributions will be made; a statement on organizations and causes which cannot be assisted; and an outline of office procedure for considering and acting on charitable appeals. If a contributions committee has been set up, its composition and duties are outlined. Policies on complimentary advertising and on memberships are often included. Statements may be made on control of in-plant solicitations, on participation of personnel on the boards of welfare organizations and in their fund drives, on contributions in kind, on branch office policy, and on other special matters which may affect the particular company.

Two representative corporation policy statements are included in Appendix F,[1] and quotations from many such statements appear in this chapter and elsewhere in this volume. The National Industrial Conference Board has collected 19 such statements in its recent publication, *Company Policies on Donations*,[2] and the American Society of Corporate Secretaries includes in its *Corporate Contributions Report*[3] 63 statements of policy based on the answers to a letter requesting information on six significant aspects of this problem.

The uses of written policies are many. The very process of reducing practice to writing is salutary in resolving borderline decisions and clarifying procedures. The document can be used for direct quotation as to company policy, and may often be the basis for a standardized but gracious letter of refusal. Consistency in policy is promoted, and this is especially important for companies with large organizations and far-flung branches. Greater efficiency is usually achieved in the internal handling of requests for contributions.

General Policy

These policy statements, written for internal use, often reflect the practical considerations behind corporate giving, as did our confidential questionnaire. Most companies accept the duty and desirability of giving, but the test of the particular cause is not likely to be an abstract moral judgment but the interests of the company. The International Harvester Company puts it succinctly:

> The first test, therefore, that should be applied to all contribution requests is: Does it benefit the Company directly or indirectly? Unless it can be demonstrated that it does, the contribution should not be made.[4]

[1] Of International Harvester Company and Commercial Investment Trust Financial Corporation. See pp. 330–341.

[2] *Studies in Business Policy*, No. 49. National Industrial Conference Board, New York, 1950.

[3] American Society of Corporate Secretaries, New York, 1950.

[4] From *International Harvester Contributions*, quoted in full in Appendix F, pp. 330–336.

The penalties of not contributing must also be considered, and sometimes dictate a departure from set policy. The *Manual* of one corporation warns:

> Regardless of policy outlined below, if the Manager believes that failure to participate in any community enterprise will be a reflection on the Company, he should make his recommendation . . . .

Various corporate directives emphasize the need for dealing courteously with applicants, the desirability of being "not the last to contribute" if a favorable decision is made, and in general of looking to the public relations aspects of the contribution program.

Advertising

Nearly all corporations that mention the subject disapprove courtesy advertising as a form of contribution, often in terms similar to Corporation 3009:

> "Good Will" advertising (space in programs, special editions, testimonials, etc.) is contrary to policy. All advertising must meet media standards and be included in the annual advertising budget.

Small local companies often do make contributions in this form, but for the larger corporation it presents serious dangers. Any good will won by a particular advertisement may be more than offset by refusals to the numerous other managers of yearbooks, labor papers, benefit programs, and the like who have observed the single advertisement and regard their cause as quite as worthy.

Personal Service

Corporations frequently include in their policy statements advice to executives and other employees on service to welfare organizations. One of the earliest statements vigorously encouraging such participation was made by Thomas J. Watson for International Business Machines Corporation in 1914:

> We want you to take time off from IBM to do a good job as citizens because communities will only be as good as the citizens make them.

We want IBM to be a real part of the citizenship of this country and the world. Keep that in mind. That is one of your duties. We are trying to develop not only IBM and develop people for IBM, but we are trying to help in our small way to develop this great country of ours.

We all owe a duty to the community in which we live, to society at large. Aside from that, it is a fine thing for a person to participate in things worth while outside his business.[1]

Many other companies have recently issued similar statements, with the Shell Oil Company pronouncement typical:

There is probably no way in which Shell's interest in public service is more clearly shown than in the participation of Shell employees in the affairs of their own communities. In a number of publications expressing company policy, employees are encouraged to accept civic responsibilities, and at present there are few, if any, communities in which Shell has a major concentration of employees that does not have Shell people in local government, in the chamber of commerce, on the school board, on committees for charitable drives, in Parent Teacher Associations, in Boy Scouts, and in Junior Achievement or service clubs.[2]

Corporations make exceedingly valuable, but untabulated, contributions to many welfare agencies in these free services of company personnel as officers, board members, directors of fund drives, and volunteers in other capacities, often on company time and occasionally with the use of company secretarial and other facilities. But sometimes this willingness to lend prominent names has not been coupled with adequate checking of the "welfare" agency; rackets have fattened on prestigeful names associated with sound companies, too carelessly lent them.

A few corporations suggest discretion in acceptance of fund-raising assignments, since in such cases support will usually be expected from the company.

[1] Quoted in "As Big Companies View Their Civic Responsibilities," *The American City*, March, 1950, with the further statement of Mr. Watson that "these policies are just as fundamental in IBM today as they were when originally formulated 36 years ago."

[2] *The American City*, June, 1949.

One corporation tries to have a major executive on the board of every agency, college, or other institution to which it makes substantial contributions. This is not so much a matter of voluntary service, however, as a means of keeping in close touch with the agency's program and being in a position to suggest activities of direct interest and value to the corporation. Such a policy leans toward controlling benefiting agencies. This may seem to the corporation a legitimate privilege of the large contributor, but the agency and its other contributors may have a different view. While most agencies seem to feel that only one taint attaches to money—'t ain't enough—contributions have on occasion been refused where even the suspicion of influence might alienate other contributors.

Types of Contributions Made

Many companies include in their statements of policy a description of the classes of contributions they are willing to make, often with mention of specific agencies. Community chests are almost universally accepted, though even here one company (in transportation) rules against such contributions. The Red Cross and hospitals are high in the acceptance categories. Chambers of commerce, service clubs, and trade associations are supported by memberships and often by added contributions; gifts to the last group are usually properly chargeable to business expense rather than the charitable budget, and practices differ on some of the other types of membership.

The various health drives are supported by some companies, ruled out by others. The same diversity applies to general welfare, character building, and recreational services. These questions are discussed at length in Part II, where the benefiting agencies are described, together with company programs relating to them.

Education, particularly higher education, is accepted with qualifications in many statements of policy, ruled out in others. A separate chapter is devoted to this important and complicated problem.

Types of Contributions Not Made

Policy statements are unanimous in ruling out political contributions, which in many jurisdictions are illegal. But even here one executive personally demurs. He points out that the American political system requires party campaigns, which in these days of radio and television have become expensive. He would have corporations contribute equally to both major parties to defray these expenses, for if they do not, "the costs will be met by individuals who expect offices if their party succeeds." The more usual attitude in this and related fields is expressed by Corporation 1123:

> We do not contribute to religious, racial, political, or other activities that are intended to benefit special groups. . . . It would be difficult to support any one such group with fairness to customers and stockholders, many of whom have conflicting interests.

Many corporations also mention in the prohibited list fraternal, labor, and veterans' organizations. But under some circumstances exceptions are made:

> *Sectarian or denominational appeals:* Contributions will be made only in cases of unusual merit when made to institutions under sectarian sponsorship which offer their services to the general public on a broad basis without regard to sectarian considerations.[1]

Similar exceptions sometimes apply to veterans' and other organizations, which are discussed in detail in Part II.

Creative Giving

This and preceding chapters have presented from the records the history, the present status, and the avowed policies of corporate giving.

The record is impressive. The corporation is already a new giant in philanthropy, more than offsetting the overemphasized decline in large individual gifts. The greater detachment and hardheadedness of this new giver are salutary in a field ruled too long by appeals to sentiment and emotion. Introduction of busi-

[1] From *Statement of the Policy of C.I.T. Financial Corporation*, quoted in full in Appendix F, pp. 336–341.

ness methods and business judgment may result in a wiser spread of contributors' dollars, helping correct the imbalance among other givers that now exists.

But, with a few honorable exceptions, corporate giving is still traditional and custom-bound. It has been pointed out that more than half of the sampled companies gave from 90 to 100 per cent of their contributions to annually recurring drives; that only 30 per cent go so far as even to set up a contributions budget; that in most companies giving is the spare-time responsibility of a single individual, although it is a job of great complication, difficulty—and opportunity.

The customary drives usually do need support, and fewer dollars are wasted on rackets and dubious causes by corporations than by individuals. But one hopes that corporations will also spend some of their funds, as a few of them already do, in new and creative patterns, using the special knowledge and resources of their particular industry toward the common welfare in ways not possible for other donors.

Every company has intimate knowledge of its own local community, and is vitally concerned in its welfare. The great foundations and national organizations cannot deal with local problems and particular situations. Local government knows the local needs, but often cannot meet them because of tax burdens and political involvements. The corporation may be the only agency with intimate knowledge of a local need and adequate resources to meet it. The Allis-Chalmers Manufacturing Company sponsored "summer and winter concerts for people in our community."[1] The Bridgeport Brass Company "arranged with the co-operation of the National Guard and the State Assembly to modernize and equip the old Armory, which has now become one of the vital community sports centers in this area."[1] In every local community dozens of special opportunities can be found, opportunities to do things which no one else can or will do, but which will contribute directly to the company through better health and living conditions for workers, and in terms of local prestige and customer good will.

[1] *The American City*, March, 1950.

In addition, each industry, even each company, has its own particular knowledge, skills, and interests. These can be applied in its philanthropic program, rendering unique service. An earlier chapter has described the Joseph Bulova School of Watch-making,[1] which serves handicapped and paraplegic veterans. Probably no more than three or four corporations in the United States, and no other agencies whatever, possessed the special knowledge to set up that particular philanthropy. Other industries also have their special knowledge and interests. Insurance companies have a natural concern for health and for accident prevention. Motor companies might profitably busy themselves with traffic problems, parking, and city planning. Travelers Aid and the YMCA would seem logical fields for railroads, buses, and airlines.

Special knowledge acquired through company medicine might be extended into a community program. One New York company has accumulated considerable experience with alcoholics in its industrial medicine section. It has developed a series of tests to determine whether the patient should have a "drying up" period in a hospital, psychiatric treatment, services of a social worker, religious aid, or be encouraged to go to Alcoholics Anonymous. Its executives think this multiple approach exceedingly useful, and are endeavoring with the aid of other corporations to establish such service on a citywide basis.

The older worker is becoming a serious problem in America, and one which only business can solve. How can the limited capacities of these workers be used in today's speeded-up, mechanized production? A satisfactory solution would contribute in at least three directions—provide a more satisfactory life pattern for the aging, keep them and their families off the relief rolls, and add to our total wealth. Such programs would be a part of employment practice, but the studies that might precede them and some of the accompanying services may be deductible philanthropy.

Similarly, the handicapped are a proper concern of industry, and a necessary one in a time of full employment. It is estimated

[1] See p. 111.

that there are 28,000,000 disabled Americans, and the Department of Labor believes that at least 1,000,000 physically handicapped persons, nonveterans and veterans, can be added to the nation's work force if they are given rehabilitation, training facilities, and an equal chance with other applicants for a job. Corporations are helping in various ways. A workshop for the handicapped has been built in Binghamton, New York, with the aid of several corporations, and its workers are executing regular business contracts. J.O.B. ("Just One Break") has been set up in New York City as an affiliate of the New York University Bellevue Medical Center—Institute of Physical Medicine and Rehabilitation. It helps train and place handicapped workers, and with the interest and aid of business firms this idea has spread to many other cities. These projects are pure business, a day's work for a day's pay. But in these areas, too, studies are needed and sometimes special services.

The range of possibilities for creative giving for corporations, in the special settings of their own communities and their particular resources, can only be suggested. Its best examples will be the inventions of the corporations themselves as each faces unique opportunities in its field.

PART II
THE BENEFICIARIES

CHAPTER 8

The Fund-Raisers

$\mathbb{F}$UND-RAISERS form the first line of attack on corporate philanthropy. Their skill or lack of it, their persistence and the pressures they bring to bear, have sometimes more to do with the direction of a company's gifts than the actual merits of the causes they represent. A first step toward wiser giving is some understanding of fund-raisers and their techniques. For fund-raising varies from the unpredictable ways of the devoted volunteer through the organized operations of the trained professional to the wiles of the racketeer.

The Volume of Appeals

All large companies, and many small ones, are bombarded constantly by appeals for funds—not only community chest, hospital, college, Red Cross, polio, heart, cancer, tuberculosis, arthritis, cerebral palsy, crippled children, the blind, firemen, policemen, veterans, church, ladies' aid, Salvation Army, Boy Scouts, Girl Scouts, and the YMCA, but by dozens and sometimes hundreds of additional special causes. Even in those communities where most of these services are "wrapped in one package" in a tight community chest or united fund, the extra appeals flood in.

Corporation 3005, in New York City, recorded 248 separate mail appeals in one year; since it contributes to the Greater New York Fund, it presumably had immunity from the 423 agencies in that Fund, except for capital appeals. Corporation 2124, also in New York City and somewhat larger than the first mentioned, reported "about 500 new appeals" for the same year together with several hundred from former beneficiaries and annually recurring drives; but even this large number represents some falling off in recent years. Corporation 2124 has a well-defined contributions policy, a staff contributions specialist, and its refusals are in the form of a letter or interview setting out so clearly what the company will and will not consider that at least some of the appeals have been effectively discouraged.

The attack takes many forms, ranging from simple telephone calls and single letters to carefully laid campaigns involving visits from executives of other companies, college presidents, important customers, or others not easily turned away, with the assault carried often to more than one officer or director in the company.

The Solicitors

Amateur fund-raisers bear much of the load, especially in smaller communities and for local causes. The variety in method is tremendous. The solicitor for the veterans' organization wants a complimentary advertisement for the program of its minstrel show. The ladies' aid would be happy with prizes for their bridge benefit. The Youth Committee needs baseball uniforms, which could carry the company name.

Larger campaigns, and those for national agencies, may also use volunteer solicitors, but the campaigns are better organized. Printed material precedes or accompanies the solicitor. Newspaper stories and radio announcements have attempted to soften up the prospect. If the company's gift is likely to be substantial, the solicitor will be from the "special gifts" flying squadron. He has in his pocket a card that tells him a great deal about the company's recent profits, its standing in the community, number of its employees, and any direct relation to this charitable project. He has a minimum gift quite exactly in mind. And he has probably been selected for this call because of a relationship to the company's business or acquaintance with its officers. Various forms of the "squeeze play" are discussed later.

Community chests form so important a segment of corporate giving that a separate chapter is devoted to them, with discussion of their drives and the special "yardsticks" for corporate giving they are currently striving to develop.

Campaigns that run into the millions, as do those for many educational institutions and national agencies, are usually conducted by professional fund-raising firms whose sole business is organizing solicitations. The weaker firms in this field sometimes work for a percentage of the funds raised, and in their efforts to increase their own income have been known grossly to misrepresent the agency and to engage in other objectionable practices. The better firms do not work on a percentage basis. They make a preliminary investigation, and if they accept a campaign, they charge a flat fee based upon the nature of the task, without consideration of final result. They claim these fees usually work out to between 6 and 9 per cent of money eventually raised.

Their fund-raising campaigns are highly organized. Operatives are often in the offices of the agency or university six months before the solicitation begins, getting into the spirit of the organization, working on lists, preparing the elaborate printing pieces and advance publicity. The fund-raising company takes no part in the actual solicitation of givers, its name appears on none of the literature, and the giver is usually unaware of its existence. But it prepares every detail of a campaign that is supposed to work with clocklike precision.

Where substantial corporate gifts are in prospect, separate attention is given to this detail. Lists of all corporations which might conceivably contribute are prepared. If a college campaign is being planned, the college affiliations of each company's principal officers and directors are probably catalogued, along with any advantages to the corporation from courses taught, laboratory facilities available, training of executives, supplies purchased, or through bringing more customers into the community. In campaigns for other types of agencies, interlocking board memberships—including those of the wives of corporation executives —are regarded as important, as well as all services advantageous to the corporations.

If corporation gifts are likely to be a large part of the total collected, it is well to have a corporation president as the chairman of the campaign committee. The enlistment of a corporation officer or director as a solicitor usually ensures a substantial contribution from that company. Care is taken to obtain, in advance of the regular solicitation, one very generous gift from a friendly corporation. This is known in the profession as a "pacesetter gift," and can be mentioned casually at the group luncheon for corporate executives and in individual solicitations.

Thirteen professional fund-raising firms are now members of the American Association of Fund-Raising Counsel, with a code of approved practices. Members of the Association are: Adderton-Johnson Associates; American City Bureau; Beaver Associates; Reuel Estill and Company; Charles W. Gamble Associates; John Price Jones Company; Kersting, Brown and Company; Ketchum, Inc.; Marts and Lundy; Pierce, Hedrick and Sherwood; Tamblyn and Brown; Ward, Wells and Dreshman; Will, Folsom & Smith.

If some of these behind-the-scenes operations of the fund-raisers seem too highly organized and coldly calculated, it should, nevertheless, be recorded that they work. Moreover, the agencies whose campaigns are undertaken by the better professional fund-raisers represent legitimate causes, about which adequate information can be obtained. Perhaps some of the steam-roller methods and heavy pressures now exerted are due to the resistance some corporations have put up against any giving. Whether these methods will remain either necessary or effective is a question for the future to decide.

The Squeeze Play

Company giving is peculiarly susceptible to special pressures. These take many forms, but the customer is frequently the villain in the piece. One company frankly lists among its considerations in determining upon a contribution: "Are important customers interested in the solicitation?" But says Corporation 3013:

> When a customer tries to exert undue pressure, the request is simply sent to the central office, which politely refuses; then the local man can report the refusal and blame the central office.

Examples of the squeeze play could be multiplied endlessly. A health agency in a community in the Middle West received a $50 contribution from a corporation which had no office there and did not contribute to this health drive elsewhere; by an interesting coincidence the chairman of the drive in that community was the wife of the company's board chairman. A large northern corporation contributed toward the building fund of a college library in the South, though it was not making contributions to colleges elsewhere for any purpose; the library was being named for the company's largest supplier. A member of the contributions committee of a national company was made solicitations chairman for a fund drive to which his company had never previously contributed; he brought the appeal to his committee, but refused to vote on it and left the room while it was discussed; no contribution was made.

Various defenses against the squeeze play are available, among which are referral of all requests to a contributions expert or committee, organization of a company foundation, issuance of a written policy on contributions. But since corporate benefit is a primary aim of corporate charity, divagations from usual policy may sometimes be expected in the direction of what one company calls "market considerations."

The Good, Doubtful, and Bad

Not all appeals for funds that reach corporations represent desirable charities. Soliciting agencies may be classified into three groups. First are the many organizations sincere in purpose, run efficiently, and attempting to raise a budget reasonably proportioned to a real need. Second are agencies that may be equally sincere in purpose but are badly run; or are directed toward a need not important or now being otherwise met; or have become involved in wasteful collection methods. Finally come the outright charity rackets, where the profit of the promoter is paramount and the cash receipts of the high-sounding cause are negligible or nothing. No corporation was caught by that classic charity, the Fund for the Widow of the Unknown Soldier, but enough have fallen prey to other rackets for the subject to merit discussion.

Some Charity Rackets

Complimentary "advertising" is usually more nuisance than racket, and has been discussed in a section under company policies.[1] But it may also be a racket, with the solicitor misrepresenting the facts.

> Long-distance telephone calls are being made to many business executives soliciting advertising for a weekly newspaper called the *Trade Union Courier*.
>
> Solicitors for the publication are alleged to have represented that they are connected with the American Federation of Labor. The publisher himself does not claim that the *Trade Union Courier* is an official A.F. of L. publication, but he does claim that it has the sponsorship of many locals of the A.F. of L. This Bureau requested the names of the A.F. of L. locals that allegedly sponsor the *Trade Union Courier*, but has never received them.
>
> William Green, president of the American Federation of Labor, [asserted]: "The *Trade Union Courier* is in no way connected with the American Federation of Labor."[2]

Patriotic appeals, because they are effective, are often abused. Veterans' organizations, and those for service to veterans, are exceedingly numerous. Some are legitimate, some are not. The National Better Business Bureau reports many complaints from business firms solicited by telephone for contributions toward purchasing equipment for Veterans Administration hospitals, for entertaining or providing gifts for hospitalized veterans, and the like. The solicitors become abusive if a contribution is denied. The Bureau obtained from the Veterans Administration in New York this general statement:

> The public is cautioned against making contributions to organizations which paint lurid pictures of veterans "languishing in veterans hospitals" and groups that propose to supply hospitalized veterans with items termed vital to their welfare which are provided in full by the government.
>
> The government, through the VA, supplies patients with everything necessary for their welfare and comfort. A number of services and conveniences which may add to the pleasure of patients are not

[1] See p. 122.

[2] *Service Bulletin*, National Better Business Bureau, Inc., June 17, 1948.

officially supplied and VA depends on cooperating volunteer organizations for these. . . .

The Veterans Administration does not endorse any project unless the endorsement is in writing. It under no circumstances endorses fund-raising projects.

What happens in some of the fund-raising drives is illustrated by this example:

A "man in uniform" association in California received $24,200 from the contributing public during a nine months' period to provide temporary relief for members in financially distressed circumstances. Files of the California Intelligence Bureau revealed that only $4,672 finally reached those in whose behalf the appeal had been made— 19 per cent of the amount raised.

Telephone solicitations are suspect, and many corporations demand that all such solicitors submit their requests in writing and by mail. Many appeals of this sort originate in a "boiler room"—a room crowded with desks and telephones where a group of men, representing themselves as "Father Callahan" or "Judge Brown," call long lists of companies and individuals and in trained, persuasive tones plead an appealing cause. A trifling amount of the money may even go to a charitable purpose to maintain some appearance of legality. The National Information Bureau reports one boiler-room operator who tried to play both ends, and frankly discussed his methods in their office:

This boiler-room operator offered to sell us the sucker list he had built up for 10 cents a name so that we could notify these persons they were on a sucker list, and offer our information service.

He put on a demonstration telephone "sale" which was a masterpiece of acting. With this pitch he had collected $1,000 from the head of a shipbuilding firm over a period of six months. He then called the man and thanked him for his helpfulness, pointing out he had given a total of $1,000 in the past half year. But since they were both such busy persons, wouldn't he send a check for $1,000 for the next six months so they would not need to bother him? The check arrived in the mail the next day.

His philosophy was that if he didn't take the money away from the sucker, somebody else would; he admitted to a certain dislike of doing it in the name of charity.[1]

[1] Letter from National Information Bureau, April 27, 1951.

The Cancer Welfare Fund, Inc., and its two officials were tried in 1951 on eleven counts of mail fraud in soliciting funds for cancer sufferers.

> The Cancer Welfare Fund was incorporated in July, 1949, with Joseph L. Brandt, who had a checkered earlier history, the leading figure in its formation. It set up palatial quarters in the Empire State Building, and started collecting funds immediately. More than two dozen prominent men, including five state governors, several judges, college presidents, columnists, and corporation presidents, were deluded into lending their names for the Fund's letterhead.
>
> One of the collection devices was the mailing of $17,000 in $1 bills to prospective contributors, asking return of the dollar with an appropriate gift. The corporation's records indicated that 50 per cent of the mailings brought gifts, 30 per cent returned the original dollar, and from 20 per cent there was no return. According to the United States attorney who prosecuted the case, the Fund after ten months of operations had collected $123,003 as contributions, but spent only $7,349 on 54 cancer sufferers, and was $75,000 in debt due to large "overhead."[1]

In this and many similar cases, the damage goes considerably beyond the wasted financial contribution of the corporation or its executives. The corporation prestige is given an unworthy organization, smoothing its path with other contributors. The carelessness with which some business executives, along with other persons prominent in public life, lend their names as sponsors of organizations not sufficiently investigated has added to the difficulties of all givers and to the "take" of many charity rackets:

> We received a number of inquiries last year from well known executives who were asked to accept honorary membership in a particularly high-sounding organization. Investigation disclosed that the promoter of the organization is an ex-convict, that he had been engaged in many questionable promotions since his release from prison, and was more recently indicted on charges of accepting money for a promised abortion. We discovered that several prominent persons including a university president, a railroad president, and a nationally-known attorney had accepted honorary member-

[1] From files of National Information Bureau and news reports.

ships and offices in the group without having made any check whatever on the person attempting to promote the organization or its method of operation.[1]

Subversive Organizations

During recent years many communist-front organizations, or agencies of other types which the Attorney General has officially branded as "disloyal or subversive," have campaigned for funds under high-sounding or misleading names. Corporations have been among their contributors, sometimes under the mistaken idea that the organization was promoting causes almost the opposite of its real intent.

A list of the organizations which have been officially declared disloyal or subversive by the Attorney General of the United States is available from his office. Names included are often close to those of quite legitimate and worthy organizations, so that careful checking is requisite. Since subversive groups sometimes "capture" legitimate organizations or, conversely, an organization on the doubtful list manages to throw out its subversive elements, dates are of importance. The Attorney General, in issuing his lists, has added this caution:

> In connection with the designation of these organizations I wish to reiterate, as the President has pointed out, that it is entirely possible that many persons belonging to such organizations may be loyal to the United States; that membership in, affiliation with or sympathetic association with, any organization designated, is simply one piece of evidence which may or may not be helpful in arriving at a conclusion as to the action which is to be taken in a particular case. "Guilt by association" has never been one of the principles of our American jurisprudence. We must be satisfied that reasonable grounds exist for concluding that an individual is disloyal. That must be the guide.

Nevertheless, when the Buchanan Committee on Lobbying Activities got under way and later published its extensive lists of corporation contributions,[2] some corporations were considerably embarrassed to discover subversives among their beneficiaries.

[1] *Work Highlights of 1950:* A Report of the National Better Business Bureau, Inc. New York, 1951, p. 8.

[2] *Expenditures by Corporations to Influence Legislation.* House Report No. 3137. Government Printing Office, Washington, 1950.

Information Agencies

The various information services are the first line of defense against rackets, and effective aids toward wiser giving. These may be national, local, or related to particular types of social agencies.

The national agency most used by business is the solicitations division of the National Better Business Bureau.[1] The National Better Business Bureau cooperates with some ninety local Better Business Bureaus which are financially and operationally autonomous, but exchange information and assistance. The National Bureau is a nonprofit organization supported by business firms "to maintain fair competition in advertising and selling; to build public confidence in business." It is perhaps best known for its efforts to correct abuses in business practice and to drive out fraudulent concerns, but it also maintains a busy Solicitations Division.

The Solicitations Division reviews national and regional appeals, and in many cases prepares factual reports on those reviewed. Over 150,000 names of organizations and persons are indexed in its files, and the Division reports that it handles annually some 10,000 inquiries from business firms on charitable appeals. Where the charity is local, the National Better Business Bureau will endeavor to get information from one of the local bureaus, if a Bureau city is involved, and in other cities often has cooperative arrangements with chambers of commerce and similar organizations. Its reports outline the general history and purpose of an organization; names and affiliations of its officers and directors; method of operation, activities, and accomplishments; fund-raising methods; percentage of income spent for fund-raising purposes, if available; and financial data reflecting the portion of funds expended for the purpose for which the organization was established. It does not specifically approve or condemn any agency, but lets the facts speak for themselves.

Also important at the national level is the National Information Bureau,[2] established in 1918 when the multiplicity of the

[1] Chrysler Building, New York 17, N. Y. Membership is by subscription, from a minimum of $100 up to $2,500.

[2] 205 East 42d St., New York 17, N. Y. Corporation memberships are available at $25 up.

appeals growing out of World War I created a serious problem. This Bureau has investigated and reported on more than 4,000 national, international, and interstate agencies. For its own legal protection it does not publish its reports, but they are available to members, and through them, often to a wider clientele. It does indicate whether or not an agency meets its standards.

The *Basic Standards in Philanthropy*, which the Bureau has set up for judging national agencies, are in so many respects standards which corporations could apply in nearly all their giving that they are presented on page 142.

The National Information Bureau believes that listing of agencies which meet its *Basic Standards* serves a double purpose. In addition to warning contributors away from doubtful causes, refusal of approval has often brought back into line an inefficient agency, or one using some objectionable practice. Agencies unwilling or unable to bring their practices up to the standards sometimes make violent accusations of bias or favoritism against the National Information Bureau, or other similar accrediting agencies.

Information on local-agency drives is often available from special agencies within the city. In New York a Contributors Information Bureau is maintained by the Welfare and Health Council. The Chicago Association of Commerce and Industry publishes annually an excellent directory of approved local civic, health, and welfare organizations, issues a weekly bulletin, and maintains a Contributors Information Bureau. In Cleveland the Chamber of Commerce supports an information service and its Committee on Solicitations issues a monthly bulletin on current appeals. In Los Angeles it is the California Intelligence Bureau. In Seattle a special citizens' committee called the Public Appeals Board performs this function. As already mentioned, the local Better Business Bureaus are available in some ninety larger cities; most of them are able to supply information on local agencies seeking contributions. The community chest, council of social agencies, or the chamber of commerce are other sources.

Information in certain specialized fields may be sought from accrediting agencies which have been set up for those fields.

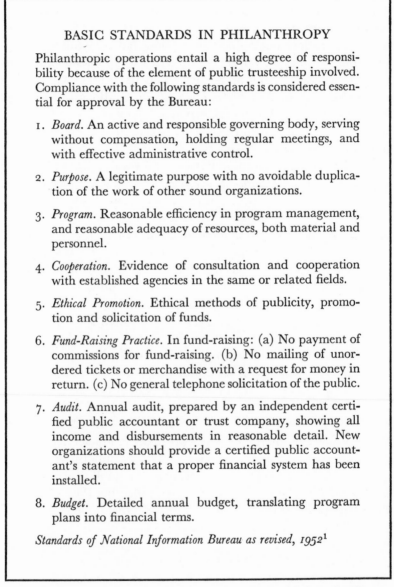

BASIC STANDARDS IN PHILANTHROPY

Philanthropic operations entail a high degree of responsibility because of the element of public trusteeship involved. Compliance with the following standards is considered essential for approval by the Bureau:

1. *Board.* An active and responsible governing body, serving without compensation, holding regular meetings, and with effective administrative control.

2. *Purpose.* A legitimate purpose with no avoidable duplication of the work of other sound organizations.

3. *Program.* Reasonable efficiency in program management, and reasonable adequacy of resources, both material and personnel.

4. *Cooperation.* Evidence of consultation and cooperation with established agencies in the same or related fields.

5. *Ethical Promotion.* Ethical methods of publicity, promotion and solicitation of funds.

6. *Fund-Raising Practice.* In fund-raising: (a) No payment of commissions for fund-raising. (b) No mailing of unordered tickets or merchandise with a request for money in return. (c) No general telephone solicitation of the public.

7. *Audit.* Annual audit, prepared by an independent certified public accountant or trust company, showing all income and disbursements in reasonable detail. New organizations should provide a certified public accountant's statement that a proper financial system has been installed.

8. *Budget.* Detailed annual budget, translating program plans into financial terms.

Standards of National Information Bureau as revised, 1952[1]

---

[1] *Giver's Guide to National Philanthropies, 1952–53.* National Information Bureau, Inc., New York, 1952, p. 3.

National Jewish agencies are reported on by the Council of Jewish Federations and Welfare Funds, Inc.[1] The National Catholic Welfare Conference[2] performs a somewhat similar service in its field. The Advisory Committee on Voluntary Foreign Aid of the United States Government[3] furnishes some information on voluntary agencies engaged in relief abroad. The Child Welfare League of America[4] will supply information on many children's agencies; and so on.

Use of These Agencies

These information services are probably unknown to many corporation givers, though used extensively by others. Our questionnaire survey included this item:

For checking on charitable appeals we use.................
name of organization(s)

Of 326 corporations, 92 failed to answer this question, and it must be presumed that substantially none of these uses any information agency. Of the 234 who replied, an additional 122 answered "None," or "No need," or, in one engaging case, "We use me." Many of the remaining 112 corporations use more than one checking agency; a few use four or five. Their choices appear in Table 22.

Only a third of the companies report using any information service. Against expectation, the largest corporations, which are bombarded by the most appeals, use such services in a smaller percentage of cases than the general average.

Only chambers of commerce and Better Business Bureaus are mentioned by more than 10 per cent of the reporting companies. In the case of the Better Business Bureau, mention of either the National or a local Better Business Bureau is counted, and it is possible that this item was included by some corporations which use the Bureau chiefly for checking on business rather than chari-

---

[1] 165 West 46th St., New York 19, N. Y.
[2] 1312 Massachusetts Ave., N.W., Washington 5, D. C.
[3] Care of Department of State, Washington 25, D. C.
[4] 24 West 40th St., New York 18, N. Y.

TABLE 22. USE OF INFORMATION AGENCIES BY SURVEYED COR-
PORATIONS[a]

Use of information agency	Number of corporations				Per cent of all corporations returning questionnaire
	Assets under $1 million	Assets 1 under 50 million	Assets 50 million or over	Total	
One or more agencies used	36	59	17	112	34
No agency used	35	63	24	122	38
Question not answered	30	44	18	92	28
Total	101	166	59	326	100
Agencies used[b]					
Chamber of commerce	19	33	6	58	18
Better Business Bureau	14	16	6	36	11
Local agencies	3	8	3	14	4
Community chest	3	4	1	8	2
Own investigators	–	4	1	5	2
National Information Bureau	–	–	3	3	1
Various	–	6	4	10	3

[a] Russell Sage Foundation Survey.

[b] Some corporations used more than one agency.

table malpractices. Also, community chests through their national organization and some city chambers of commerce hold
memberships in the National Information Bureau, so that use of
these local services may have brought to the company data available from this national agency.

Legal Protection

Some protection against the worst abuses is afforded by law—
local, state, and federal—and more legislation is pending. In
many cities organizations intending to raise funds must get a
license, which permits at least some examination of their purpose,
auspices, and officers.

In New York City, for example, such licenses must be obtained
from the Bureau of Public Solicitations of the Department of
Welfare except for "religious corporations," which are exempt.
This has proved a dangerous loophole, since in New York State
any seven persons may band together, declare themselves a
religious corporation, and avoid the licensing provision.

In other cities the licensing of charitable drives may be en-
trusted to the police department or to an independent board. In

Cincinnati no person or organization may solicit the public unless its registration application has been approved by the Public Solicitations Commission—who also review financial reports which must be submitted within ninety days of the conclusion of any drive. In St. Louis a Charity Solicitations Commission of nine persons passes on appeals. The mayor of Detroit issues permits on the basis of recommendations made by a Solicitation Authority Committee. In Chicago charitable solicitations are not subject to licensing, but for the "tag day" type of solicitation an order of the City Council is required.

These local licensing procedures are not better than the laws on which they are based and the sometimes perfunctory personnel charged with enforcement. Further legislation controlling solicitation is being attempted at the state level. One such law[1] limits solicitations within the state (except for purely local agencies or those soliciting only from their own memberships) to organizations "holding a valid license for such purpose from the state board of public welfare," issued for only one year and after due study of "proof of the worthiness of the cause, chartered responsibility, the existence of an adequate and responsible governing board to administer receipts and disbursements of funds, goods, or other property sought, the need of public solicitation, proposed use of funds sought, and a verified report . . . to show reserve funds and endowment funds as well as receipts and disbursements."

Neither state nor local laws cover appeals by mail, in newspapers, or by telephone, unless a messenger is used to pick up the contribution. However, charity rackets which attempt to use the mails come under general provisions of the postal laws relating to frauds and swindles:

> Whoever, having devised or intending to devise any scheme or artifice to defraud, or for obtaining money or property by means of false or fraudulent pretenses, representations, or promises . . . knowingly causes to be delivered by mail . . . any such matter or thing, shall be fined not more than $1,000, or imprisoned not more than five years, or both.[2]

[1] General Statutes of North Carolina 1943 (1949 Cum.Supp.), §108.80–108.86.
[2] 18 M.S.C.A. (1950 Ed.), §1341.

This is another reason corporations insist that telephone solicitors submit their proposals by mail.

Marginal Causes

Corporations probably do not lose much money to outright rackets. Their business sagacity, procedures for getting the judgment of several persons, and the information services save them from many of the schemes which filch millions from the purses of private donors.

Much more serious, in terms of money wasted, are the vast sums that go every year to honest, well-intentioned organizations that can pass any financial audit, but achieve little social benefit with the funds they spend.

The very purpose of the organization may be outmoded. If a manufacturer does not keep up with improvements, and demand for his product falls off, he fails. But voluntary welfare agencies do not necessarily "fail" when people no longer need the kind of service they offer; trustees and staff, bound by tradition or desirous of keeping their jobs, may obtain enough contributions by appealing to old loyalties to maintain a service for which there is little use.

Unnecessary duplication may exist. During World War II, 596 different agencies were registered for foreign relief! Of course, some duplication may be desirable and useful. If only one corporation were making automobiles, it is by no means certain that the American public would have cheaper or more serviceable cars than under reasonable competition. Two competing colleges are probably each better for the presence of the other. Many separate attacks on a research problem are sometimes required before a solution is reached. But duplication can be carried to needless extremes.

Management may be wasteful. This is a fault that sometimes needs drastic correction even in business enterprises, which are under the watchful eyes of directors and stockholders intent on profits. In voluntary welfare agencies some of that watchfulness may have to be undertaken by contributors. Here the corporation, with its understanding of financial statements and its experience with personnel problems, is often in a position to render useful service. The corporation, too, is more likely than the individual donor to see that "free" help for skilled tasks may be an extravagance as compared with adequately paid professional personnel.

Costs of solicitation may be too heavy, or some of the methods objectionable. The National Better Business Bureau report on a nationwide puzzle contest conducted by an organization seeking scholarship funds included this information:

> The first public appeal for funds was made through a nationwide contest conducted in 1949. That contest was completed and prizes awarded in July 1950. Both this Bureau and some local Better Business Bureaus have received a number of complaints from persons who participated in that contest. Many of the complainants contended that they had been unable to get satisfactory replies, if any, to questions concerning the scores of tie-breaker puzzles upon which the prizes were awarded, etc. . . . The direct expenses of conducting the 1949 Contest amounted to 69.2 per cent of total proceeds.

The prizes—which may be regarded as money returned to the contributors—amounted to less than 7 per cent of the gross income from the Contest. Therefore the contributor of one dollar had an average chance of getting 7 cents back in a prize and was actually contributing no more than 30.8 cents for the orphans. There is no evidence, in this case, that any of the remaining 62 cents was misappropriated. It was simply a very expensive way to "give" scholarships.

The size of the individual agency budget with relation to other needs in the community is a subject on which leaders of a particular cause can seldom be expected to have objective judgment. Since a corporation is usually the target for appeals from nearly all the agencies in its community, it must make some decisions on relative needs.

The Corporation as a Raiser of Standards

No sound estimate can be given of the money lost to useful work through actual charity rackets; they flourish in the dark, keep few records, some go undiscovered, and variations must be great from year to year. For New York City, amounts between $25 and $30 million a year have been cited by authorities close to the situation. Nationally, the round figure of $100 million is often used, but with little statistical evidence to support it.

Even this amount is not large in proportion to total philanthropic giving of about $4 billion. But charity rackets diminish regular giving by planting doubts in the minds of contributors. It is especially desirable that corporations do not lend their prestige or the names of their chief officers to such causes. In their own interest, and in the public interest, it is important to discover, expose, and starve out of existence all such endeavors.

With respect to the much more serious losses through marginal causes the corporation can play an even more useful part. As one of the larger prospective donors, it can require balance sheets and other needed information from all agencies seeking its financial aid. It can consult the appropriate information services. It can take an intelligent and continuing interest in the organizations it does assist. In so doing the corporation will not only make certain that its stockholders' money is more effectively spent; it will help raise standards in the field.

CHAPTER 9

Community Chests and United Funds

An IMPORTANT development in fund-raising was the formation of federations, of which community chests are the outstanding example. Such federations often have functions of planning and community organization of great significance, but their operations in raising and distributing funds are the necessary focus of this chapter. Community chests merit special attention because they are the recipients of so large a portion of all corporate giving.

The Federation Idea

In essence, the community chest ("fund" and "federation" are alternative names) is a contributor-and-agency-controlled organization whose principal duties are acquiring and spreading information on welfare needs, coordinating the work and reviewing budgets for the participating agencies, campaigning for contributions to meet the chest's accepted share of these budgets, and disbursing these funds to the agencies.

Chest executives believe that this plan results in wider public participation in both the planning and the support of social agencies. Usually all contributors are "members" of the chest, entitled to vote at the annual meeting, and most chests are now careful to include on their boards of directors industrialists and representatives of labor. These board members, as well as the

149

many thousands of individuals who are drawn in as volunteer solicitors for the highly organized annual campaign, gain intimate knowledge of the activities of local agencies and their budgeting problems. Publicity on the agencies and their work is broadcast to the whole community during the campaign, usually in the fall, and in the better-organized chests is a year-round responsibility.

Community chests are manned chiefly by volunteers. In small communities there may be no paid personnel, except possibly for secretarial services during the period of the active campaign. In larger communities the chest has usually a paid all-year executive and sometimes a small staff. If the chest is combined with the council of social agencies, a larger staff is probable.

Most chests endeavor to include all local fund-collecting agencies of approved status, and local chapters of national agencies that conduct local programs—as for example, the Boy Scouts and the YMCA. Many of them invite state and national agencies, and under recent prodding by business, which sees great advantages in "once-for-all" campaigns, they have sometimes exerted strong pressures to bring them in. The welfare war that has sprung up over this issue is discussed later.

The chest reviews the proposed budgets of the participating local agencies (usually with a written presentation and a conference with the budget committee and the right of appeal to the board of directors), considers relative need, and sets its goal.

When national agencies are included, the situation is more complicated. The budget committee of Middletown's community chest is not capable of determining the national need for cancer research and treatment, or how that need is related to requirements with respect to heart disease, or what proportion of either is the equitable share of Middletown's industry and citizens. But answers are necessary.

In an effort to handle such problems, Community Chests and Councils of America reactivated a National Budget Committee that had been formed in 1942 to consider war appeals. Beginning operations in 1946, this Committee since 1947 has been sponsored jointly by Community Chests and Councils and the National

Social Welfare Assembly. Neither sponsoring organization has any right of review over its decisions. National organizations seeking funds from the public are invited to submit their proposed budgets, but cannot be compelled to do so. The 32 organizations submitting their budgets in early 1952 for review to the National Budget Committee were:

American Hearing Society
American Heart Association
American Relief for Korea, Inc.[1]
American Social Hygiene Association[1]
Big Brothers of America, Inc.
Boys' Clubs of America, Inc.
Camp Fire Girls, Inc.
Child Welfare League of America, Inc.
Community Chests and Councils of America, Inc.
Family Service Association of America
Girls Clubs of America, Inc.
International Conference of Social Work, U. S. Committee
International Social Service, American Branch
Jackson (Roscoe B.) Memorial Laboratory
Muscular Dystrophy Association
National Association for Mental Health
National Child Labor Committee

National Committee on Alcoholism
National Conference of Catholic Charities
National Conference of Social Work
National Federation of Settlements
National Legal Aid Association
National Organization for Public Health Nursing, Inc.
National Probation and Parole Association
National Recreation Association[1]
National Social Welfare Assembly
National Travelers Aid Association
National Urban League
United Cerebral Palsy Association, Inc.
United Community Defense Services[1]
United Defense Fund
United Service Organizations, Inc.[1]

Several of the largest fund-collecting agencies are conspicuously absent.

As a necessary adjunct to the National Budget Committee, a National Quota Committee is charged with determining the percentage that should be raised in each of the states. These giving-ability ratios are based on 13 factors, ranging from number

[1] Agency of the United Defense Fund.

of households to individual income taxes, passenger automobile registrations, telephones, effective buying income, retail trade sales, and admission taxes. Apportionment within the states can then be made by state or local bodies, with a slightly different weighting if chest areas only are to be considered. Table 23 presents the current findings of the National Quota Committee

TABLE 23. STATE RATIOS FOR BASIC GIVING ABILITY

State	Per cent of total for United States	State	Per cent of total for United States
Alabama	1.08	Nebraska	.96
Arizona	.38	Nevada	.13
Arkansas	.65	New Hampshire	.32
California	8.56	New Jersey	3.49
Colorado	.92	New Mexico	.27
Connecticut	1.57	New York	14.27
Delaware	.25	North Carolina	1.49
Dist. of Columbia	.85	North Dakota	.35
Florida	1.50	Ohio	5.73
Georgia	1.41	Oklahoma	1.17
Idaho	.33	Oregon	1.04
Illinois	7.64	Pennsylvania	7.26
Indiana	2.55	Rhode Island	.57
Iowa	1.91	South Carolina	.71
Kansas	1.26	South Dakota	.41
Kentucky	1.17	Tennessee	1.39
Louisiana	1.16	Texas	4.32
Maine	.49	Utah	.40
Maryland	1.48	Vermont	.20
Massachusetts	3.55	Virginia	1.50
Michigan	4.53	Washington	1.76
Minnesota	2.02	West Virginia	.87
Mississippi	.62	Wisconsin	2.22
Missouri	2.73	Wyoming	.18
Montana	.38	Total	100.00

Source: National Quota Committee, April, 1952.

on basic giving ability; it may prove helpful as a guide to large corporations in their own nationwide distributions, where such other factors as plant locations, distribution centers, and number of employees are not primary considerations.

Community chests believe that programs of participating agencies are favorably affected by their requirement of annual review and this degree of budgetary control. Duplications with other agencies are often eliminated, economies in operation effected, and sometimes needed extensions of service suggested. In addition, the service agencies do not themselves need to devote staff time and money to fund-raising; they can concentrate their attention upon program.

Agencies that do participate must agree not to conduct within the given year other fund-raising drives in the community, with exceptions sometimes permitted in behalf of drives for capital expenditure, such as a new building, and appeals to their own membership. The contributor is therefore promised "immunity" from further solicitation by these agencies. In recent years this picture has been confused by two opposing trends, a multiplication of new agencies most of which are outside the chest, and strong pressures brought by business, labor, and some individual givers for more inclusive chests with elimination of, or at least strict limitation on, outside drives.

Chests have usually welcomed these pressures for wider federation, though they themselves have sometimes been gobbled up as just one among several agencies in a new superchest, often called a "united fund." But problems face them. Agencies already within the chest sometimes resist the "open door" policy of including all qualified additional agencies for fear their own proportion of the total that can be collected will be reduced; and a final question remains as to whether adequate funds can be collected, and the many agencies sufficiently individualized for maximum appeal, through any single-fund technique, however efficient.

The types of agencies to which chests contribute and the proportion of chest income given to each type differ from city to city, and in some cases have changed radically in the past year or two because of wider inclusions. However, for a chest disbursing $1,000,000 the distribution might approach the generalized figures of Table 24, which can be translated into percentage by pointing off four places. This sample chest is not a "united fund" including numerous national agencies, but 7.3 per cent is budgeted for the United Defense Fund.

TABLE 24. DISTRIBUTION PATTERN FOR A COMMUNITY CHEST

Type of service	Amount
YOUTH: Boys' Clubs, Boy Scouts, Camp Fire Girls, Girl Scouts, neighborhood houses, summer camps, YMCA, YWCA, etc.	$335,000
FAMILY: Assistance to handicapped, the aged, transients, legal aid, adult vocational and employment aid	164,000
CHILD CARE: Protection, foster home care, children's institutions, day nurseries, maternity homes, vocational training for children	137,000
HOSPITAL CARE	44,000
OTHER HEALTH SERVICES: Visiting nurses, clinics, medical, social service, mental hygiene, child guidance, fresh air and health camps	77,000
COMMUNITY WELFARE PLANNING: Information centers, social service exchange, other common services	36,000
UNITED DEFENSE FUND: Service to armed forces, including USO, defense communities, foreign aid	73,000
MISCELLANEOUS: Safety leagues, Americanization activities, interracial committees, etc. National and State services except United Defense Fund	13,000
Administrative	
YEAR-ROUND ADMINISTRATION	34,000
CAMPAIGN	50,000
Reserve for Collection Losses	37,000
Total	$1,000,000

SOURCE: Adapted from Community Chests and Councils' preliminary analysis of 1952 chest budgets.

Growth of Community Chests

The historical chapter noticed the origin of community chests, springing chiefly out of the war chests of 1917–1918.[1] Apparently the name, community chest, was first applied by Harry P. Wareham in 1919, in Rochester, New York, where he had entered this field at the urging of George Eastman. In that year 32 cities had such organizations, known under a wide variety of names, and chiefly survivals of the war chests.

By 1925, there were 240 chests recorded, which raised $58 million. Their later growth to the present total of about 1,500 is indicated in Table 25. For reasons already mentioned, New York does not have a community chest of the usual pattern. Aside from this largest city, all cities in the United States with a population of 50,000 or more are served by community chests except

[1] See p. 32.

Hoboken, New Jersey; many small cities also have them, or are served by a neighboring chest. Very few corporations, indeed, are in communities where the chest-type of federated giving is not practiced.

TABLE 25. AMOUNTS RAISED BY ALL RECORDED COMMUNITY CHESTS, 1925 TO 1952

Chest year[a]	Number of campaigns	Amount raised	Per cent of goal
1925	240	$58,003,965	94.0
1926	285	63,677,235	94.7
1927	308	66,432,072	94.4
1928	314	68,664,042	96.2
1929	331	73,276,688	95.9
1930	353	75,972,555	95.5
1931	386	84,796,505	98.7
1932	397	101,377,537	96.8
1933	401	77,752,954	83.7
1934	399	70,609,078	83.2
1935	406	69,781,478	87.2
1936	429	77,367,634	91.8
1937	452	81,707,787	93.8
1938	475	83,898,234	93.3
1939	523	82,771,362	91.2
1940	561	86,297,068	95.3
1941	598	90,379,099	98.0
1942	632	104,575,890	99.6
1943	649	162,334,486	107.0
1944	703	210,415,187	100.9
1945	772	221,272,950	101.9
1946	798	197,048,839	89.8
1947	841	168,521,984	96.6
1948	1,010	177,082,356	95.3
1949	1,152	188,061,328	91.9
1950	1,318	192,933,988	93.1
1951	1,498	212,987,292	94.9
1952	1,500[b]	240,000,000[b]	94.0[b]

[a] Year in which funds are to be expended. In most instances the campaign was conducted the previous fall, but collections continue through the chest year.

[b] Preliminary.

SOURCE: Community Chests and Councils of America, Inc.

Although Table 25 indicates a fairly steady growth in both number of chests and amounts collected, closer analysis presents a much less favorable picture. In 1924 (chest year 1925) chests in only 240 communities collected $58 million, or 8 cents out of each $100 of the total national income of $69 billion. Collections for chest year 1951 were $213 million, but were made by more than six times as many chests, covering a much larger proportion of the population, and the relation to the national income of $239 billion was still less than 9 cents to $100. Using disposable personal income as a criterion, which eliminates personal tax and any nontax payments to federal, state, or local government, the records of 180 chests reporting continuously from 1940 through 1951 indicated a substantially larger increase in such income in that period of twelve years than in chest contributions.[1]

How Much Corporations Contribute

Chests, from their earliest beginnings, have been favorite channels for corporate giving. Combining many types of local services, chests provide a convenient means through which much of the corporation's responsibility as a local "citizen" can be met with a single contribution. Some chests and united funds now also include many of the national appeals.

Of course, individual corporations show wide difference in their policies toward chests. They range all the way from the flat statement "We do not contribute to community chests" and the practice of another company that matches from company coffers the total amount the employees contribute to the chest, to the policy of several companies to contribute only to the community chest.

Ordinarily, companies do not consider any further appeals from agencies already aided through a chest contribution, though exceptions may be made for building funds or other special drives. But when one large corporation recently added a contributions expert to its staff, this man discovered, first, that the company had been treating the combined appeal made through the chest as just another of many appeals to which a standard-sized small contribution was given; second, that it was making many contributions to solicitors from agencies included in the chest.

Sometimes the chest idea appeals so strongly to corporate executives, not only for their company giving but for plant solicitations, that they use company contributions as a lever to make

---

[1] *Trends in Community Chest Giving, 1951*. Bulletin 157. Community Chests and Councils of America, New York, 1951, p. 12.

the chest more inclusive. Says the policy statement of the General Electric Company:

> It is the desire of the Company to promote the community chest idea because it saves time and expenses in solicitations by many different organizations among our employees. In general, it will be the policy of the Company not to contribute to organizations of the type ordinarily included in the community chests which remain outside of community chest campaigns for the respective communities.

But some companies, particularly those in trade or dealing otherwise directly with consumers, feel that a chest contribution does not give them advertising value equal to a similar amount distributed in smaller gifts among the individual agencies.

Records of corporate contributions to community chests are sparse until 1946, when Community Chests and Councils of America began collecting them with some care. But even now only a small proportion of the chests segregate company from other contributions, so that percentages must be based on small samplings. These samplings for various years, and the total probable corporate contributions to chests if one assumes the same percentages will prevail for all chest contributions, appear in Table 26.

Evidence from other sources suggests that this table does not overstate either the rising proportion of support chests are deriving from business or the total dollar amounts. Records are available of corporate contributions to 34 identical chests in 1929 and 1951. The total amount raised by these chests increased in these twenty-two years from $16.5 million to $32.1 million, substantially doubling; but the amount received from corporations almost quadrupled, rising from $3.5 million to $12.7 million, bringing the corporate percentage from 21.5 to 39.6 per cent.

In the 1941 sampling of 108 chests, the nine cities in which the chests received 40 per cent or more of their totals from corporations were all relatively small: Honolulu 51 per cent, Newport News 45 per cent, and between 43 and 40 per cent, in order, East St. Louis, Spokane, Pontiac, Salt Lake City, Elgin, Racine, and Saginaw. More recently, the better-organized large-city chests

TABLE 26. CORPORATION CONTRIBUTIONS TO COMMUNITY CHESTS FOR CERTAIN YEARS, 1920 TO 1951

Dollar figures in millions

Year	Chests reporting corporate gifts			All reporting chests		
		Corporation contributions			Total amount raised	Estimated amount raised from corporations
	Chests	Amount	Per cent of total raised	Chests		
1920	13	$2.5	23.8	–	–	–
1925	94	9.0	21.9	240	$58.0	$12.7
1929	129	13.0	22.0	331	73.3	16.1
1937	11	–	34.9	452	81.7	28.5
1941	108	7.3	27.2	598	90.4	24.6
1946	71	8.6	34.2	798	197.0	67.4
1947	104	12.9	35.1	841	168.5	59.2
1948	122	17.9	37.2	1,010	177.1	65.9
1949	85	17.1	38.5	1,152	188.1	72.4
1950	64	14.9	40.2	1,318	192.9	77.6
1951	69	10.9	39.5	1,498	213.0	84.1

SOURCE: Data for chests reporting corporation gifts: 1920 to 1929, Williams and Croxton, *Corporation Contributions to Organized Community Welfare Services*, National Bureau of Economic Research; 1937, Irving Weissman, mimeographed report, Social Planning Council of St. Louis; 1941, *Bulletin 108*, Community Chests and Councils of America; 1946 to 1951, Correspondence, Community Chests and Councils of America. Data for all reporting chests from Table 25. Estimate obtained by applying percentages for chests reporting corporate gifts.

usually secure a greater percentage in corporate contributions than smaller chests.

The Survey Record on Chests

The Survey questionnaire asked all responding corporations to report community chests as a separate item under "welfare agencies." Their answers are analyzed in Table 27.

The $2.5 million these particular corporations contributed to chests represented considerably more than a third (36.2 per cent) of their total contributions. The percentage was even higher (40.8 per cent) for the very large corporations, but dropped to less than a quarter of total contributions for those in the asset class $1 under $50 million.

The picture changes radically, however, if chest contributions are measured as a proportion of net income. On that basis small corporations contributed to chests at the rate of 0.54 per cent of net income, the intermediate companies dropped to 0.22, and the high asset group to 0.18, with an over-all rate of 0.19 per cent.

TABLE 27. CONTRIBUTIONS TO COMMUNITY CHESTS OF 326 SUR-
VEYED CORPORATIONS, BY AMOUNT OF CORPORATION
ASSETS, 1950[a]

Dollar figures in thousands

Asset class (millions)	Corpora-tions	Contributions			Net income	
		Total	Amount to chests	Per cent to chests	Total	Per cent contributed to chests
Under $1	101	$ 104	$ 31	29.8	$ 5,728	0.54
1 under 50	166	1,734	406	23.4	181,032	0.22
50 and over	59	4,951	2,019	40.8	1,137,964	0.18
Total	326	$6,789	$2,456	36.2	$1,324,724	0.19

[a] Russell Sage Foundation Survey.

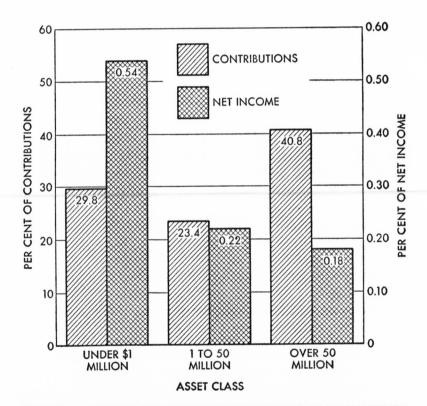

FIGURE 8. COMMUNITY CHEST CONTRIBUTIONS OF 326 SURVEYED
CORPORATIONS

Although warnings have been given against the assumption that findings for this sample will necessarily hold for all corporations, it is interesting to observe that application of this rate of 0.19 per cent to the $34.6 billion of compiled net profits of all corporations in 1948 results in an estimate of $65.7 million contributed to chests in that year, which is almost identical with the estimate of Table 26, derived from entirely different data.

It is clear from these figures that community chests now depend heavily for their present support on business contributions. In addition, business encourages employee contributions to chests through permitting plant solicitations, often with payroll deductions. Pointing out that chests receive more than two-thirds of their funds from corporations and their employees, Stanley C. Allyn, formerly president of Community Chests and Councils of America, declared recently that "the success of individual chests depends more upon the attitude of corporate management toward chest contributions than upon any other one factor."

Yardsticks for Chest Giving

Both corporations and community chests have experimented for many years with yardsticks as a means of measuring equitable shares in chest quotas, and both have sometimes resisted such measures.[1] Advantages and disadvantages of quotas in general from the corporation's point of view have been discussed in Chapter 4; but recent developments in the chest field deserve notice.

A corporation devised one of the earliest chest yardsticks. In 1936 Gerard Swope announced that the General Electric Company, of which he was then president, would bear in each of its "factory" communities "the same proportion of the community chest that we do in the taxes we pay to the community," but with the reservation that if the gifts of G.E. employees in that community were less than the Company gift, the Company would

[1] For an excellent discussion see Sturges, Kenneth, *Yardsticks for Corporation Gifts to Community Chests*, Bulletin 160, Community Chests and Councils of America, New York, 1952, from which many of the facts in this section are taken.

either decrease its own local gift or warn the Chest of that danger unless it did a better job of selling itself to individual contributors. A somewhat similar plan was developed for General Motors Corporation by Donaldson Brown at about the same time.

But neither this formula nor others proved wholly satisfactory. Any yardstick was in danger of being used as a club. The wiser chests saw to it that corporation executives had a part in devising the measuring stick and stressed friendly relations with corporate donors above any rigid formula. The Community Chest of Buffalo and Erie County pointed out that because welfare needs grow when payrolls and profits shrink, a formula should have place for the heart impulse and charitable-mindedness of corporate executives and directors. The Greater St. Paul Community Chest and Council informed national corporations of the costs to chest agencies of services in behalf of their local employees, which in one case were six times the corporation's contribution.

The fact that many corporations do not wish to reveal some of the profits and sales data needed for measuring a corporation's fair share has been met by the Rockford (Illinois) Community Chest in an interesting way. It adopts as its yardstick the *average* of one day's over-all payroll, 0.1 per cent of annual sales, and 1 per cent of annual net profit before taxes. The company may calculate the result for itself, without revealing any of the figures. This Chest's "Guide for Giving" card presented to both company officials and employees is reproduced on page 162.

Nearly all formulas recognize in varying degrees the three factors, *ability* to give as measured by net profits, gross sales, or other similar indices; *responsibility* to the community as measured usually by number of employees, or possibly tax liability; and *inclination* to give, as measured by past gifts. The Los Angeles formula, described in Chapter 4, recognizes the highly practical aspects of the last of these, and gives it great emphasis with provision for gradual adjustment toward the other two factors. The Greater New York Fund, on the other hand, accepts the highly logical first two factors as the chief criteria, and gives substantially no weight to past experience. Cleveland is cur-

ROCKFORD COMMUNITY CHEST
Guide for Giving

General Employees . . .
   Give a minimum of six hours pay.

Executive, Administrative, or Professional . . .
   Senior Executives, 1% of your annual income.
   Junior Executives, ½ of 1% of your annual income.

Corporations, Partnerships, and Individual Proprietors . . .
   Your fair share is easily figured this way:
   (Use 1950 figures, unless your fiscal year ended in 1951—
   in that event, use the figures for the fiscal year, please.)

1. Put down here one day's average overall
   payroll. Leave out overtime, of course—
   but include all payroll other than over-
   time. . . . . $. . . . . . .

2. On this line enter 1/10 of 1% of your an-
   nual sales. . . . . $. . . . . . .

3. Your annual profit, before income taxes.
   Please write 1% of that amount here. . . . $. . . . . . .
   _____

   Add these three amounts
   Now, divide by three. . . . .   3)_____

   And you have YOUR COMPANY'S
   FAIR SHARE of the 1952 Community
   Chest. . . . . $. . . . . . .

rently experimenting with a modification of the Los Angeles
formula, using past experience as an important factor, but
endeavoring to bring contributors much more rapidly up to the
level indicated by a yardstick based on profits and number of

employees adjusted into a per capita rating for the various trade groups. Certain industries and companies were necessarily given individualized treatment.

As business contributions to chests continue to grow both in dollar amounts and in relative importance in total chest budgets, objective standards are increasingly important. The search for a suitable yardstick received much emphasis at the 1952 biennial meeting of Community Chests and Councils in Milwaukee.

Federation in Large Cities

In our greatest cities the usual community chest pattern encounters difficulties. The amounts needed, the tasks of organization, and the vast numbers and varieties of agencies that have to be considered are staggering problems. Chicago and New York have solved these problems in diverse ways.

The Community Fund of Chicago is classified as a chest, though it is unable to follow the chest pattern in all respects. For 1952, the Fund included 188 local agencies with expenditure budgets aggregating $28.1 million, to be financed by $10.5 million from earnings and endowment income, $10.1 million from contributions raised by the agencies, and $7.7 million from the Community Fund. The Fund raised $8.5 million, the difference representing allocations to the United Defense Fund, administrative and campaign expenses, and an allowance for shrinkage.

The Chicago Community Fund therefore differs from the usual community chest pattern in urging its agencies to seek contributions from individuals; it does cover corporations and employee groups, offering them the usual immunity.

New York is not classified as a chest city. Its Greater New York Fund helps support most of the city's voluntary hospitals, health and social agencies. Such agencies numbered 423 in its 1951 campaign. The expenditures of these agencies for 1952 were estimated at $202 million, of which $157 million would be earned by services or received from endowment income and similar sources. Of the remaining $45 million "need," the Greater New York Fund set out to raise from business firms and employee groups $9 million. (It raised $5.9 million, mostly from corporations.) Unlike the Chicago Fund, the Greater New York Fund does not solicit from individuals except as members of employee groups. It does not even accept individual contributions of more than $100 in employee group gifts, so as to leave the field of solicitation for large individual gifts open entirely to its agencies.

Other Federated Funds

While the community chest, serving a single town or one town and its immediate neighborhood, is the best-known form of fund-collecting federation, many other types exist.

In larger cities hospitals sometimes unite for fund-raising purposes. New York's United Hospital Fund, for example, collected $2.7 million for the 1951 needs of its members.

Various national and state educational funds are discussed in Chapter 11, including the United Negro College Fund, the National Fund for Medical Education, and the mushrooming statewide college funds.

Many religious agencies are federated on a sectarian basis, and these are discussed in Chapter 12. Among examples are such organizations as the Federation of Protestant Welfare Agencies in New York City; Catholic Charities, organized in more than a hundred separate dioceses of this Church; and the United Jewish Appeal, with its affiliates.

The state, rather than either the local community or the nation, is the basis for some experiments in federation. This has logic in the fact that the state is the important unit in certain welfare activities, as when the federal government participates in supplying funds; where state planning or legislation may be involved; and in assigning local quotas for nonlocal appeals. Michigan has gone farthest in the development of a state chest in the United Health and Welfare Fund of Michigan. This organization, one of the few survivors of the state organizations that functioned under the National War Fund of World War II, conducted its fourth campaign in the fall of 1951. In many Michigan cities the local chest conducted a single campaign for its own local agencies and the state and national agencies included in the United Health and Welfare Fund "package."

The United Defense Fund

The emergencies of the defense period resulted in formation of a special national agency, the United Defense Fund. It collects funds for United Service Organizations, Inc. (USO), United Community Defense Services, American Social Hygiene Association, National Recreation Association, American Relief for Korea, and United Seamen's Service. This "federation for financing national voluntary health and welfare services made necessary by the defense effort" plans to use the greater part of its income for the armed forces; smaller amounts go to services for communities congested by the defense effort, and to helping provide used clothing and blankets for needy Koreans.

Organized late in 1950, the United Defense Fund conducted its first extensive fund-raising campaign in the fall of 1951, usually as part of the regular community chest or united fund campaigns. Its national budget was $18.6 million for 1952, and each chest was asked to accept its proportional share as determined by the National Quota Committee formula. More than a thousand chests did so, sparking their campaigns for substantially increased contributions with special notices of the addition of UDF.

Direct contributions of corporations to UDF were credited back to cities, in proportions specified by the corporations. In cities where chests did not accept the UDF for inclusion, separate campaigns were usually attempted. To reach rural and other areas not covered by city chests, statewide chests similar to those already existing in Michigan and Oregon were being organized or under consideration in many states in early 1952. The United Defense Fund realized about $12 million, substantially all from chest campaigns and the nonchest effort in New York City. The 1953 goal is $19.5 million.

Industry Funds and Plant-Level Federations

The historical chapter noticed a different kind of federation, a Manufacturers' Chest in Cambridge, Massachusetts. That experiment had a recent revival in Beloit, Wisconsin, in the Community

Relations Fund. A group of firms belonging to the Beloit Association of Commerce have agreed to make contributions only through the Community Relations Fund. Solicitors for charitable appeals or complimentary advertising are directed to the Fund, where they are required to fill out a "solicitations information request" on the background and purposes of their organizations. A committee of the Fund considers all applications and, if it approves, directs that a single contribution in the amount it determines be made to the organization for the current year in behalf of all the members of the Fund. The recipient must agree not to solicit those firms, whose names are sent along with the check.

Two Long Island (New York) counties began experimenting in 1951 with a Long Island Industry Fund, organized by industrial leaders to gather funds for local hospitals from both employee and corporation donations. By May, 1952, the Fund had collected $160,000.

Los Angeles has developed an AID plan (Associated In-Group Donors). Companies may participate if at least 51 per cent of their employees give by payroll deduction an amount representing their earnings for at least twelve minutes each week. The total is accumulated in a common fund, and disbursed not only to the community chest, but to all other accepted philanthropic drives. The contributor refers solicitors to AID, to which he has already contributed. Though announced only in the fall of 1951, by the spring of 1952 this plan had enrolled 50,000 employees and raised $1.6 million.

In the past several years a great number of individual plants have organized plant-level federations. Such a federation is a "plan by which the employees of a firm or plant subscribe at one time to two or more appeals, one of which is the Chest; the proceeds being then distributed among the agencies in a manner determined by the group itself."[1] In many instances the company makes its own charitable contributions chiefly through this fund, which may then be controlled by a combined labor-management

[1] *Experiments with More Inclusive Federation*, Part III, Plant Level Federated Funds. Community Chests and Councils of America, New York, 1951, p. 2.

committee. At least 535 plant-level federations were known to chests in 1951.

Such a plan offers both advantages and problems from the company viewpoint. Solicitations are reduced to a single annual drive, and where a "continue-until-notice" payroll deduction slip is signed, only new employees require attention. The accounting nuisance of payroll deduction is necessary if the plan is to succeed. If the chest and other benefiting agencies rest on their assured income and fail to keep their services dramatically before the contributors, interest wanes and the deduction becomes just one more form of resented taxation. If the company contributes to the same fund, joint administration may become a source either of friction or of better understanding between management and labor.

Finally, plant-level federation leaves to a committee within the company the difficult task of deciding which causes should receive help, and how much. Since few companies have the special knowledge needed for budget reviews, some rule-of-thumb is often applied. The Phoenix (Arizona) Endorsement Council, which is promoting in Phoenix the formation of such federations under the name, Community Services Fund Plans, recently suggested these percentages:

    65 to the Community Chest
    25 to the Red Cross
    10 for all other (The specific amounts to be determined by the
        Committee.)

It would seem highly undesirable to apply such rounded percentages to the quite different situations in various cities, or to freeze them into the giving pattern of any one city.

The chests, which believe their programs of community planning and budget review offer a sounder basis for distributing gifts, have sometimes opposed, sometimes tolerated, and sometimes actively promoted plant-level federations, which usually have substantially increased employee giving. They would prefer, of course, a chest-centered united fund. Efforts in that direction, and resistance to them, need next to be examined.

Growth of United Funds

The struggle between the groups favoring greater federation in fund-collecting and the agencies desiring to run independent campaigns may almost be called a welfare war. Though in the heat of battle extreme positions have been taken, both sides have powerful arguments and both are sincere in believing that their opposite courses will reach the goal each seeks, maximum income for needed social services.

The independents challenge the ability of federated fund-raising to collect enough money for the manifold needs of today. Some of these independents are very large. The American National Red Cross, to cite the extreme example, raised in its own campaign $232 million in war year 1945, as against $221 million for that year in all the chest campaigns, most of which included special wartime appeals. The National Tuberculosis Association has in its Christmas seals a special fund-raising device that has become widely accepted.[1] Several other health organizations have more recently begun to collect large amounts in national drives of various sorts. The "big six," which to varying degrees have resisted federated fund-raising, are the American Cancer Society, American Heart Association, American National Red Cross, National Foundation for Infantile Paralysis, National Society for Crippled Children and Adults, and National Tuberculosis Association.

In addition to the argument that spaced special appeals draw out dollars that would not be contributed in a single federated drive, these and similar organizations point out that emergency demands (Red Cross), epidemics (polio), and other special conditions make advance budgeting and restriction to that budget unsuitable; that the independent drives, while costly, are themselves useful in public education; and that since no cause receives as much as it could usefully employ, there should be no restriction on expanding that sum by ingenious collection methods, with appeals for particular needs to individual sympathies of donors.

[1] The tuberculosis Christmas stamp sale was sponsored by the Red Cross from 1907 to 1919; by the National Tuberculosis Association since 1919.

The goal of the proponents of federation has already been indicated—a joint appeal, seeking gifts in proportion to ability to give, to be distributed as nearly as possible in relation to need. But so far as business was concerned, the decisive factor was probably the nuisance and expense to business of multiple campaigns.

Detroit became the storm center. In 1949 industry, led by Henry Ford II and other industrialists, and with the support of the labor unions, helped organize a drive limited to Detroit industrial plants under the name, United Foundation of Detroit, which "invited" all national fund-collecting agencies to join, with notice that no other plant solicitations would be permitted. It listed various diseases, including cancer and polio. The American Cancer Society refused to come in; a contribution was made to the Michigan Cancer Foundation. The National Foundation for Infantile Paralysis announced in advance it would neither participate nor accept any money from this drive; a payment was made to the Sister Elizabeth Kenny Foundation.

The movement spread to other industrial centers. Several of the large national agencies resisted strongly, warning their local chapters of suspension if they made any move to join the federated drives. Court actions against the united funds were threatened. The skirmish in Hutchinson, Kansas, was fairly typical:

> A new organization, the United Community Chest, was set up to conduct the federated campaign. . . . General Marshall, President of the American Red Cross, sent a telegram to the executive director of the drive, demanding that the name of the Red Cross be removed from all campaign literature, and the public be informed that no funds were being raised for the benefit of the Red Cross. To this the Executive Committee replied that they were not illegally representing themselves to be agents for the Red Cross, but that individual donors have the right to make the Hutchinson United Community Chest their trustee to receive funds for the agencies they designated. Although it was expected that the Red Cross would at once resort to court action, the matter was closed by a telegram from Marshall to the President of the local Red Cross chapter requesting that the people of Hutchinson withhold their Red Cross gifts for the regular March campaign.[1]

[1] *Experiments with More Inclusive Federation*, Part II, Summary of Community Experience. Community Chests and Councils of America, Inc., New York, 1951, pp. 9–10.

In August, 1951, the American National Red Cross revised its national policy to permit chapters to cooperate with community fund campaigns by joint solicitation of industrial plants and business firms where only one fund drive a year was allowed, but with special provisions including "recognition of the Red Cross as a principal in the solicitation on an equal footing with, and not as part of, the fund-raising agency." Some communities found this formula workable for their 1952 solicitations; in others the "equal footing" provision, which logically could be demanded by all other participating agencies, was regarded as unmanageable. In Philadelphia the Red Cross was not included in the United Fund Campaign, and its general chairman indicated that "when the Red Cross comes around in March we will suggest that employees of our local firms be solicited at home." The March, 1952, drive fell far short of its goal in the Philadelphia area.

Highly industrialized communities will increasingly insist that at least plant solicitations be limited to a single annual drive. A completely satisfactory solution for inclusion of the Red Cross and other national agencies has not yet been worked out.

Meanwhile, the trend toward united funds made such large strides in some cities that the community chest itself was swallowed up. Leaders felt that some new organization was needed which would connote the sudden great increase in inclusiveness; the former chest was either abandoned or it became just one of a number of organizations participating in the new fund. But experienced chest personnel was usually prominent in the new setup, however named.

For the 1952 chest year, at least 166 campaigns included the Red Cross or some other national agency not previously participating. Most of these were true "united funds," though names varied widely. In Akron it was the Give Once-For-All Campaign; in Bay City, United Chest and Red Cross; in Columbus, Georgia, United Givers, Inc., but in Columbus, Ohio, United Appeals and Red Cross, Community Chest, USO, Heart Association and Cancer Society Campaign! "United Chest" or "United Fund" were common names, though in quite a few cities the old community chest name was retained for the bigger package; the familiar "red feather" was kept as the symbol for most campaigns, and sometimes appeared in the new name, as in Lansing's United Red Feather Campaign.

Of 38 larger "united funds" for which records are available, just half reached their expanded goal, but all except one collected more than in 1951, and two collected more than twice as much. Eight which became "united funds" within the year increased aggregate collections 21 per cent over the amount raised by all the agencies the preceding year. The experience of the United Fund of Greater New Haven is illustrative:

> The Community Chest, as such, went out of existence so that when the United Fund came into legal existence it had no member agencies. The former Community Chest agencies (thirty) were given the opportunity to withdraw at this point, but were all invited to join the new United Fund. All the former Chest agencies joined the United Fund immediately. In addition fifteen new agencies and causes were added before the first United Fund campaign.
>
> Although the campaign goal of $1,459,000 was not reached, the following were achieved:
>
> 1) Excellent, aggressive young leadership was obtained as a result of the United Fund. . . .
>
> 2) Over 60 per cent more was raised than in the Community Chest campaign of last year.
>
> 3) Almost 17 per cent more was distributed to all the former Community Chest agencies.
>
> 4) All the new agencies and causes received as much or more than they had raised in separate campaigns the year previously.[1]

How far the "united fund" tide will run is not yet certain. The ultimate decision will be made, not by the embattled agencies, but by givers. Since communities differ widely in their organization and in traditional attitudes, it is probable that small residential and rural communities may support chests in the older pattern, covering local and a few state and national agencies but with toleration for a number of independent drives, while alongside them industrialized communities will enforce the united

[1] *United Fund Campaigns for 1952.* Community Chests and Councils of America, Inc., New York, 1952, p. 8.

drives, with single plant solicitations and periodic wage deductions.

Corporations have in general supported the united fund principle. If it is to prevail, even in industrial communities, it must prove its ability to raise adequate funds for local and national agencies not merely in the first year or two, when collections are high under fresh enthusiasm and the dramatic challenge of a new idea, but in the longer run. In addition, no superchest attempts to cover all fields of philanthropy, or even in its own fields all genuine needs, such as building funds, sudden emergencies, special causes. Great opportunities will remain for corporations, as well as private donors, and only if these opportunities also are adequately met will the "united fund" method prove satisfactory.

CHAPTER 10

Voluntary Welfare Agencies

WITH GOVERNMENT increasingly oper-
ating in various fields of health and welfare, it became necessary
to distinguish between agencies run by the government and those
supported by private initiative—and contributions. At first these
were respectively called "public agencies" and "private agencies," but "private" seemed misleading since most such agencies
offer their services widely to the general public. For want of a
better term, "voluntary" is now in common use. A voluntary
welfare agency is one organized by private initiative and usually
supported by voluntary contributions. It may or may not have
"volunteer" (unpaid) workers.

Public vs. Private Support

The vast expansion of governmental services in the past two
decades has affected nearly every field of voluntary philanthropy.
The ratio between government and voluntary support for welfare
purposes will differ with definitions of "welfare purposes," but it
is estimated that government expenditure (including federal,
state, and local) is now about nine times voluntary giving for
purposes which a generation or two ago would have been considered within the field of private "charity."

In America some areas, such as religion, are wholly in the field
of private enterprise. Others, such as punishment for crime, are

restricted to government. But prevention of crime, in terms of combating juvenile delinquency or supplying desirable character-building and recreational opportunities, is largely in the hands of voluntary agencies, as are efforts at rehabilitating former prisoners. The changing picture in education, where elementary instruction is almost wholly state-supported while higher education is about half public, half private, is examined in the next chapter.

The longest stride ever made in bringing into government's orbit services that were formerly first charges upon private philanthropy was the Social Security Act, passed in 1935 but broadened by later amendment. It touches most closely the traditional fields of "charity" in its provisions, in which the states participate, for the needy aged, dependent children, the needy blind, and the permanently and totally disabled. Expenditures by government for these four categories and for general assistance, in which the federal government does not now participate, amounted to $192 million in January, 1952, which is an annual rate of $2.3 billion. At least five million persons were benefited from state and federal funds in these programs.

The need for charitable relief is also much reduced through new vast social insurance programs, particularly old-age and survivors' insurance and unemployment insurance, under the Social Security Act. In January, 1952, benefit payments went to some 4,433,000 beneficiaries under the first of these programs; to 1,384,000 in an average week under the second. These funds were accumulated from obligatory contributions by business and the benefiting employees rather than from general taxation, but if the systems prove actuarially unsound, general taxation may need to help out. The new "health and welfare funds" that are a part of many recent union contracts are not collected by government, but closely resemble a tax for welfare purposes in their impact on industry.

The proposed federal budget for 1953 includes the items shown in Table 28 relating to welfare expenditures; they are compared with 1941, the last prewar year, and 1951.

It will be noted, perhaps with surprise, that the "social security, welfare, and health" category has risen less than 5 per cent

TABLE 28. CERTAIN WELFARE EXPENDITURES OF THE FEDERAL GOVERNMENT IN FISCAL YEAR 1941 COMPARED WITH 1951 AND THE BUDGET PROPOSED FOR 1953

Dollar figures in millions

Budget number	Purpose	Fiscal years ending June 30		
		1941 actual	1951 actual	1953 budget
	SOCIAL SECURITY, WELFARE, AND HEALTH			
201.	Retirement and dependents' insurance	$ 143	$ 614	$ 726
202.	Public assistance	8[a]	1,187	1,242
203.	Aid to special groups	725	137	168
204.	Work relief and direct relief	1,575	—	—
205.	Accident compensation	5	27	37
206.	Promotion of public health	53	304	341
207.	Crime control and correction	39	109	133
208.	Defense community facilities and services	—	—	15
	Subtotal	2,548	2,378	2,662
	HOUSING AND COMMUNITY DEVELOPMENT[b]			
251.	Public housing programs	333	124	94[c]
252.	Aids to private housing	*198*[c]	462	39
253.	Research and other general housing aids	—	7	38
254.	Provision of community facilities	*4*[c]	6	41
255.	Urban development and redevelopment	—	2	25
257.	Defense housing, community facilities and services	—	—	274
258.	Disaster insurance, loans, and relief	—	—	17
	Subtotal	131	601	340
	EDUCATION AND GENERAL RESEARCH			
301.	Promotion of education	26	51	574
302.	Educational aid to special groups	12	6	8
303.	Library and museum services	5	10	12
304.	General-purpose research	24	48	29
	Subtotal	67	115	623
	MISCELLANEOUS WELFARE-RELATED ITEMS			
101.	Veterans' education and training	—	1,943	701
102.	Other veterans' readjustment benefits	10	163	111
105.	Veterans' hospitals and medical care	104	745	802
405.	Recreational use of natural resources	14	30	33
	Subtotal	128	2,881	1,647
	Total	$2,874	$5,975	$5,272

[a] The 1941 "social security administration" has been entered here; but see also 203 and 204.

[b] Omitting "civil defense," which appeared in 1953 only, at $339 million.

[c] Credit, repayments exceeding expenditures.

SOURCE: *The Budget of the United States Government for the Fiscal Year Ending June 30, 1953*, pp. 1202–1203, and earlier data.

in the past twelve years—much less than the population growth and with no allowance for the monetary inflation. The great increase has been in the war-related items of payments for veterans' education and medical care. However constituted, a federal budget of $5.3 billion ($3.7 billion without the veterans items) for welfare-related services is an impressive total when compared with $1.9 billion a year[1] receipts of all philanthropy except churches from all private sources—business, individuals, and bequests. Governmental welfare services and agencies also receive substantial support from state and local taxation.

In broad generalization, tax-supported agencies undertake to meet, more or less adequately, basic economic, health, and educational needs; in some cases for the whole population, in others for only certain specific classes of the disadvantaged. To voluntary agencies remain the important tasks of filling in gaps and inadequacies in these fields, of establishing standards and checking the work of public agencies, of covering many additional needs not now met by government, and of doing most of the exploratory, experimental, and research work in the welfare field.

But we are in a period of transition. Relations between public and voluntary agencies in philanthropy have been changing rapidly. The extent to which voluntary agencies survive the trend toward wider governmental services will depend not only upon judgment as to relative efficiency and usefulness but upon their ability to collect adequate funds.

National Voluntary Agencies

Nearly every cause to which one could possibly wish to contribute, from the treatment of alcoholics to the maintenance of zoos, is represented by at least one national voluntary agency. Many, but not all, have local branches or counterparts. This multiplicity is sometimes confusing, but the agencies can be classified, and there are useful guides through the maze.[2]

[1] Estimate from *Philanthropic Giving*, p. 73.

[2] *Social Work Year Book, 1951*, edited by Margaret B. Hodges, American Association of Social Workers, New York, 1951, is one such guide. Its directory section describes 422 national voluntary agencies in the welfare field.

Organizationally, national agencies are of three main types. Some are very loose associations, created by local agencies to perform certain advisory, research, and coordinating functions, with the national office closely controlled by the local member agencies.

Others, usually organized before their local members, retain strong control in the national office, dictating program and policy to local chapters chartered by the national organization. Local chapters may participate in policy formation through annual conventions or councils.

Finally, some national agencies have no local affiliates. They may be study or planning groups, operating only on the national level, or not yet large enough for local chapters. In some cases they are organizations of national organizations.

For example, the need for central consultation and planning in the whole field of social welfare resulted in formation in 1922 of the National Social Work Council, reorganized and broadened in 1945 as the National Social Welfare Assembly. This Assembly, which calls itself "the welfare council of the national community," includes 66 affiliate organizations, of which 15 are government bureaus.

For financial support, some national organizations run nationwide campaigns, and are known to all givers. Others appeal to selected groups, or are supported by dues or service fees of member agencies; the local giver may support them, but so indirectly that he may not even know their names. Some national agencies have endowments or other sources of income adequate for their needs, and make no appeals for funds. Collectively, national agencies represent a wide range of choice for givers, with usually more emphasis upon research, policy formulation, and administration than on meeting individual needs.

The American National Red Cross

The largest nonsectarian agency, in terms of the contributions it annually receives, is the American National Red Cross. Organized in 1881 by Clara Barton as the American Association of the Red Cross, it remained relatively small until World War I, when it engaged in the great financial drives already noted. Contributions from corporations were emphasized during that war, but after its close the Red Cross returned to main reliance upon the traditional membership "roll call" for support. Membership variation was immense. In 1914 it had only 16,000 members. In 1918 at the height of the war effort there were 20 million. By 1925 the membership was only 3 million, which rose gradually to 7 million by 1939.

With World War II this membership leaped to 56 million (of which 20 million were junior members) in 1945, and collections in that peak war year amounted to $232 million. The five major campaigns of World War II realized a total of $785 million, called by the Red Cross "the greatest freewill offering in history." To achieve such totals the emphasis on membership was modified in favor of larger individual gifts, and corporation contributions were vigorously sought.

After the war the Red Cross lowered its contribution goals and met some expenses from the surplus accumulated in the over-subscribed war drives; but it did not return to prewar levels nor abandon drives for corporate contributions. With Korea, new demands were placed upon it and budgets again rose.

In 1952 the Red Cross sought $85 million. The amount raised by the end of April was approximately $81 million. Current activities of the Red Cross are indicated by the 1953 budget, for which the 1952 drive was conducted:

Purpose	Budget (millions)
Services to the Armed Forces, veterans, and their families	$38.4
Disaster preparedness and relief	5.4
National blood program	13.3
Health, nursing, and safety services	7.4
Junior Red Cross	2.1
Service and financial assistance to chapters	3.8
International activities	.3
Other community projects	.5
Fund-raising supplies and expense	4.3
Public information	1.8
General management—planning and administration	10.9
Total	$88.2

Our Survey did not treat statistically any individual agency, but correspondence and other sources indicate that most corporations include the Red Cross in their contributions budget, and its gift is likely to be exceeded only by the community chest. National companies usually arrange to have their contributions made by their various branches to local Red Cross chapters, or, if given nationally, credited by the Red Cross office to their local branches.

TABLE 29. CONTRIBUTIONS TO AMERICAN NATIONAL RED CROSS, 1941 TO 1952, WITH PARTIAL DATA ON CORPORATE CONTRIBUTIONS

Dollar figures in millions

Year[a]	Total contributions	Contributions of 1,352 leading corporations to 113 Chapters	All corporation contributions as per cent of total contributions to 112 Chapters
1941 to 1942	$71	–	–
1942 to 1943	147	–	–
1944	216	–	–
1945	232	–	–
1946	118	–	–
1947	79	$3.4	31.5
1948	73	3.2	31.1
1949	68	2.9	29.7
1950	64	2.7	27.5
1951	78	3.4	29.4
1952	81[b]	–	–

[a] Fund drives began in November until 1944, when March became Red Cross Month.

[b] Preliminary.

SOURCE: Office of Statistics, American National Red Cross.

Until recently corporation contributions were not separately tallied by the American National Red Cross, but were not large except during World War I and during and after World War II. Table 29 presents data on total collections of the Red Cross for recent years and scattered information on corporate contributions for some of these years. In 112 Chapters, including nearly all the large cities (but not New York or Boston), the ratio of corporate to total contributions was about 30 per cent, with some decline from 1947 to 1950. Information is too fragmentary to apply these percentages nationally with much confidence, but they suggest a total of possibly $19 million contributed by corporations to the Red Cross in 1950. This and other evidence indicates that most of the sums reported in our Survey as given to "national health agencies (polio, cancer, Red Cross, etc.)" actually represented Red Cross receipts.

"American Way" Organizations

The expansion of governmental agencies and controls during recent years brought at first resentment and resistance on the part of business. Then, when popular support for most of these changes became evident, a wide variety of publicity and educational campaigns began to appear in support of what was variously called "the American way," the "free enterprise system," and the like.

A host of organizations sprang up, all promising to advance these ends. Some were research or public relations agencies soundly conceived and well managed. Others appear to have been set up by promoters who, in the words of one business critic, "would have promoted with equal vigor birth control for Eskimos, if they had seen as much money in it." At the height of the movement a group of business firms set up a Central Information Bureau, now discontinued, as a clearinghouse on these programs and organizations; an executive of this Bureau asserted that at least 500 organizations of this type were currently in existence. *Fortune* estimated in a blistering article that for 1950 the Free Enterprise campaign "will probably account for at least $100,000,000 of industry's ad budget and an unknown but hefty share of its employee-relations expenditures. . . . And it is not worth a damn."[1]

At the urging of business executives, we included in our questionnaire a special item on agencies supporting "the American way." Among 326 replying corporations, 4.5 per cent of total contributions were given to such agencies. The corporations of moderate size (assets $1 under $50 million) gave less than this average, 3.8 per cent; the largest corporations somewhat above it, at the rate of 4.7 per cent; but the highest rate was among the

[1] "Is Anybody Listening?" *Fortune*, September, 1950, p. 78.

small corporations, 5.4 per cent. These totals do not reflect amounts which may have been spent by corporations in their own advertising for this purpose. Indeed, Corporation 1865 reported:

> We have a special section of our Sales Department which is spending its entire time supporting the American Way with agencies and groups doing likewise. We have made no effort to indicate the total amount of such expenses in the space provided for that purpose on the form.

Corporation 1946, sadly reporting a loss of $98,000 for the year, made no deductible charitable contributions. Nevertheless, or possibly because of its situation, it gave $80 to "American way" agencies.

If the percentage found in the Survey sample can be applied to the 1948 total corporate giving of $239 million, the corporate contribution to "American way" organizations may have approximated $11 million for that year.

No attempt is made to evaluate these agencies, since appraisal would be needed of both the correctness of the precise economic doctrine each preaches and the effectiveness with which the preaching is performed. Among organizations of this type known to have received substantial support from corporations are the American Economic Foundation, American Heritage Foundation, American Viewpoint, Americans for the Competitive Enterprise System, Committee for Constitutional Government, Foundation for Economic Education, Freedoms Foundation, Harding College, and Spiritual Mobilization.

Recently a Crusade for Freedom was organized, seeking substantial funds to tell the American story, not chiefly to the American people, but abroad, as a means of "fighting Communist propaganda with the truth."

A House investigating committee discovered that the Committee for Constitutional Government paid its executive secretary a commission on all receipts.[1]

[1] *General Interim Report of the House Select Committee on Lobbying Activities*, 81st Congress. House Report No. 3138. Washington, 1950, p. 65.

Voluntary Health Agencies

Annual expenditures in the United States for medical care of civilians has been estimated at $11 billion. Patients pay about 70 per cent of this through doctor and hospital bills or prepay it through insurance plans. Tax funds supply about 25 per cent. The remainder comes from business and philanthropy.

Certain business expenditures in this field—in-plant medical services, workmen's compensation insurance, payments toward employee medical insurance plans—are not properly "contributions" and are therefore merely mentioned here. But corporations do contribute substantial sums to health agencies, chiefly national, and to hospitals. Table 30 from our Survey indicates that more than a quarter (26.6 per cent) of all the reported corporate contributions went to health agencies.

TABLE 30. CONTRIBUTIONS TO HEALTH AGENCIES OF 326 SURVEYED CORPORATIONS, BY AMOUNT OF CORPORATION ASSETS, 1950[a]

Dollar figures in thousands

| Group | Amount of contributions to health agencies | | | | Per cent of total corporation contributions |
	Assets under $1 million	Assets 1 under 50 million	Assets 50 million or over	Total	
Hospitals	$ 18	$ 254	$ 733	$1,005	14.8
National health agencies	11	108	574	693	10.2
Other health agencies	2	20	84	106	1.6
Total to health agencies	$ 30	$ 382	$1,392	$1,804	26.6
Total contributions	$104	$1,734	$4,951	$6,789	100.0

[a] Russell Sage Foundation Survey.

The total health contribution was a nearly uniform percentage for corporations of various asset classes. But the companies of intermediate size were below the general average in contributions to all health agencies and considerably below it in supporting national health agencies. For purposes of the Survey national health agencies were explained as "polio, cancer, Red Cross, etc." Two respondents questioned inclusion of the Red Cross among health agencies, but it seemed difficult to place its diverse program under any closer category. Probably most of the contributions here reported went to the Red Cross. Corporation 1586 reported that its total contribution of $29,030 to "national health agencies" went wholly to the Red Cross: "We make no cash donations to polio, cancer, heart drives, etc."

The progressive "fractionating" of the human body among separate agencies, most of whom conduct aggressive fund-raising drives, has become a major headache for the corporate contributor. One editor suggests:

> It does not seem to be too much to ask all the people who are worried about the ravages of one particular disease or condition to the exclusion of all others, to get together and worry a little about the sum total of human health, and the sum total of the public's ability to stand the strain of an increasingly expanding number of drives.
>
> There are just too many diseases for each to have its own special organization, complete with radio hitchhikes, sponsored ads, expensive brochures, pledge cards, team captains and collection envelopes.[1]

Nearly all the health agencies have joined the National Health Council, which has 42 members—33 active (national agencies), 3 advisory (all governmental agencies), 4 associate, and 2 "sustaining" business firms. But this Council, while it renders many useful coordinating services, has found no formula for a united health drive. With a few exceptions, these organizations are unwilling even to submit their budgets for review to the National Budget Committee. Each regards its cause as of unique importance, and feels able to raise more money by the special appeals it has developed than it might receive from a united drive.

One result is distribution of funds in the health field more nearly in proportion to the "heart appeal" of the cause and the technical skill of the fund-raisers than to relative need. Agency executives themselves have sometimes pointed this out:

> Not many know that only 32 persons died from polio last July during what was considered a severe polio epidemic, while 4,562 persons died of heart diseases in the same month.[2]

[1] *Advertising Age*, March 19, 1951, p. 12.

[2] Elliott V. Bell, chairman of the Board of Directors, New York Heart Association, February 15, 1950.

But to such comparisons the polio people might have replied that polio did not receive all the funds it could effectively use, and if there had been no separate March of Dimes there is no assurance that those particular dimes and dollars would have been given at all to health services.

Table 31 indicates the multiplicity and something of the dimensions of fund-raising campaigns in the health field.

TABLE 31. FUND-RAISING CAMPAIGNS OF CERTAIN NATIONAL HEALTH AGENCIES, 1951, 1952

Dollar figures in millions

Organization	Campaign month	1951		1952	
		Sought	Raised	Sought	Raised
American Cancer Society	April	$14.6	$15.0	$16.0	$16.0[a]
American Heart Association	February	8.0	5.6	8.0	6.1[a]
American National Red Cross	March	84.7	77.6	85.0	81.0[a]
American Social Hygiene Association	Note b.	0.6	0.4	0.6	—
Arthritis and Rheumatism Foundation	Nov.–Dec.	2.0	1.0	3.5	—
Muscular Dystrophy Associations of America	Nov.–Jan.	—	—	1.0	—
National Foundation for Infantile Paralysis	January	—	33.3	—	41.0[a]
National Multiple Sclerosis Society	Dec.–Apr.	—	—	0.4	0.1[a]
National Society for Crippled Children and Adults	Easter	—	6.1	6.5	6.3[a]
National Tuberculosis Association	Nov.–Dec.	—	21.7	—	—
Sister Elizabeth Kenny Foundation	Aug.–Oct.	1.7	1.5	2.1	—
United Cerebral Palsy	May	—	2.1	5.0	—

[a] Preliminary.   [b] In United Defense Fund in 1952.
SOURCE: Correspondence with the organizations.

In addition to organizations conducting national campaigns, a number raise funds by special appeals to business, individuals, and foundations. Examples of these are National Safety Council, of obvious interest to many industrial groups, and the various national agencies for the blind, the hard of hearing, and other handicapped groups. Local agencies also are sometimes large, and perform important functions, as for example the Lighthouse of the New York Association for the Blind. Health-planning councils have been organized in no fewer than 32 states and 1,190 local communities, and the number is growing.

Corporate support for these health services, and more particularly toward the organized drives of the national agencies, has varied widely. The two sample corporation policy statements cited in Appendix F happen to take quite opposite positions on this subject, the one approving contributions to "cancer, tuberculosis, infantile paralysis, heart and other similar health campaigns, etc." while the other states it will not contribute to *"Specialized Health Appeals,* such as campaigns to combat heart, cancer, tuberculosis, infantile paralysis, cerebral palsy, alcoholism, etc., etc. Because of long standing social custom, an exception will be made to permit nominal purchases of Christmas Seals on a local basis." One industrial group so strongly opposes the multiplicity of health drives that its members were planning, when interviewed, to create for the industry "one general health fund and redistribute it to the various health drives." They were less clear on how this distribution was to be apportioned.

Sometimes a company makes a direct health contribution, as in the various health services of life insurance companies, the support of sheltered workshops for the handicapped through offering regular business contracts, or the Allis-Chalmers Manufacturing Company's mechanical kidney:

> We have been fortunate, in the past year, in that we have been able to work with outstanding medical men in the building of a successful mechanical kidney. This machine, which snatched a man from death's door, proved so effective that two more were made, one for a medical school and one for a large clinic. The first machine, which was manufactured at considerable expense, was donated to the community.[1]

Hospitals

Even before permissive legislation on corporate giving existed, hospital contributions were regarded as clearly in a company's interest when employees would make substantial use of the facilities.

Hospitals remain by long odds the most important among the local health resources supported by corporations. As Table 30

[1] Reported in *American City,* March, 1950.

indicates, more than half of all corporate contributions for health go to hospitals, rising to two-thirds of the health contributions of the corporations of intermediate size. In addition, the amounts shown here are not all the corporate dollars that reach hospitals, since in many cases a portion of the operating expenses of local hospitals is met from community chest contributions.

Some companies contribute to operating expense budgets only, others only to special building campaigns, and many to both purposes. Replies to our question on capital contributions indicate that a very large portion of the totals reported there went for hospital construction. One company notes that it makes an exception to its rule against contributions to religious agencies in favor of hospitals under religious supervision if they "serve the general public." Usually contributions are limited to hospitals used by employees and their families, but the International Harvester Company recently broadened its policies to include "other hospitals in works cities either to help relieve the patient load upon the hospital which we use for industrial purposes, or for public relations reasons."

Currently, there are about 6,600 registered hospitals in the United States with 1.5 million beds. About half these beds are in mental hospitals, 40 per cent in general hospitals, the remainder in various other types. Some 78 per cent of all hospital beds are in hospitals operated by federal, state, or local government, but most of these hospitals are restricted to special groups (such as veterans) or to patients hospitalized for particular diseases, such as mental illness or tuberculosis.

Building costs range from $15,000 to $20,000 or more per bed, making a 300-bed institution cost upwards of $4 million. The 315-bed Methodist Hospital in Houston, Texas, for example, was reported to have cost $4.5 million when dedicated in late 1951. In larger cities, the aspirations of hospitals need to be subjected to citywide planning if costs are to be kept within reasonable bounds.

Inflation has severely affected the operating costs of voluntary hospitals. According to the American Hospital Association, the 1951 cost per patient day was $18.01. Reports from 2,922 nonprofit, general hospitals to the Association show total income of $1,746 million, of which patient income totaled $1,551 million. The remaining $195 million came from endowments; allotments from city, county, and state governments for care of indigents; and from contributions of individuals, corporations, foundations, and some miscellaneous sources.

In most cases funds are collected by individual hospitals, though in an increasing number of cities federated campaigns are conducted after appraisal of hospital needs of the given population. In New York City 83 hospitals join in an annual United Hospital Campaign, which in 1951 asked for $3.5 million, and collected approximately $2.7 million.

Family Services

Various services to families form an important part of the welfare program of all but the smallest communities. They are customarily performed by local agencies, and fortunately for contributors, usually derive their support from a community chest rather than from separate drives.

The most notable change among these voluntary agencies has been their shift from direct relief to guidance and supporting services. The extent to which public agencies have taken over responsibility for meeting most of the primary needs of "bread and milk and medicine, of shelter and clothing" is noted in a *New York Times* editorial, which goes on to say:

> But now the equally important needs of the mind and the spirit and the individual personality are at last being given scientific attention. In this new sphere of moral and psychological assistance that is as much preventive as it is curative the private agency continues both to pioneer and to perform a service that is indispensable. Private charity formerly helped its beneficiaries to exist. Now it helps them to live, and to become useful, productive and happier members of society.[1]

These services are of great variety. They may include family and premarital counseling, adult vocational and employment aid, legal aid, assistance to various groups of the handicapped,

[1] *New York Times*, December 9, 1951.

aid to the aged, to transients, housekeeper services, income supplementation for special needs, family budgeting, and a wide variety of services for children—day nurseries, child protection, foster home care, children's institutions, maternity homes, vocational training. In smaller communities two or three agencies may attempt to cover all these needs; in large cities the organizations may run into the hundreds, counting the separate homes and institutions.

In such service agencies it is obvious that the older concept of giving—seeing that nearly all the gift reaches persons in need in actual dollars and cents, with a minimum for "overhead," "service," or staff salaries—is no longer applicable. We have pointed out elsewhere:

> It might seem a commendable act (and would show up irreproachably on the annual report) for an agency to give a breadwinner who has lost his arm $20 a week toward support of his needy family. Instead, this agency may interview the man, his friends, his former employer; take the facts discovered to a specialist in employment for the handicapped; and send him to a school to be fitted for a job where his handicap will not seriously interfere with his ability to earn. Soon he may again be supporting his family, with self-respect and interest in living revived. All of this is service and "overhead," but in the end it will cost vastly less even in cold cash than continuing weekly aid, and do vastly more for the man and his family.[1]

Overhead does need to be examined, and agencies that are substandard or have outlived their usefulness should be eliminated. But business, better than the private donor, understands the eventual economy of adequate and skilled service.

Recreation and Character Building

A considerable group of agencies, chiefly for youth, may be classified as related to recreation and character building. Examples in the youth field include American Youth Hostels, Boy Scouts of America, Boys' Clubs of America, Camp Fire Girls, 4-H Clubs, Girl Scouts of the United States of America, Junior

[1] *Philanthropic Giving*, p. 119.

Achievement, the YMCA, YWCA, the several Catholic and Jewish youth programs, and the National Federation of Settlements and Neighborhood Centers. These are all "national" organizations, but the local branches provide the actual service under varying degrees of guidance and control from the national organization. Sometimes purely local groups are developed to serve similar purposes.

Recreational agencies often have no age limitation. The founding fathers put recreation among the "unalienable Rights" in the Declaration of Independence in terms of the "pursuit of Happiness," but only in the past few decades has recreation become highly organized. Many of our leisure-time facilities are now provided out of tax funds—national, state, and local parks; playgrounds, public libraries, museums, swimming pools, civic centers, and the like. Many others are commercially provided— professional baseball, football, boxing, racing, motion pictures, sponsored radio and television, the theater. But even in these fields voluntary agencies have often been needed to perform advisory and other services. The National Recreation Association, for example, gives itself a broad mandate to "promote a program whose purpose is that every child in America may have a chance to play, and that all persons, young and old, may have an opportunity to find the best and most satisfactory manner of using leisure time." There is a National Industrial Recreation Association[1] serving as a national clearinghouse for information on programs for employee recreation, to which some 270 companies currently belong.

Many companies contribute to some or nearly all of these recreation and character-building agencies in their plant communities and sometimes, as in Junior Achievement, lend special aid to their programs. Not infrequently they sponsor ball teams, supplying uniforms, paying incidental expenses, and perhaps contributing to maintain a ball field or lending such facilities on company property. In New York City the Police Athletic League conducted a drive in 1952 among corporations and others for $969,000 to operate 75 youth centers, 75 play streets and play-

[1] 203 N. Wabash Ave., Chicago 1, Ill.

grounds, and 2,300 baseball, softball, and basketball teams, as well as its summer camp and many other activities for young boys and girls.

One exception should be noted to the otherwise universal welcome accorded to corporation gifts in these fields. Distillers report that they are usually unable to contribute to youth organizations for fear it will be considered an attempt to influence the drinking habits of young people.

Sometimes companies contribute recreational facilities themselves, or join with an organization in providing them. The Standard Oil Company of Indiana in 1926 gave Wood River, Illinois, a park including a swimming pool and "Round House," where teen-agers conduct their social activities under supervision of an adult council.[1] The Trumann (Arkansas) Community House was built by the men of Trumann in their spare time, with materials donated by the Poinsett Lumber and Manufacturing Company. The Southern Railway supplied the station for the miniature railway the City of Birmingham, Alabama, placed in its new park.

Cultural and Community Activities

Corporations often contribute to general cultural or other community facilities, sometimes through national or local agencies, sometimes in a program of their own devising.

The "public" library—there are now some 7,500 public and an additional 4,000 school and special libraries in the United States—is one of the most widely spread of such facilities. Unlike the public school, it is seldom built and wholly supported by taxes. Andrew Carnegie alone, by the time of his death in 1919, had given a total of 2,811 library buildings at a cost of $60 million. He made these gifts, however, on condition that the community should furnish a suitable site, and should guarantee an annual support for the library of not less than 10 per cent of the cost of the building. Probably most library buildings in smaller com-

[1] This and the two following examples are cited from *Community Relations: Being a Good Neighbor*, A Report Prepared for Metropolitan Group Policyholders by the Policyholders Service Bureau, Group Division, Metropolitan Life Insurance Company, New York, 1949.

munities are private gifts, memorials, or the result of a special subscription.

Companies contribute toward such building campaigns, or toward book collections. Occasionally the connection is direct and obvious, as when the New York Public Library invited a group of leading businessmen to aid in its 1951 drive for $400,000 for its special reference library. General contributions to libraries are justified by many companies on the basis of use by employees and their families, or simply as good citizenship. The Libby-Owens-Ford Glass Company, for example, gave Rossford, Ohio, $50,000 toward a new public library in recognition of the co-operative relationship between the community and the Company. An organization of Greek ship operators presented 1,500 volumes of Greek classics in English to the Columbia University libraries.

There are about 3,000 museums in the United States, of which nearly half are historical, and one-third devoted to science; the remaining sixth, however, includes the art museums, which are among the largest and most heavily endowed. Companies often contribute toward special museum collections, especially in the science museums, and sometimes toward general expenses or building funds. Traveling exhibits or collections closely related to the company's product are usually excellent advertising, properly chargeable as a business expense, though also a cultural contribution.

To commemorate its hundredth anniversary in 1951, Corning Glass Works at Corning, New York, built a Glass Center, including the Corning Museum of Glass, which preserves glass of scientific and historic importance and encourages the study of glass and glass-making. The museum is a separate corporation, controlled by a board of trustees that includes educational and civic leaders who represent the public. Contributions to it are tax-exempt.

Corporations support a wide variety of other cultural activities and interests in communities in which their employees live. These include symphony orchestras, outdoor theaters, band concerts, adult education in many forms.

In a few instances the community contribution is not made to a voluntary agency, but to the community as a unit of government. The subsidizing of master plans for towns in which the company is located is a growing practice. In 1951 the Nixon Nitration Works gave a dam and 48 acres of land, providing New Brunswick, New Jersey, with water storage capacity for 95 million additional gallons.

One of the most unusual examples of this sort was the gift the day after Christmas, 1951, of $100,000 in cash to the Town of Northbridge, Massachusetts, by the Whitin Machine Works in recognition of a "very good year" and a desire to "show our interest in the town." No conditions were attached, and at last report the use of this money was to be decided by a town meeting.

CHAPTER 11

Education and Research

TRADITIONALLY, philanthropy has played the major part in the support of education. An early example is the Academy near Athens. Before Plato died in 347 B.C., he directed that the natural income from his own fields should be devoted to the perpetual support of the Academy; it survived nearly 900 years, being finally suppressed by the Christian Emperor Justinian in A.D. 529 for teaching "pagan" doctrines.

All early American colleges were founded and chiefly supported by philanthropists, and were usually under religious auspices. About a century ago the elementary schools, until then largely private, began to be supported by taxation. But in many states, particularly in the South, free public schools were not plentiful until after the Civil War. Now public education, usually through high school and sometimes including two or even four years of college, is available everywhere in the United States.

Higher Education Today

With elementary and secondary education now largely in the hands of the state and tax supported, the philanthropic problem centers in higher education. Under present conditions parents cannot in many cases pay the mounting costs of a college education for their children; and even when they can, their payments do not fully reimburse the college. A glance at backgrounds will be revealing.

193

TABLE 32. POPULATION 18 TO 21 YEARS, STUDENTS IN INSTITU-
TIONS OF HIGHER EDUCATION, AND NUMBER OF SUCH
INSTITUTIONS, 1900 TO 1950

Year	Population 18 to 21 years (thousands)	Students in institutions of higher education (thousands)	Students as per cent of population 18 to 21 years	Institutions of higher education		
				Private	Public	Total
1900	5,931	238	4	—	—	969
1910	7,335	355	5	—	—	866
1920	7,344	598	8	627	414	1,041
1930	9,033	1,101	12	890	519	1,409
1940	9,754	1,494	15	1,141	610	1,751
1944	9,776	1,155[a]	12	1,061	589	1,650
1946	9,537	1,677	18	1,144	624	1,768
1948	9,273	2,616	28[b]	1,158	630	1,788
1950	8,979	2,659	30[b]	1,203	665	1,868

[a] Includes 278 thousand full-time military students.

[b] Percentage not comparable because of inclusion of many veterans from older age groups.

SOURCE: *Biennial Survey of Education, 1946–1948*, and *Circular 326*, August, 1951, Office of Education.

The problems of higher education mushroomed in the period between the two world wars. From 1918 to 1940 the total population of the country increased from 104 to 132 million, a mere 27 per cent; but in the same period students in higher education increased from 440,742 to 1,494,203, an increase of 239 per cent! Then in war year 1944 the enrollment was down to 877,000 regular students, plus 278,000 full-time military students. When World War II was over, the enrollment bounded up to the unprecedented height of more than two and a half million college students, many of whom were older veterans, who might never have gone to college had it not been for the government aid available under the GI Bill of Rights.[1] Table 32, reflecting these

[1] Servicemen's Readjustment Act, Public Law 346, 78th Congress.

Notes to Table 33

[a] Related to instructional departments, as dairy products, etc.

[b] Residence and dining halls, intercollegiate athletics, printing and other industrial plants, etc.

[c] Includes student aid, prizes, promotion, interest on debt.

[d] Almost wholly for endowment.

[e] Includes annuity funds.

SOURCE: *Circulars 326* and *332*, August and December, 1951, Federal Security Agency, Office of Education.

TABLE 33. FINANCIAL DATA FOR INSTITUTIONS OF HIGHER EDUCATION, SCHOOL YEAR 1949–1950

Dollar figures in millions

Data for institutions of higher education	Private institutions		Public institutions		All institutions	
	Number	Per cent of all institutions	Number	Per cent of all institutions	Number	Per cent of all institutions
Number of institutions	1,203	64	665	36	1,868	100
Students (thousands)	1,304	49	1,355	51	2,659	100
Faculty (thousands)	124	50	123	50	247	100
	Amount	Per cent of receipts	Amount	Per cent of receipts	Amount	Per cent of receipts
Receipts for current operation:						
Student fees	$ 293	26	$ 102	8	$ 395	17
Federal government	278	24	246	20	524	22
State governments	28	2	464	37	492	21
Local governments	1	—	60	5	61	3
Endowment earnings	87	8	9	1	96	4
Private benefactions	99	9	19	2	118	5
Organized activities[a]	48	4	64	5	112	5
Miscellaneous sources	20	2	15	1	35	1
Auxiliary enterprises[b]	265	23	247	20	511	21
Other noneducational income	17	2	13	1	30	1
Total receipts	$1,136	100	$1,239	100	$2,374	100
	Amount	Per cent of expenditures	Amount	Per cent of expenditures	Amount	Per cent of expenditures
Expenditures for current operation:						
Administration and general expense	$ 130	12	$ 83	7	$ 213	9
Resident instruction	366	33	415	36	781	35
Organized research	109	10	116	10	225	10
Extension	12	1	75	7	87	4
Libraries	29	3	27	2	56	3
Plant operation and maintenance	112	10	113	10	225	10
Organized activities[a]	50	5	69	6	119	5
Auxiliary enterprises[b]	241	22	236	20	477	21
Other noneducational expenditures[c]	43	4	20	2	63	3
Total expenditures	$1,092	100	$1,154	100	$2,246	100
	Amount	Per cent of all institutions	Amount	Per cent of all institutions	Amount	Per cent of all institutions
Receipts for plant expansion	$ 129	24	$ 400	76	$ 529	100
Expenditures for plant expansion	141	34	276	66	417	100
Private gifts and grants for nonexpendable funds[d]	62	93	5	7	67	100
Property:						
Physical plant and plant funds	$2,386	45	$2,887	55	$5,273	100
Endowment and other nonexpendable funds[e]	2,202	85	399	15	2,601	100
Student loan funds	29	67	14	33	43	100
Total property	$4,617	58	$3,300	42	$7,917	100

195

extraordinary changes, highlights the problems of colleges in fitting plant and instructional staff to so volatile a situation. Final 1951–1952 figures are not in, but preliminary data indicate a drop in enrollment of some 10 per cent, because of the ending of GI scholarships and the new draft affecting regular students.

A comprehensive view of present support for higher education is given by Table 33, but allowance must be made for the fact that this table represents the school year 1949–1950 when a substantial veteran contingent was still in the colleges. Of the federal government's contribution of $524 million, $307 million was for veterans' education.

In the field of higher education, while there are almost twice as many private schools as public, most private schools are smaller; in the two groups, the numbers of students and of faculty are nearly equal, as are current income and expenditures. Public institutions have a slightly more valuable physical plant, and it is increasing more rapidly; private institutions have almost all of the available endowment.

Receipts for current operation were at a new high of $2.4 billion, and if receipts for plant expansion and for nonexpendable funds (chiefly additions to endowment) are included, total income approximated $3 billion for the year. Expenditures, including those for plant expansion, amounted to about $2.7 billion.

Student fees no longer meet a major part of this enormous budget, though the private college does get 26 per cent of its money for current operation from this source, and an additional 23 per cent from auxiliary enterprises, mainly paid by students.

The contribution of government at its three levels is worth emphasis. For all institutions it amounted to 46 per cent, and for public institutions, nearly two-thirds. Even private colleges got $307 million for current operation from government (26 per cent), but $180 million of this was for veterans' education, an item being rapidly reduced; the remainder is for other services rendered, including especially research.

As Table 34 indicates, the total educational and general income of colleges and universities trebled in the decade 1940–1950. The amounts received from state governments—heavy contributors to the great state universities—rose in about the same proportion, as did the contribution of local government. But the federal contribution rose from $39 million to $524 million, increasing more than 13-fold. Without the veterans' education item, the 1950 federal payment was $217 million, a fivefold increase in the decade.

TABLE 34. CONTRIBUTIONS TO HIGHER EDUCATION FROM FEDERAL, STATE, AND LOCAL GOVERNMENTS, CERTAIN YEARS, 1940 TO 1950

Dollar figures in millions

Year	Contributions from governments				Total educational and general income[a]	
	Federal	State	Local	Total	Amount	Per cent from governments
1940	$39	$151	$24	$214	$571	37
1944	308	175	27	510	864	59
1946	197	225	31	453	925	49
1948	526	352	48	926	1,538	60
1950	524	492	61	1,077	1,834	59

[a] Omits auxiliary enterprises and other noneducational income from "receipts for current operation."

SOURCE: *Biennial Survey of Education, 1944–1946*, and *1946–1948*, and *Circular 332*, December, 1951, Office of Education.

The proportion of educational and general income which higher education receives from all governmental sources has risen from 37 per cent in 1940 to approximately 60 per cent in recent years. Privately controlled institutions receive a negligible amount of the sums voted by state or local government, but somewhat more of the federal funds than the publicly controlled institutions. These sums are not subsidies, but are paid for specific services rendered, including education of veterans.[1]

Philanthropy contributes a smaller portion of current funds of colleges and universities than is generally realized—about 9 per cent. In 1950 this amount was divided nearly equally between endowment earnings representing past philanthropy, totaling $96 million, and current private benefactions of $118 million. But

[1] For a detailed study of federal educational contributions, see Russell, James Earl, *Federal Activities in Higher Education After the Second World War*, King's Crown Press, New York, 1951.

philanthropy should also be credited with $67 million given during the year in private gifts for nonexpendable funds, chiefly endowment, and about 40 per cent of the $417 million for plant expansion. In addition, philanthropy has built up the $2.6 billion in "endowment and other nonexpendable funds" belonging to all institutions and most of the $2.4 billion plant of the private institutions, and shares in various other forms of educational aid. An examination of the schedules of reporting colleges suggests also that these figures are not complete.

The Stake of Business in Education

The picture thus far presented is not deeply disturbing. Clearly, colleges have had a tremendous job in keeping up with the jump in enrollment after World War II. With the aid of quonset huts and overcrowded classes they managed in some fashion, and that bulge is now past. Financial statistics for 1949–1950 indicate operations at unprecedented dollar levels, but with receipts exceeding expenditures by a comfortable margin, both for budgetary items and for plant expansion, and with modest additions to endowment.

Unfortunately the 1950 data, the latest yet available from the government, do not reflect present conditions. The Korean military situation has brought a severe inflation which greatly increases college expenditures, even though faculty salaries have not kept pace with rising prices. It also resulted at first in wholesale enlistments and disarrangements in student bodies; the situation in the academic year 1951–1952 was not so catastrophic as had been predicted, but a loss of about 10 per cent in registrations is indicated. Endowment earnings have not substantially increased.

Most colleges believe they cannot further raise student fees. "Private colleges will soon be forced to admit only the economically privileged," warns one authority,[1] unless government subsidies or additional funds from private donors become available. Even the state universities are now in most cases charging sub-

[1] Hollis, Ernest V., "Federal Aid for Higher Education," *School and Society*, January 8, 1949, p. 20.

stantial student fees, a development stimulated by government payments for GI's.

A *New York Times* survey[1] at the beginning of the 1951–1952 school year reported that 50 per cent of the private colleges in the United States are operating on a deficit. Business leaders have become deeply concerned. Among those who have made recent statements on the stake of business in the survival of private higher education are three board chairmen, Irving S. Olds of the United States Steel Corporation, Frank W. Abrams of Standard Oil Company (New Jersey), and Alfred P. Sloan, Jr., of General Motors Corporation. Mr. Olds' statement is typical:

> Capitalism and free enterprise owe their survival in no small degree to the existence of our private, independent universities. Both are not only important to each other—they are dependent upon each other. . . . I want to say emphatically that—in my opinion—every American business has a direct obligation to support the free, independent, privately-endowed colleges and universities of this country to the limit of its financial ability and legal authority.[2]

Such pronouncements mark a reversal in the attitude of American business. Traditionally, money had been granted only when a substantial relationship to the company's interest has been obvious. Such programs included scholarships for children of employees, fellowships in the field of the company's operations, contract research or even fundamental research, but in the general area of company activities, and sometimes support of local colleges. But nearly all the older company policy statements opposed general contributions to higher education where no such relationship was clear. These paragraphs from two policy statements[3] were typical:

> Contributions will be made only when the institutions render direct service to C.I.T. through courses of instruction for our employees, specific research activities or other similar functions.
>
> C.I.T. FINANCIAL CORPORATION

[1] Reported by Benjamin Fine, September 30, 1951.
[2] From an address at Yale University, October 19, 1951.
[3] Presented in full in Appendix G.

Educational Institutions: Many educational institutions today seek corporation financial support. Such support to educational institutions, we think, can be looked upon as a proper expenditure of corporation funds where it brings direct or indirect benefit to the Company. We believe such support must be limited to assistance of specific research projects, scholarship and fellowship programs and loans of, or discounts on purchases of, machinery and equipment of these institutions, provided any crops that may be produced by the institution are not sold in competition with crops produced by our farmer customers.

We follow the policy of not making contributions to tax-supported public educational institutions, except in rare instances where public funds may not be available for some special project that is of great interest and potential direct benefit to the Company's business.

INTERNATIONAL HARVESTER COMPANY

Many policy statements were even more pointed. "Contributions for general education are to be discouraged." "Contributions should not be made to educational institutions nor for endowment or scholarship purposes." But, says Corporation 54, "This problem of corporate assistance to higher level education is an extremely interesting one and I think that all businesses are going to have to develop a philosophy on it."[1] Our personal interviews conducted in 1951 and 1952 revealed a new and keen interest on the part of many of the large corporations, with much questioning as to how effective giving to general colleges could be done.

The Survey Record

The Survey, reflecting 1950 giving, shows a low level of educational support. The analysis of contributions under education included four subdivisions: scholarships and fellowships; research in colleges; institutional aid, schools and colleges; agencies supporting "the American way." The last of these was placed under education in default of a more suitable classification; but the moneys so spent had seldom any relation to support of institu-

[1] *Corporate Contributions Report.* American Society of Corporate Secretaries, New York, 1950, p. 32.

tions of higher education, and should be largely discounted for purposes of this discussion.

Contributions of the small corporations to education were nearly negligible. Of the amounts they did give, as much went to agencies promoting the American way as to scholarships, fellowships, research, and collegiate institutional aid combined.

TABLE 35. EDUCATIONAL CONTRIBUTIONS OF 326 SURVEYED CORPORATIONS, BY AMOUNT OF CORPORATION ASSETS, 1950[a]

Dollar figures in thousands

Purpose	Amount of contributions to education				Per cent of total corporation contributions
	Assets under $1 million	Assets 1 under 50 million	Assets 50 million or over	Total	
Scholarships and fellowships	—[b]	$47	$140	$187	2.8
Research in colleges	—[b]	49	370	420	6.2
Institutional aid, schools and colleges	$4	308	213	524	7.7
Aid to agencies supporting "the American way"	4	68	234	306	4.5
Total to education	$ 8	$472	$957	$1,437	21.2
Total contributions	$104	$1,734	$4,951	$6,789	100.0

[a] Russell Sage Foundation Survey.   [b] Less than $500.

Corporations of moderate size gave much more heavily to education than other businesses, and two-thirds of their contributions were for institutional aid. Many such companies find only one or two local colleges within their area of immediate interest, simplifying their problem. Their characteristic gift of direct institutional aid is of most benefit to the ailing college budget.

The largest corporations concentrated their educational giving on research, with more modest amounts for institutional aid, for scholarships and fellowships, and to the "American way" agencies.

In addition to the dollar amounts reported to the Survey, various companies indicated contributions in the form of equipment, discount on educational sales, and gifts of educational materials, which in one case were valued at "slightly over $10,000 in 1950."

Examination of the individual schedules disclosed that only 196 of the reporting 326 corporations gave at all to education. Forty per cent did not give any money to education in any form.

If the distributions found in this sample are applied to the 1948 total giving of corporations, the dollar picture would look like this: Total corporate contributions, $239 million. Total to all forms of education, $51 million,[1] distributed as follows: scholarships and fellowships, $7 million; research in colleges, $15 million; institutional aid to schools and colleges, $18 million; agencies supporting the "American way," $11 million. As noted, little of the "American way" money went to colleges. Also, the research funds were mostly earmarked for projects related to the corporation's own interests and usually barely paid their own extra costs; scholarships, too, helped students but seldom the college budget. That leaves the $18 million in institutional aid, which is about 1 per cent of the colleges' educational and general income.

Scholarships

Aid to students may be offered as a scholarship, usually for undergraduate work; a fellowship, awarded usually to scholars of proved ability for work in a special field; or a student loan.

The total number of scholarships now available is not known, but the United States Office of Education recently reported 141,554 scholarships from all sources in 1,198 colleges. Under present trends in student costs, scholarship aid is an important factor in making higher education possible for many students. The situation at Oberlin College is illustrative, and may be reasonably representative for the private college:

> About 530 students, or 25 per cent of the total student body, are receiving scholarship aid from special scholarship funds or from general college income. About 15 per cent of the total tuition of all students in the College is covered by scholarships.

[1] The Commission on Financing Higher Education urges 0.5 per cent of net income before taxes for education. On 1948 income, that would have amounted to $173 million. *Higher Education and American Business*, The Commission, New York, 1952, p. 3.

In addition over 700 students, or about 30 per cent of the student body, are working their way through college in whole or in part, through part-time jobs in dining halls, dormitories, laboratories, etc., averaging over $200 each per year from such work.[1]

Although scholarships offered by business firms are not yet numerous, an increasing number of companies support such plans. Sometimes these are limited to employees or employees' children. In such cases the field is usually not specified and the operation is best described as employee relations. Indeed, a few companies appear to be avoiding such programs for fear they may become a fringe benefit in union negotiations. But at least a hundred companies do have scholarship plans, widely varying in liberality and in detail.

One carefully considered plan is operated by the Ford Motor Company Fund. In 1951 and again in 1952 this Scholarship Program offered some 70 scholarships to sons and daughters of Ford employees who receive base pay of less than $675 per month. The applicant must be a high-school senior in the top third of his or her class, and is chosen on the basis of competitive tests and the judgment of a board of educators. Winners get full tuition and academic fees together with 80 per cent of the prevailing average rate for local room and board up to a maximum of $750 per year for such living expenses if the students do not live at home; 40 per cent of local room and board up to $300 for students living at home. Scholarships continue for four years if satisfactory personal and scholastic standards are maintained. A unique and important feature of the Ford plan is the granting of an additional $500 a year to the general educational budget of the college or university each such scholar selects, provided it is not tax-supported. By this means the Company makes a direct contribution to the private colleges of the nation without the onus of selection; the scholars do the choosing. When in full operation this program may cost some $350,000 annually, of which possibly $70,000 will go to the colleges, depending somewhat upon the proportion of private colleges chosen by the winners.

[1] Statement on behalf of Oberlin College before the House of Representatives Ways and Means Committee, February 10, 1950.

The General Electric Company has an education assistance program financed in part from income from a million dollar Educational Fund. Scholarships and loans for employees or their children are available for undergraduate study. The candidate applies for "undergraduate financial assistance" which may be either in the form of a scholarship or a loan. Seventy $500 scholarships and twenty $250 loans are available. Additional loans for study at Union College are also available through the Gerard Swope Loans. Thirty $500 scholarships, mostly in engineering, are also awarded each year to outstanding juniors to help them complete their senior year. These awards are not restricted to employees, and recipients are recommended by professors who have attended the GE summer professors' conference.

A word of caution is needed with respect to student loans. Such arrangements appeal to many donors as a means of making the money go farther, the original fund being presumably paid back and used time and again. Repayment, however, is not always accomplished and efforts to collect create severe problems. Such loans are not popular with students, many of whom prefer to combine work with study rather than mortgage their future. Some colleges report that loan funds already in their hands are more than adequate for the demand.

Electrical contractors and the union which are members of the Joint Industry Board of the Electrical Industry in New York City are granting scholarships worth $4,260 each at Columbia University or Barnard College to sons and daughters of workers in Local 3 of the International Brotherhood of Electrical Workers, AFL. This particular plan is financed by the contractors, the number of scholarships varying with the number of firms which reach an agreed profit level in the given year. For 1952–1953 some 25 scholarships will be available. Similar plans are sometimes jointly financed by industry and labor, and a few by labor alone.

Other scholarship plans are open to the general public, at least in a given region. In such cases the field is usually specified, and the purpose is to increase trained personnel.

The most famous of these plans is the Annual Science Talent Search financed by the Westinghouse Educational Foundation and administered by Science Clubs of America. The 1952 contest attracted some 15,000 contestants. The 40 finalists receive a five-day trip to Washington. The winner there selected gets a "Grand Scholarship" of $2,800, the runner-up a $2,000 scholarship, eight get $400 scholarships, and thirty others $100 each. However great the publicity value—to the sponsoring company, to the award winners, and toward emphasizing science in high schools—it must be pointed out that when only $11,000 is appropriated for the four-year college expenses of 40 persons, the average per college year is less than $69. Westinghouse's ten annual scholarships for boys in engineering, chemistry, or physics at Carnegie Institute of Technology are on the more liberal basis of $2,850 each.

Companies sometimes endow individual scholarships at particular colleges, often devoted to a subject related to the company interest and honoring a company official or scientist. For example, Merck and Company, of Rahway, New Jersey, in 1951 established the Merck Directors' Scientific Award, bestowing $75,000 in scholarships and lectureships in chemistry to institutions selected by the three Merck scientists so honored. On the other hand the Lehigh Portland Cement Company of Allentown, Pennsylvania, gave Princeton University $15,000 to endow a scholarship not restricted to any department or course of study, "a departure," notes the University, "from the usual corporation gift made on the basis of a clear *quid pro quo*."

Other scholarship plans exist in wide variety.[1] Radio Corporation of America currently finances 11 scholarships worth $600 per year in 11 named universities for undergraduate work in the pure sciences or in various branches of engineering, especially electrical, radio, and electronic. The Kroger Company in 1951 awarded 86 scholarships worth $200 each for freshman students in agriculture and home economics in cooperation with the land-

[1] On this and related fields, see Watson, John H., III, *Industry Cooperation with Education*, Studies in Business Policy, No. 34, National Industrial Conference Board, New York, 1949. Also, *Scholarships for Employees and Their Children*, Policyholders Service Bureau, Metropolitan Life Insurance Co., New York, 1950.

grant colleges of 17 midwestern and southern states in which the Company operates retail food stores. Sears, Roebuck and Company finances through the Sears-Roebuck Foundation some 900 scholarships for farm boys entering agricultural colleges from every state in the United States. While the program is designed to give boys a leg-up for the first year in college, provision is made for a continuation of the scholarship for a small percentage with exceptionally high grades. The program was begun in 1936 and to date 10,164 scholarships have been awarded. The Company reports that 67 per cent of Sears scholarship winners go through college and more than 87 per cent go into farm or farm-connected work.

While most plans which offer student aid to the general public base selection on scholarship, character, leadership, future promise, or financial need, one chain of retail stores awards its scholarships on the votes of customers, an extreme example of shaping aid to education into a merchandising device.

Scholarship programs financed by business should probably be kept fluid. Federal scholarship aid has just been extended to Korean veterans and might later be offered in connection with Universal Military Training. Proposals are also before the Congress for extensive federal aid to higher education through a general scholarship program. If a high percentage of prospective students secure financial help in any of these ways, the need for business-financed scholarships will decrease.

Fellowships

Fellowship programs for specialized graduate study and research have long been supported by corporations. National Research Council reported for 1929 a total of 95 fellowships and grants from 56 companies; in 1946 their compilations showed 302 companies supporting 1,800 "fellowships, scholarships, or grants for research." Indeed, in many cases the distinction between a fellowship and a grant for research is a mere matter of definition.

E. I. du Pont de Nemours and Company has been financing fellowships since 1918. For the academic year 1952–1953 $510,000 has been appropriated for 75 postgraduate fellowships in 47 universities, and for research grants to 15 universities to "stock-pile" knowledge. Each of the fellowships pays tuition plus $1,400 for a single person or $2,100 for a married person, together with an award of $1,200 to the university. Forty-five of these fellowships are in chemistry, 15 in chemical engineering, the others in related sciences. "It is expected," says the Company, "that the program will help maintain the flow of technically trained men and women into teaching and research work at universities and into technical positions in industry." The fellows are chosen by the universities to which the fellowships are granted, and there is no obligation with respect to later employment by Du Pont.

The Frank B. Jewett fellowships offered by the American Telephone and Telegraph Company are not merely graduate but post-doctoral, designed to stimulate the work of outstanding young scientists in the physical sciences. The five awarded for 1952–1953 give $3,000 to each recipient and $1,500 to the institution at which he chooses to do his research.

The General Electric Company offers science fellowships for high-school teachers. These recently have covered all the expenses, including travel, for six weeks' summer refresher courses for 50 teachers each at Union College and Case Institute of Technology. The purpose is to "return the teachers to their homes and schools with the raw material for more enlightened and inspired instruction."

Individual fellowships are usually granted for attack on a specific problem of interest to the donor. However, the Merck Postdoctoral Fellowships in the Natural Sciences were established to assist young scientists who had mastered one field of specialization to become proficient in a second, related field, thereby developing a broader perspective toward any scientific problem.

Fellowships may be financed by a trade association instead of individual companies. The American Pharmaceutical Manufacturers' Association, through the American Foundation for Pharmaceutical Education, is financing two $2,500 fellowships in pharmacy and drug law, respectively. Findings of these fellows will be in the public domain, but obviously of chief use to the donors.

Research, Basic and Applied

The genius of the twentieth century has been scientific research, and in the first half of the century most of it was financed by business. Lately government has seized the financial leadership with such immense projects as research and development in atomic energy, for which the President's proposed budget for 1953 is $1.8 billion, but business expenditures remain large. The Steelman Report[1] estimated contributions to research in the natural sciences (the social sciences were not included, but the amounts were small) at amounts from various sources, 1930 to 1947, as shown in Table 36 and Figure 9.

TABLE 36. SUPPORT OF RESEARCH IN THE NATURAL SCIENCES FROM VARIOUS SOURCES, IN CERTAIN YEARS, 1930 TO 1947

Dollar figures in millions

Year	Amount from				Total	Per cent from	
	Federal government	Industry	Universities	Other[a]		Government	Industry
1930	$23	$116	$20	$7	$166	14	70
1932	39	120	25	7	191	20	63
1934	21	124	19	8	172	12	73
1936	33	152	25	8	218	15	70
1938	48	177	28	11	264	18	67
1940	67	234	31	13	345	19	68
1941–1945 average	500[b]	80	10	10	600[b]	83	13
1947	625[b]	450	45	40	1,160[b]	54	39

[a] State governments, private foundations, research institutes (including nonprofit industrial institutes).

[b] Excluding atomic energy.

SOURCE: Steelman, John R., *Science and Public Policy*, vol. 1, Tables 1 and 2.

Though the industry *proportion* dropped, the amount rose to about $450 million in 1947. Most of these millions are not generosity but good business; useful inventions and improved techniques have flowed from the laboratories with profitable regularity.

Scientific research may be divided into two main types, basic (sometimes called "fundamental" or "pure") and applied. Basic research attempts to uncover new facts (e.g., Is an atom divisi-

[1] Steelman, John R., *Science and Public Policy*, vol. 1. The President's Scientific Research Board, Government Printing Office, Washington, 1947, pp. 10–12.

ble?) without immediate concern for their use. Applied research takes a known fact (atomic fission) and tries to put it to a practical use (powering an ocean liner) or else it tries to solve a specific problem by a variety of controlled experiments.

Most research financed by business has been applied research. Whether it was conducted within plant walls or, for convenience, in the laboratories of a college, it aimed directly at profits and was charged as a business expense. True, when college facilities

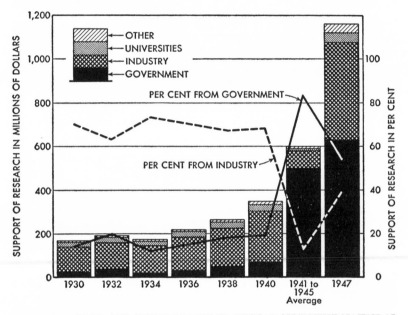

FIGURE 9. SOURCES OF SUPPORT FOR RESEARCH IN THE NATURAL SCIENCES, 1930 TO 1947

were used it may have financed graduate study for needy students, augmented a professor's salary, added to laboratory equipment, or in some liberal contracts contributed to general educational overhead. But it was money spent for value received, not philanthropy.

In a thousand ingenious ways applied research has been turning our store of fundamental knowledge into practical uses and cash dividends. But we have been adding too little to the storehouse. Business is becoming aware that basic research must be increased, and basic research not only in the physical sciences, but in the social sciences. For we must also know more about the men and women who run the machines, and the people who use the products.

Business has been increasingly supporting this basic research, some of it in the social sciences. Whether such sums should be charged to business expense or the philanthropic budget depends upon the degree of relationship. Certainly colleges received from business more than the probable $15 million indicated by our Survey as given for research from the philanthropic budget. For the 1949–1950 college year a *New York Times* survey of only 200 large educational institutions reported $25 million from private industry. In one field alone, business and economic research projects, the United States Department of Commerce recently listed 1,188 separate projects[1] in colleges and universities, most of them financed directly or indirectly by business; 175 were studies of industries, 133 of labor relations, 85 of public finance and taxation, 73 of management.

The University of Chicago recently reported that industry was supporting its Institutes for Basic Research in natural sciences to the amount of $600,000 a year. Massachusetts Institute of Technology issues a brochure, entitled *Business Statesmanship*, which invites "not charity . . . but a substantial appropriation to its $20,000,000 Development Program as a legitimate charge against operating expense, with the reasonable expectation of beneficial returns," and these "returns" are later elaborated in terms of "men, fundamentally trained," and "ideas in the realm of scientific discovery."

Sometimes the contribution is toward a technical school or a whole broad interest field. In December, 1951, Columbia University announced receipt of $100,000 from Socony-Vacuum Oil Company toward its $22 million engineering center. The University of North Carolina received in the fall of 1951 $100,000 for establishment of a professorship in banking—from the Wachovia

[1] *Survey of University Business and Economic Research Projects.* Department of Commerce, Washington, 1949.

Bank and Trust Co. The University of Chicago's Industrial Relations Center, which conducts research both at the Center and in individual plants, has as "members" some 62 companies ranging from steel and oil to department stores.

Sometimes an industrial group works together. For instance, the Nutrition Foundation set up in 1941 by food manufacturers and related companies[1] has disbursed $2.7 million to 69 universities and medical centers for research, in addition to carrying on its own educational programs. Similarly, the Life Insurance Medical Research Fund, supported by 141 life insurance companies in the United States and Canada, has announced $783,835 in grants and fellowships for research in heart disease in 1952. Organized in 1945, the Fund's awards already total $4.7 million, all for this same purpose.

Contributions toward basic research seldom have strings attached, beyond broad designation of the field. But where a research project is likely to result in a patentable finding, arrangements in wide variety are possible. For example, Princeton University advances three basic requirements with respect to patent rights in its research contracts: (1) Some consideration to the inventor; (2) Some return to the University; (3) Protection of the public interest. The business sponsor may in some cases receive a royalty-free license exclusive[2] for the general technical field of the project but nonexclusive for other fields; in other cases, a nonexclusive license under any resultant patents at terms as favorable as granted to others and a percentage of all royalties up to a certain maximum.

The University of Chicago, on the other hand, has a provision in its statutes that it "will not profit financially from research by means of patents, royalties or licensing agreements. . . . The University will cooperate with industrial organizations by conducting fundamental research projects financed by grants from such organizations, and will make research reports to the grantors, but it will retain the right to publication of the results."

[1] See pp. 110–111.

[2] But none was in effect in March, 1952, and the University was reported "increasingly reluctant to give exclusive licenses."

Research at several universities is conducted by separate organizations, of which the Lehigh Institute of Research set up at Lehigh University in 1924 is an example. In such cases the research personnel may include not only members of the teaching staff and graduate students of the University, but the scientific staff of the Institute and temporarily assigned employees of the sponsor. Research programs (the current annual budget is about $500,000) are largely in basic sciences and do not look toward patentable discoveries. However, contracts of Lehigh's Institute may vary all the way from the outright business arrangement in which all rights to publication and profits reside in the sponsoring agency to research sponsored without restriction except as to general field, and with no immediate or direct financial profit to the sponsoring company.

From the viewpoint of business, cooperation with colleges in research has many advantages and some limitations. Laboratories and research personnel are available in the colleges; to set up equal facilities outside would often be prohibitively expensive. The training of additional research people through the universities is in itself of no small importance to industry. But the graduate students who perform most of the research are interested primarily in obtaining an advanced degree, turnover is large, and the researchers are apt to be inexperienced in the practical aspects of business projects. Many businesses report that the colleges are more useful for basic research than for special projects.

From the viewpoint of the college, business-sponsored research is not an unmixed blessing. It expands the graduate program, and helps pay professors' salaries in some cases. But except in contracts which provide a grant to the university for general overhead, it may pay only its own specific costs, actually increasing the general deficit. Sponsors are not plentiful for the basic research in which the university itself may be primarily interested. The many millions which corporations pour into college treasuries earmarked for research and research fellowships are welcomed, but they go primarily to a small number of the larger universities.

The Roots of the Problem

The various forms of aid to colleges thus far discussed are useful to both parties, but they do not reach the roots of the problem. Dr. John D. Millett, executive director of the Commission on Financing Higher Education, outlines "five broad types of choice which a corporation has in channeling funds to institutions of higher education":

1. Grants for promotion of basic research
2. Fellowship awards for the training of specialized personnel
3. Scholarship awards for broad undergraduate education
4. General operating or capital grants based upon
    a. Common location of business and institution in a community
    b. Common interest in the advancement, let us say, of business education, engineering education, or medical education
    c. General interest, such as improvement of race relations and educational opportunities for Negroes
5. Compensation for special services rendered, such as institutes for discussion of professional problems in banking, journalism, labor relations and other fields where the persons benefiting from the service are the present employees of the corporation[1]

All these channels are useful, and may have a logical and important place in a corporation's program. With the exception of the fourth, however, they contribute chiefly to the student or to college extras. Colleges complain, "We can always get more money for frills and extras, but we get less and less for salaries and running expenses, the heart of our educational program."

Companies may be willing to contribute to the general expenses of liberal arts colleges, but they find it difficult. The contributions specialist of Corporation 3005 reports in a desk-side conversation:

We're for such contributions; the Board, my distribution committee, and I am, personally. But we've given not one penny. Why? There are some twelve hundred private colleges. We have employees and distribution centers in all the forty-eight states, and in most

[1] In "Corporation Philanthropy and Higher Education," an address delivered to the Educational Advisory Committee, National Association of Manufacturers, October 29, 1951.

cities of any size. How can we know which colleges are good and which should be let die, which are really needy, which to pick, and how much to give? If we help one, the other eleven hundred and ninety-nine will be at my desk next week, mad as hornets. We've got money we're willing to give, but somebody else, perhaps the colleges, must solve the distribution problem for us.

No completely satisfactory solution to this problem has been found, but certain recent developments deserve notice.

The Local College

Contributions to the local college from local industry, or local branches of national industry, solve a portion of the problem, and are being increasingly made. Business has no difficulty in justifying such support. The president of an industry with 12 small factories in the Middle West, reporting such contributions, gives a typical picture:

> Private business should support our private colleges. We selected a college in one of our plant towns as a natural. Another is located 20 miles from a plant town and three others, not quite as close in miles, have many alumni working for us and a sizable number of students living in cities where we have plants. We visit the campuses of those colleges and select outstanding students to work for us. We invite their economics classes to visit us and otherwise maintain a close relationship.

In 1951 Remington Arms Company gave $33,500 to the University of Bridgeport (Connecticut) and Bridgeport Brass Company gave $50,000; both pointed out in their letters of gift the values of local higher educational facilities to the company, and to employees and their children.

Such examples could be multiplied, but this solution has limitations. The large private universities are almost without exception in great population centers, where such intimate relations do not prevail. As for the smaller liberal arts colleges, the Commission on Financing Higher Education points out:

> The majority are located in more or less isolated, predominantly rural areas, such as Hanover, Williamstown, Northampton, Clinton, Suwanee, Delaware, Greencastle, Northfield, Grinnel, and Claremont. These colleges cannot make much of a purely local appeal to

business corporations, because there are no business corporations of great wealth in their particular community.[1]

Statewide College Funds

In many states the colleges are endeavoring to meet the corporations' distribution problem, and at the same time simplify their soliciting task, through statewide college funds and foundations. The first of these was organized in Indiana in 1948. In 1951 campaigns to industry were conducted by variously titled state college funds in Indiana, Michigan, Minnesota, Missouri, Ohio, and Oregon. By the spring of 1952 similar organizations had been created in Illinois, New York (the Empire State Foundation of Independent Liberal Arts Colleges), Pennsylvania, West Virginia, and Vermont, and were in the survey stage in southern California, Georgia, Kentucky, Maryland, Nebraska, Oklahoma, South Carolina, and Virginia. New England colleges, led by Dartmouth, were contemplating a regional organization.

Membership qualifications vary. Frequently only private (as distinguished from tax-supported) and accredited institutions are eligible. In Indiana 11 of the 29 colleges participated in the joint solicitation, but the contribution blank listed all 29, including the 4 tax-supported. The Ohio Foundation of Independent Colleges was incorporated in 1950 and limits membership to non-tax-supported colleges which are accredited by, and hold membership in, the Ohio College Association. Twenty-two of the 36 colleges eligible in Ohio were members in early 1952.

Organization and solicitation procedures are still experimental. Indiana, Missouri, and Oregon operate on an informal basis, with routine work parceled out among members and soliciting done usually in pairs, either by two college presidents or a president and a business executive. The Michigan Colleges Foundation employs professional fund-raising counsel. The Ohio Foundation has a full-time director.

No consensus prevails on how the funds collected should be distributed. Indiana asks the corporation to specify the percentage of the total gift for each designated college, leaving with

[1] *Corporation Contributions to Higher Education.* Staff Study, unpublished. The Commission, New York, 1951, p. 24.

business a chore it has often tried to avoid. The Minnesota College Fund Association divides all receipts 50 per cent share and share alike, and 50 per cent in accordance with full-time student enrollment. The Ohio and the Vermont Foundations of Independent Colleges distribute gifts 60 per cent evenly and 40 per cent on the basis of student enrollment.

As a return service for contributors, the Ohio Foundation of Independent Colleges offers to circulate the personnel needs of contributing corporations among the placement officers of all its member colleges.

Changes in memberships and in methods are certain, and may be rapid. Organization of such state college funds was a subject of lively interest at the 1952 sessions of the Association of American Colleges, which has a Commission on Colleges and Industry, and the finance section of the American Council on Education.

National College Funds

At the national level, the United Negro College Fund was organized in 1944, and its successful operations have to some extent been a pattern for the state funds. Beginning with a total of $765,000 raised in 1944 of which $229,000 (30 per cent) came from corporations, the Fund raised in 1951 for its 32 participating colleges a total of $1,311,000 of which corporations contributed $420,000 (32 per cent). The campaign chairman was Thomas I. Parkinson, president of the Equitable Life Assurance Society. The Fund distributes 45 per cent of the net proceeds equally among member institutions; 45 per cent in the proportion of the income from gifts, grants, and endowments for the preceding five years of each of the member colleges; and 10 per cent proportioned to their five-year average enrollments.

A more recent and highly important national college fund is the National Fund for Medical Education, which went into operation in 1951, though planned some years earlier.

Medical education is the severest financial problem of most universities which include medical schools. The Commission on Financing Higher Education reports[1] that the 72 four-year medi-

[1] *Financing Medical Education:* A Statement by The Commission on Financing Higher Education. New York, 1951.

cal schools of the United States cost $70 million in 1950; all but 9 of these schools are part of a university. In spite of this large outlay, a deficit totaling $9.5 million was shown by 48 of these schools one recent year, and the Public Health Service reported that "a minimum of another $40 million a year is needed to cover the medical schools' operating expenses at present enrollment levels" with "even more money required to expand the physical facilities needed to teach medicine."

One survey indicates that the cost of a medical education has risen from about $2,000 before World War I to $10,000. Average tuition is now $600 per year, and cannot be much increased without danger of keeping out all but the economically privileged. Money for specialized research is plentiful, but medical school deans say they are "research money" poor; even the Public Health Service limits its "indirect" project grants to 8 per cent of direct expenditures, with actual costs often three or four times as much. Government subsidy has been suggested, but is resisted vigorously by the American Medical Association, many of the schools, and others.

As one means of working out a solution, the National Fund for Medical Education was organized with the specific objectives of making the financial needs of medical education known to the American people, raising a minimum of $5 million a year from private sources, and distributing these sums to the schools. The Fund seeks the financial support of "business and industry, labor, the medical profession and the general public." Doctors, through the American Medical Association Foundation, make contributions, and it has been suggested that if they would contribute an average of $100 a year to support medical schools, nearly $18 million in new income would be provided. Because industry has a large stake in health standards, intensive efforts are being directed at various industrial groups to secure contribution pledges for not merely a single year but as a continuing amount.

The Fund collected $1.5 million in 1951, and is now greatly broadening its appeal. Distributions are made in the form of grants in three classes: Class A grants are uniform amounts awarded to each accredited four-year medical school and uniform lesser amounts to each accredited two-year basic medical science school, to be used without restriction for the support of the instructional budget. Class B grants are amounts awarded to the same schools, similarly unrestricted, but in proportion to the number of full-time undergraduate students regularly enrolled. Class C grants will be awarded only when substantial sums are in hand, and will be determined by the trustees on the basis of special needs and problems of individual medical schools.

A similar national fund for the liberal arts colleges has been discussed. Conceivably, it could be set up as an independent agency by the colleges themselves, by one of the foundations with a special interest in education, or by industry. Certain objections have been raised, however. Though such an organization would relieve business contributors of the difficulty of deciding on allocation of educational funds, it would have to undertake that task itself. This would create a new bureaucracy which might destroy the very diversity and freedom which private support of higher education desires to preserve. If such a central bureau were formed by a group of corporations there would be the additional danger of charges that "big business" was attempting to control education.

A Changing Situation

No single pattern emerges as the best way business can aid higher education. The educational situation is fluid, and the interests and resources of corporations differ. Many forms of educational aid will prove mutually helpful.

Some corporations can supply instructional aids relating to their own operations for college classes, or permit plant visits, to mutual advantage. Colleges can arrange business or technical courses of special value to business personnel, and permit instructors to serve as consultants.

Research offers a wide variety of possibilities, ranging from bought-and-paid-for contract research conducted in college laboratories, through fellowships with one eye on possible findings in an area of interest and the other on building up trained researchers, to support of pure research designed primarily toward building up man's storehouse of knowledge, with only the remotest relation to any present return.

Scholarships, particularly if there is an accompanying grant to the college, are an attractive way of aiding students and educational institutions. If granted to employees or children of employees, they improve employee relations; if granted in a field of corporate interest, they increase future available manpower; if open to the general public, they are a community or public service.

In a period of rapid college expansion, grants toward new buildings or equipment are of special value. In periods of financial stress, contributions toward general expenses are most useful for the college. For the national company, the problem of apportioning gifts has not been satisfactorily solved, but various experiments are under way.

CHAPTER 12

Religious Agencies

R̲ELIGION is the mother of philanthropy. Relief for the poor, education of the young, care of the sick—nearly all the welfare services of the present day had their origins in the church, and in certain periods the church was the chief almoner, and sometimes the only one, for many of these causes. Though we often characterize the present period as highly secular, membership in the 67 larger religious bodies in the United States, including Catholic, Jewish, and Protestant, was estimated at over 85 million in 1950. Giving to religious agencies, approximating $1.9 billion in 1949, is almost precisely half the total estimated for all voluntary giving. But while individuals give half their charitable dollars to religious agencies, chiefly for church support, the patterns of corporate giving are radically different.

The Survey Record

In response to our Survey question on giving to "religious agencies (include churches, Salvation Army, YMCA, etc.)" the responding corporations reported only 4.1 per cent of their total gifts going to such agencies. Table 37 details the findings.

Wide differences appear in the contributions of corporations of varied asset size. The largest corporations gave least liberally to religion—less than 3 per cent of their total contributions, and only 0.01 per cent of net income. Companies of moderate size, $1 to $50 million in assets, gave somewhat more, proportionately: about 7 per cent of their total contributions, and 0.07 per cent of net income. The pattern of giving for the under $1 million asset group was entirely different. They gave to religious agencies more than 15 per cent of their total gifts, and 0.28 per cent of their net income. It may be presumed that many of these smaller companies were closely held or family corporations, where ownership was probably all of one faith and where in some cases personal gifts could be made by company check, with the substantial tax advantage explained in Chapter 14.

TABLE 37. CONTRIBUTIONS TO RELIGIOUS AGENCIES OF 326 SURVEYED CORPORATIONS, BY AMOUNT OF CORPORATION ASSETS, 1950[a]

Dollar figures in thousands

Asset class (millions)	Corporations	Contributions			Net income	
		Total	Amount to religious agencies	Per cent to religious agencies	Amount	Per cent to religious agencies
Under $1	101	$ 104	$ 16	15.4	$ 5,728	0.28
1 under 50	166	1,734	120	6.9	181,032	0.07
50 and over	59	4,951	142	2.9	1,137,964	0.01
Total	326	$6,789	$278	4.1	$1,324,724	0.02

[a] Russell Sage Foundation Survey.

The percentage for all groups found in our sample, if it can be applied with some validity to total corporate giving, would indicate a contribution to religious agencies of under $10 million out of 1948's $239 million in gifts. But even this relatively small amount was in many cases not considered a contribution to "religion." Several corporations protested this classification. Said Corporation 1586, "Your term is misleading. We do not consider Salvation Army and YMCA 'religious agencies.'" Corporation 1073 entered a contribution in this line only after crossing out "churches." And Corporation 1835 carefully noted, "YMCA in our community is the community center."

Attitudes Toward Religious Giving

Publicly owned corporations face difficulties in making contributions to religious agencies. The statement of International Harvester Company is typical:

Because our stockholders, employees and customers represent all religious groups, the Company does not contribute to strictly sectarian or denominational religious organizations, such as churches, missionary groups, etc.[1]

However, exceptions are frequently made in behalf of such organizations as the YMCA and Salvation Army, which render services in recreation, housing, rehabilitation, and other areas; for nonsectarian services of religious organizations, such as hospitals or colleges open to those of all faiths; and for organizations that are interfaith or at least interdenominational.

Nominal gifts raise no problem. One corporation, prohibiting, in general, gifts to any form of religious endeavor, exempts small payments for church events, which are regarded as "a community gesture" and range usually from $5 to $10. The Southern Railway System found no difficulty, and much advertising value, in contributing to churches of many denominations, white and Negro, some 64 bells from steam locomotives that were being scrapped.

Some corporations, instead of avoiding or limiting their religious contributions, regard them as the most important part of their giving program. Corporation 2161, engineering contractors, gave $10,500 to religion, constituting 92 per cent of its total gifts. Corporation 1328, manufacturing nuts, screws, and machine products, gave about 50 per cent to religion and added a footnote: "We believe the church donations are more beneficial to company."

Certain Religious Agencies

The YMCA, as Chapter 2 indicated, was the earliest recipient of substantial corporation gifts, and it remains high on the list of agencies to which companies contribute. The Young Men's Christian Associations of the United States of America presently include some 1,726 local Associations with a membership of nearly two million individuals. They "minister to the needs of boys and young men, by giving them opportunities for greater

[1] Appendix F, p. 333.

self-development of body, mind, and spirit." Local city Associations usually provide dormitory facilities for unmarried young men and a wide program of recreational, cultural, and religious activities. The orientation is Protestant, though persons of all faiths are included in its membership.

The National Council of the YMCA is supported chiefly by contributions from the local Associations, though drives are sometimes conducted for special projects. But the local Association is the usual focus of fund-raising efforts. These may be toward current support—"Y" activities, particularly for younger boys, often cannot carry their costs—or, less frequently, a major drive for a new building. Amounts sought vary with the local situation. Contributions to 1,632 reporting YMCA's for current purposes were $22.4 million for 1951, of which $14 million came through community chests. Approximately $10 million were added to the capital assets of these Associations in 1951. In New York City a Centennial Fund of $10 million is being sought, with 1957 the closing date.

In addition to the local YMCA's and the National Council, there is an International Committee of the YMCA's of the U.S.A. and Canada which is conducting in 1952 a $1.8 million campaign for world services, including restoration of war-damaged "Y" buildings in other countries, aid to impoverished workers, refugees, and others.

The Young Women's Christian Association of the United States of America, functioning under a National Board, offers similar services for young women. Contributions to local Associations are not centrally tabulated. Gifts to the National Board, either through local Associations or directly, totaled just over $1 million in 1951.

The Salvation Army is much more evangelical in its program than either of the "Y's," but it also offers a wide welfare program, ranging from transient shelters and men's hotels, summer camps and nurseries, children's homes and hospitals to Christmas dinners, prison visitation, and the ubiquitous open-air and indoor religious services. It is supported almost entirely by voluntary contributions, which in 1951 were reported at over $30 million.

Beginning with its special services to soldiers in World War I, the Salvation Army has attracted many corporate contributions.

The United Jewish Appeal, which has ethnic as well as religious characteristics, has set one of the most remarkable contribution records in American philanthropy. Beginning with collections of $15 million in 1939, it passed $100 million in each of the years 1946 through 1949, approaching $150 million in peak year 1948. The UJA raised $86 million in 1950 and $85 million in 1951. The "goal" for 1952 has been set at $151.5 million. A large part of the funds of the United Jewish Appeal is devoted to programs of settlement and reconstruction in Palestine. However, Jewish giving for local needs is also liberal. The Federation of Jewish Philanthropies of New York City called its 1950 pledges and contributions of $14.5 million "the largest ever raised for the annual maintenance of a locally supported network of philanthropic institutions." This "network" includes 116 affiliated agencies in the New York area.

Catholic Charities, organized in more than a hundred separate dioceses of the Roman Catholic Church, support a wide range of social services, including care of children, family casework, recreation, care of the chronically ill and the aged; they are designed primarily to serve Catholic communicants, but do not exclude people of other faiths if they may be served without slighting the primary beneficiaries and "without offense to religion." They have great local autonomy, each conducting its own local campaign, to which the community chest may sometimes contribute.

The more than 200 Protestant denominations also maintain, in many cases, welfare agencies of various types, but these are not so numerous in proportion to church membership as Roman Catholic institutions, nor so closely integrated with the churches. Protestants pioneered in the establishment of many types of social agencies in their communities, particularly those for child care, homes for the aged, and hospitals. But even where these remain under the control of the individual church or the denomination, disunity among Protestant bodies in the same community has usually prevented the closer coordination, for fund-raising and other purposes, that has been achieved by Jewish and Catholic agencies. A few federations of Protestant welfare agencies have been organized, but there has also been resistance against the attempt to put social welfare in general under denominational auspices.

Where federations of all three groups—Jewish, Catholic, and Protestant—exist in a community, corporations may give to all three groups, thereby minimizing criticism. They also contribute more readily to agencies working for interfaith cooperation, such as the National Conference of Christians and Jews. The Ford Motor Company Fund, for example, granted $1 million to this organization in 1951 for a permanent "World Brotherhood Headquarters" in New York City.

One important step toward Protestant unity was taken in 1950 in the formation of the National Council of the Churches of Christ in the United States of America, representing 29 Protestant and Orthodox communions with 33 million members in 143,959 local churches. This united enterprise has begun vigorous efforts to secure corporate contributions in support of some or all of its programs related to communities and the armed services. In 1951 it received contributions ranging from $10,000 to $100 or less from 835 corporations and business foundations, totaling $110,689; among these contributors were 97 of the nation's largest corporations.

A Case for Religious Giving

Religious leaders urge that business has a much more substantial stake in the agencies of organized religion than is represented by the present meager contributions. Says one group:

> Our religious, political, personal and business freedoms are all tied up in one bundle. Freedom of worship, freedom of speech, freedom of the press, freedom of communication, freedom for inventive genius, freedom of business initiative, freedom to own property, freedom to move from place to place; the free school, the secret ballot, the inviolability of the person, the sanctity of the home—all these freedoms express our belief in the inherent dignity and worth of every individual in the sight of God. . . .

The real question confronting directors of corporations today is whether they can afford *not to support financially* the element which most strongly reinforces our freedoms, including those indispensable to the survival of private business enterprise.[1]

They point out that the church is one of the few institutions that have successfully resisted the trends toward state control, and must therefore rely upon voluntary contributions rather than partial or complete tax support. On the propriety of religious rather than secular auspices for certain welfare services, they maintain that the religious ministry is itself a part of the service which should be offered, that the sick and the aged should be cared for "in the faith of their fathers," and that the law itself in most states specifically requires that dependent children who become wards of the state shall be assigned to homes and institutions, or in charge of persons, of the same religious faith as the children.

With respect to the practical difficulties for the publicly owned corporation of allocation among Jewish, Catholic, and Protestant agencies, they suggest making a fixed appropriation for religious purposes later to be divided either (a) on the merits of specific appeals; (b) in proportion to the members of those faiths on the payroll or in the population; or (c) equally among the three groups.

[1] *Religion and Corporate Giving.* National Council of the Churches of Christ in the U.S.A., New York, 1952, p. 7.

PART III
LEGAL AND TAXATION FACTORS

CHAPTER 13

The Law

WHAT LEGAL right do directors of a corporation have to contribute corporate funds to charitable causes? The law varies among the states and sometimes with the type of corporation. New permissive legislation has been enacted in a majority of the states within the past few years, but some doubt remains in certain states as to the validity of these statutes for corporations whose charters antedate them. Interpretive court decisions exist, but sometimes they seem to be contradictory and recent citations are scarce. The decision in each case will depend upon the applicability of a specific statute or upon the available facts. The reader is warned that actions regarded as invalid a few years ago may be accepted today, and may go unquestioned tomorrow.

The Classic Case

The classic case, from which lawyers have taken the oft-repeated dictum, "Charity has no business to sit at boards of directors *qua* charity," originated in England in 1883 and had nothing whatever to do with philanthropy as the layman would define it. The West Cork Railway Company was being dissolved, its business being taken over by the Bandon Company. A general meeting of the West Cork Company, in closing up its affairs, voted to pay a portion of the settlement money to its retiring directors for past services. A stockholder objected that, since these retiring directors could render no further service to the company, such a payment was a mere gift and therefore illegal. He was sustained and the opinion of Lord Justice Bowen was so happily phrased it has become a classic for the whole field of corporate donations. Portions of it merit quotation:

> It seems to me you cannot say the company has only got power to spend the money which it is bound to pay according to law, otherwise the wheels of business would stop, nor can you say that directors . . . are always to be limited to the strictest possible view of what the obligations of the company are. They are not to keep their pockets buttoned up and defy the world unless they are liable in a way which could be enforced at law or in equity. Most businesses require liberal dealings. The test there again is not whether it is *bona fide*, but whether, as well as being *bona fide*, it is done within the ordinary scope of the company's business, and whether it is reasonably incidental to the carrying on of the company's business for the company's benefit.
>
> Take this sort of instance. A railway company, or the directors of the company, might send down all the porters at a railway station to have tea in the country at the expense of the company. Why should they not? It is for the directors to judge, provided it is a matter which is reasonably incidental to the carrying on of the business of the company, and a company which always treated its employees with Draconian severity, and never allowed them a single inch more than the strict letter of the bond, would soon find itself deserted—at all events, unless labour was very much more easy to obtain in the market than it often is. The law does not say that there are to be no cakes and ale, but there are to be no cakes and ale except such as are required for the benefit of the company. . . .
>
> It is not charity sitting at the board of directors, because as it seems to me charity has no business to sit at boards of directors *qua* charity. There is, however, a kind of charitable dealing which is for the interest of those who practice it, and to that extent and in that garb (I admit not a very philanthropic garb) charity may sit at the board, but for no other purpose.[1]

Although this is a British opinion, and nearly seventy years old, it graphically illustrates principles with respect to corporate donations which have in general prevailed in American common law.

[1] *Hutton* v. *West Cork Railway Company*, 23 The Law Reports, Chancery Division, 1883, p. 654.

The Developing Doctrine

A corporation can exercise only powers expressly granted by its charter, or powers incidental to these. Until legislation expressly permitting donations was passed by the various states, corporate philanthropy had to rely upon the increasingly liberal interpretation of these "incidental" powers. Says Ray Garrett:

> It was the traditional rule that a donation of its property by a corporation not created for charitable purposes was *ultra vires* [beyond the powers] and in violation of the rights of the stockholders. This was based upon a strict interpretation of charter powers and made no allowance for possible justification of donations under incidental powers. Out of this strict rule there evolved many years ago through scattered American and English decisions the concept of direct corporate benefit as justification for a corporate donation. Courts modified the traditional rule by sustaining donations under incidental powers where some direct benefit to the corporation could be demonstrated.[1]

The growing scope of a corporation's incidental powers was noted as early as 1896 in an important decision. If the act—

> . . . is one which is lawful in itself, and not otherwise prohibited, is done for the purpose of serving corporate ends, and is reasonably tributary to the promotion of those ends, in a substantial, and not in a remote and fanciful sense, it may fairly be considered within charter powers. The field of corporate action in respect to the exercise of incidental powers is thus, I think, an expanding one. As industrial conditions change, business methods must change with them, and acts become permissible which at an earlier period would not have been considered to be within corporate power.[2]

But the early history of corporate donations was checkered. The Metropolitan Life Insurance Company could donate to a special tuberculosis hospital for the care and treatment of its employees,[3] and Corning Glass Works[4] could deduct for income

[1] Garrett, Ray, "Corporate Donations to Charity," *Proceedings* of the Section of Corporation, Banking and Mercantile Law, published in *The Business Lawyer*, November, 1948. Mr. Garrett is legal consultant for this study and this chapter leans heavily on his advice and writings.

[2] *Steinway* v. *Steinway & Sons*, et al., 17 Misc. Rep. 43, 40 N.Y. Supp. 718 (1896).

[3] *People* ex rel. *Metropolitan Life Insurance Co.* v. *Hotchkiss*, 136 App. Div. 150, 120 N.Y. Supp. 649 (1909).

[4] *Corning Glass Works* v. *Commissioner*, 37 Fed. (2d) 798 (1929).

purposes a donation toward construction of a general hospital in a city where employees and their dependents comprised two-thirds of the population; but a donation for a hospital for the benefit of a whole community was not sufficient grounds for an income-tax deduction.[1] When Henry Ford tried to limit dividends of the Ford Motor Company to 5 per cent *monthly* and put the remaining profits back into the business "to employ still more men, to spread the benefits of this industrial system to the greatest possible number, to help them build up their lives and their homes" the court directed otherwise, stating:

> The discretion of directors . . . does not extend to a change in the end itself, to the reduction of profits, or to the nondistribution of profits among stockholders in order to devote them to other purposes.[2]

A corporation doing business in Buffalo could contribute to the endowment funds of a college and a university in that city with a view to setting up the first college-level courses in that city in "the science of business"[3] but E. M. Holt Plaid Mills was disallowed for tax purposes even a small educational contribution as a business deduction when direct corporate benefit was not proved.[4]

Nearly all the earlier cases were without benefit of special state statutes legalizing charitable contributions under various conditions; they therefore tested whether the corporation directors had the power to make such a contribution at all, or whether the particular contribution was closely enough related to the business interests of the corporation to be deductible as a business expense for tax purposes. One writer summarizes the confused and changing picture in these words:

> . . . corporation donations may be made to charity where such gifts tend reasonably and directly to promote the corporate purpose. The modern tendency of decision is to a broader view so that gifts that would formerly have been considered *ultra vires* are now held to

[1] *Alfred J. Sweet, Inc.* v. *United States,* 66 Ct. Cls. 654 (1929).
[2] *Dodge* v. *Ford Motor Co.,* 204 Mich. 459, 170 N.W. 668 (1919).
[3] *Armstrong Cork Co.* v. *H. A. Meldrum Co.,* 285 Fed. 58 (1922).
[4] *E. M. Holt Plaid Mills, Inc.* v. *Commissioner,* 9 B.T.A. 1360 (1928).

be proper. Certain gifts may be held improper for special reasons of public policy, but the general rule is that a corporation may carry on its business by the method and means commonly used in its field of activity. The more restrictive of the earlier decisions must now be considered as obsolete because of their conflict with this principle.[1]

However, recent decisions are too few in number[2] to support a generalization that earlier decisions are obsolete. The important fact is their fewness; since the decision against the Ford Motor Company in 1919 quoted above, only six significant law cases have been brought to trial, and all of these were decided in favor of the contributor. Undoubtedly the growth of permissive legislation in many of the states has much to do with this decline in challenges.

State Permissive Legislation

Our historical chapter[3] sketched early attempts to meet the legal problem through such devices as Red Cross Dividends and pressure for legislation, state and national. Since corporate directors derive their powers under charters subject to the corporation laws of the various states, permissive legislation in the states seemed the logical means for clarifying this situation.

As early as 1917 Texas passed a law which came at the subject backhandedly. Under "Acts Prohibited" it had "provided that nothing in this Article shall be held to inhibit corporations from contributing to any bona fide association, incorporated or unincorporated, organized for and actively engaged for one year prior to such contribution in purely religious, charitable or eleemosynary activities. . . ."

Slowly, other states began passing permissive legislation—New York in 1918, Illinois in 1919, Ohio in 1920, Tennessee in 1925, New Jersey in 1930, Massachusetts in 1933, Michigan in 1935. Also in 1935 came the Revenue Act which permitted deduction of charitable contributions from federal corporate income tax up

[1] Cousens, Theodore W., "How Far Corporations May Contribute to Charity," *Virginia Law Review*, vol. 35, May, 1949, p. 423.

[2] Our tabulation of all significant United States cases shows only one law and 10 tax cases since 1936. See Appendix D.

[3] See pp. 22–39.

to 5 per cent of net income beginning in 1936. This federal law added nothing to the actual powers of corporations to make such contributions, since such powers were under state control. But by recognizing contributions as a category of tax deductibles quite separate from the direct business expense items deductible under 23(a) it gave moral support to a broader interpretation of existing state laws and the common law, and doubtless some impetus toward the passing of new or revised legislation.

Missouri joined the parade in 1937, Delaware in 1941. But the great surge toward state permissive legislation came after the beginning of World War II, when pressures from needy agencies were heavy and corporations themselves were eager to give, perhaps in part to take advantage of the charitable "bargains" available under the combination of deductibility and high tax rates. Four states adopted new legislation in 1945 alone, another plus the Territory of Hawaii in 1947, five more states in the legislative year 1949, and six in 1951.

Strong influences in the postwar peak of legislation were the efforts of a committee of the American Bar Association and Community Chests and Councils of America. Ray Garrett, chairman of the American Bar Association's Committee on Business Corporations, addressed a section of the Association's 1948 meeting on "Corporate Donations to Charity." The following spring his Committee devised a very brief, unrestrictive model statute and sent it to secretaries of state and to presidents of state bar associations and larger city associations. Meanwhile a committee of Community Chests and Councils was working on the same problem, telling its list of selected chests early in 1949 that:

> Of course the issue of the right to contribute to Chests is relatively dormant in most areas. However, the question does becloud the thinking in at least two important industries, namely utilities and railroads. . . . Other corporate support of Chests is customary, and often taken for granted. Nonetheless there are indications that this support could sometimes be seriously challenged in the absence of definite permissive legislation.[1]

[1] Memorandum from Community Chests and Councils of America, Inc., January 19, 1949.

This committee urged pressure on state legislatures wherever permissive legislation did not exist, and attached copies of the Colorado and Pennsylvania laws as possible models. Two months later, having learned of the parallel activities of the American Bar Association Committee, it joined in recommending the simple model statute prepared by that Committee. This model statute was adopted by two states in 1949, five states in 1951, and with slight modification by two other states in 1951.

By the close of the 1951 legislative year permissive statutes of some sort were on the books of 26[1] states and the Territory of Hawaii. The covered states include all the industrialized area from which corporate contributions are substantial. According to the 1941 geographical breakdown of contributions,[2] the 26 states and one territory now covered contributed in that year 90 per cent of the total reported corporate contributions in the United States.

Nature of the State Laws

Unfortunately, the situation is far from being as satisfactory as this 90 per cent presumed coverage suggests. The laws differ widely in their provisions, and a final question may remain in some states as to whether they apply to corporations chartered before the respective dates of enactment.

First, an examination of the permissive sections of the laws themselves is in order. They are quoted in full in Appendix C[3] as they stood at the close of the 1951 legislative year, and some of their characteristics are summarized in Table 38.

In many states banking and other financial institutions, railroads, insurance companies, and sometimes utilities and non-profit corporations, are organized under special acts rather than the general corporation law. Permissive legislation on contributions attached to the general corporation law does not necessarily cover these special categories. As the table indicates, 16 states and

[1] Now 29. Kentucky, Mississippi, and Rhode Island passed permissive legislation only in 1952, as this book was going to press.

[2] Table 10, p. 61.

[3] See pp. 293–316.

TABLE 38. CHARACTERISTICS OF STATE LEGISLATION PERMITTING CHARITABLE CONTRIBUTIONS

State	First legislation passed	Latest amendment	Applicability	Special limitations	Retroactive clause	New model law
Arkansas	1951	–	A	–	–	X
California	1949	–	A	–	–	X
Colorado	1947	–	A	–	RV	–
Connecticut	1951	–	A	–	–	X
Delaware	1941	1951	F	–	–	X
Hawaii	1947	–	A	E	V	–
Illinois	1919	1949	FU	–	–	X
Indiana	1949	–	FU	I	–	–
Kansas	1951	–	A	–	–	X
Maine	1951	–	A	–	–	X
Maryland	1945	1951	F	P	–	–
Massachusetts	1933	1946	A	CL	V	–
Michigan	1935	1947	FU	–	–	–
Minnesota	1949	–	A	–	RV	–
Missouri	1937	1945	FU	B	–	–
New Jersey	1930	1950	FU	DS	V	–
New Mexico	1951	–	FU	–	• –	X
New York	1918	1951	A	DJS	V	–
North Carolina	1945	–	A	IP	–	–
Ohio	1920	1945	A	BDJ	–	–
Oklahoma	1949	–	A	BJ	–	–
Pennsylvania	1945	1947	U	–	R	–
Tennessee	1925	1943	A	P	–	–
Texas	1917	1943	A	–	–	–
Virginia	1945	–	T	–	–	–
West Virginia	1949	–	A	I	R	–
Wisconsin	1951	–	A	–	–	X

KEY: *Applicability:* A =all general business corporations; F =not applicable to certain financial corporations; T =applicable only to utilities; U =not applicable to certain utilities.

Special limitations: B =to promote corporate purposes or interests; C =to agencies approved by commissioner of public welfare; D = 1 per cent of capital and surplus, otherwise notice to stockholders; E =on vote of stockholders; I =income-tax deductibility test; J =to joint enterprises; L =to local agencies; P =out of profit; S =beneficiary may not hold substantial amount of donor's stock.

Retroactive clause: R =ratifies previous contributions; V =does not prejudice validity of previous contributions.

SOURCE: Appendix C.

Hawaii cover substantially all business corporations—though even among these Oklahoma excepts land companies and agencies. The Virginia law applies *only* to certain public service corporations. For the remaining states, the exceptions are noted in the table.

In a few cases the legislators wrote into the law special limitations. Maryland grants permission to make "reasonable gifts or contributions out of profits." Tennessee specifies that they shall be "made out of the earnings of such corporations, and shall be charged to operating expenses." North Carolina goes still further, limiting such gifts annually to "five per centum of its net income . . . provided, further, that the assets of the corporation exceed its liabilities immediately after any such contribution or gift is made." In these states it would appear that in a depressed period contributions could not be continued at all by corporations which had no net profit for the period concerned.

New Jersey, New York, and Ohio have a different type of limitation on amount, which in each case may not exceed in any calendar year "one percentum of the capital and surplus" of a stock corporation, unless further proposed expenditures are brought to the attention of stockholders and then, if holders of 25 per cent or more of the stock have objected, authorized by a meeting of the stockholders.

Several states obviously fear that stockholding philanthropies may vote benefits to themselves. New Jersey and New York forbid contributions "if at the time of the contribution or immediately thereafter the donee institution shall own more than ten per centum of the voting stock of the donor corporation or one of its subsidiaries." Ohio and New York at certain periods required reporting of the names of recipient agencies, but these provisions were repealed.

Phrasing of the legislation in several jurisdictions would seem to limit contributions to going operations to which others are also contributing, possibly forbidding an independent venture. The Ohio law is typical:

> Any corporation may cooperate with other corporations and with natural persons in the creation and maintenance of funds or credits for aiding community growth or development or for aiding charitable, philanthropic or benevolent instrumentalities, conducive to public welfare. . . .[1]

[1] Section 8623–119, Ohio General Code.

Massachusetts limits contributions to "any fund being raised by a relief committee or agency approved by the commissioner of public welfare, as evidenced by a writing filed in his office, and formed for the purpose of raising money to be used for the betterment of social and economic conditions in any community in which such corporation is doing business." Hawaii is the only jurisdiction in which it is provided that donations "may be authorized by the affirmative vote of the holders of a majority of the stock of any such corporation," with the presumption that other donations are *ultra vires*.

Illinois includes "donations to associations and organizations aiding in war activities" in time of war. New York has a special Section 35 authorizing the corporation to contribute to the American National Red Cross "as a proper part of the expense of its business," but in the case of utilities such contributions cannot be considered for rate-making purposes. Indiana defines permissible contributions in terms of deductibility under the federal Internal Revenue Code. Texas includes a strong prohibition against contributions toward political parties, campaigns, or candidates, or for propaganda directed toward legislation. Michigan has the shortest permissive clause of all, and one that may prove inadequate: "To make contributions for public welfare."

Much of the recent legislation attempts to validate, or at least not to invalidate, previous corporate beneficence. The Minnesota provision is typical:

> Sec. 3. This act shall not be construed as invalidating any such contributions or gifts heretofore made by any such corporation and all such contributions or gifts made by such corporations prior to the enactment hereof shall be as valid as if made after the effective date hereof.

Colorado, Minnesota, and New Jersey specifically declare it to be the public policy of those states to recognize such donations as their statutes describe.

The Model Law

The American Bar Association's Committee on Business Corporations in its 1949 memorandum recommended that "business corporations be empowered by statute to make donations for the public welfare or for charitable, scientific or educational purposes without regard to direct corporate benefit and without limitation as to amount." It pointed out the restrictions in much of the existing permissive legislation and the dangers of relying upon court decisions in jurisdictions where only the common law prevailed. It thought that the grant of power should be broad, its exercise should be left to the discretion of corporate management, and saw no logical reason for regulating by statute the amount that can be donated. Mr. Garrett's Committee suggested "for use in statutes that enumerate the general powers of corporations" this form:

(_____) To make donations for the public welfare or for charitable, scientific or educational purposes.[1]

The Committee suggested that in other statutes the same simple form be the basis for a new section consistent with the form and style of the statute.

In the two legislative years 1949 and 1951 this simple model statute has been adopted by Arkansas, California, Connecticut, Maine, New Mexico, and Wisconsin, and as an amendment to previous laws by Delaware and Illinois; the Kansas statute adopted in 1951 is not materially different.

The Immutable Contract Doctrine

As this summary indicates, great strides have been made, particularly in the past four years, toward clarifying the legal right of corporations to make contributions. Permissive legislation of some sort exists in all the industrialized states, and many others; and the recent acts are usually broad, without troublesome restrictions.

One difficulty remains. Some responsible legal opinion supports the immutable contract doctrine. According to this doctrine, the new permissive legislation applies only to corporations which receive charters after the date of the legislation. It is held

[1] Memorandum from the Committee on Business Corporations of the Section on Corporation, Banking and Mercantile Law of the American Bar Association, February 15, 1949.

that a corporate charter is a contract between the state of incorporation and the corporation and between and among the stockholders themselves. In this view the state cannot by legislation confer new powers on corporations organized prior to such legislation. The doctrine's extreme form holds that the corporation itself cannot alter its charter, nor the state accept such alteration, if there is even a single dissenting stockholder.

Other legal opinion holds that the state as the creating agency retains the right to alter the powers conferred upon corporations by their charters. This view is supported by Mr. Garrett, chairman of the Committee on Business Corporations of the American Bar Association, and it seems the reasonable view. But it is possible that the strict doctrine would be upheld in some jurisdictions.

However, even under the strict interpretation the matter reverts simply to the common law.

> Here the absence of recent cases makes it hard to demonstrate that the courts have become more liberal toward corporate giving. Nevertheless it seems safe to say that many gifts once invalid would now be sustained, and this is so for several reasons. It is today more apparent that the welfare of a particular corporation is intimately connected with the general welfare and the private charitable institutions of the community in which it operates. Perhaps even more significantly businessmen seem today to regard an active concern for community welfare and private charity as good business, both because of this economic relation and because of the benefits which flow, business-wise, from community good will and favorable publicity. It is even arguable that the relevant community for many businesses is the nation, and, for some, the world. A modern court can reasonably be expected to look to these changed circumstances and to the current opinions of businessmen generally in determining what is a direct corporate benefit within the rule of the common law.[1]

It seems most unlikely that any court would decide against a power neither specifically granted nor withheld in the face of clarifying legislation granting it to other corporations. The bugaboo of illegality has been largely laid. Corporations which in the past used it to frighten off undesired solicitors are sometimes

[1] Quoted in a letter from Ray Garrett, Jr., New York University Law School, March, 1952.

finding it difficult to rid themselves of the doubts they induced, but in the light of recent developments their fears seem nearly or quite groundless. Corporations can give to philanthropic causes if at least some direct relation to their own interests can be demonstrated.

Court Decisions

Court decisions significantly affecting corporation giving show a wide variety over the years. Appendix D[1] presents brief digests of 106 law and tax cases, believed to be substantially all the important cases in the United States. They make interesting but sometimes confusing reading. In the tax case of Bishop Trust Company in 1937 a donation to the Hawaiian Bureau of Governmental Research was disallowed; but in *American Factors, Ltd.* v. *Kanne* in 1947 a contribution toward maintenance of the same Bureau was approved. Decisions concerning contributions to hospitals show wide variety, but even the earliest years evidence a strong tendency for approval if employees and their dependents make up a large proportion of the hospital's probable patients. Nearly all projects bearing directly on employee welfare were approved.

In each case many attendant circumstances must be considered, particularly the date. Was permissive legislation in effect in that state, in the general law cases, at the time of the decision? It has already been pointed out that no significant law case has been decided against the contributor since 1919.

In tax cases 1936, when contributions first became deductible, is the significant date. Only ten tax cases decided since that date are noted. Four of these were decided against the contributor, one being the Hawaiian Bureau of Governmental Research already noticed, the other three involving contributions to organizations of the community chest type. But in each of the community chest cases the corporation had claimed the deduction as a business expense for a year preceding 1936, when contributions became deductible.

[1] See p. 317.

A decision on the immutable contract doctrine in New Jersey is pending. Unless that decision proves unfavorable to the donor, it can be said that few obstacles remain to the corporate giver in either statute or recent judge-made law.

National Banks

National banking associations were in 1940 granted broad powers to contribute to philanthropic objectives if located "in a state the laws of which do not expressly prohibit state banking institutions from contributing to such funds or instrumentalities." The pertinent section of the National Banking Act is cited in full at the end of Appendix C.

Railroads and Common Carriers

Railroads and common carriers are sometimes organized under special state legislation rather than the general corporation act. Under this circumstance the permissive legislation already noticed does not always extend to them. Among the 26 states with permissive legislation listed in Table 38, Illinois, Indiana, Michigan, Missouri, New Jersey (if operating within the state) and New Mexico (unless organized for operation outside the state) exclude railroads from coverage under the conditions noted.

Aside from the question of express powers, giving by railroads is hampered by Interstate Commerce Commission accounting rules regarding inclusion of contributions among operating expenses. Under the Commission's interpretation of these rules a railroad may charge to operating expense those items which "have a direct or intimate relation to the protection of the property of the carrier or to the development of its business or to the welfare of its employees." Examples include "donations to local fire department" and "donations to Y.M.C.A., and similar institutions." Presumably donations of a more general character might be disallowed as an operating expense, though they could still be charged to the profit and loss account.

Government Contracts

Contributions and donations cannot be included as cost items in government contracts based on a cost formula according to the contract cost principles of the Joint Regulations of the Armed Forces.[1] Regulations with respect to renegotiation of government contracts were liberalized in the revised 1951 Renegotiation Act as follows:

Section 1459.8(b)—Charitable and other contributions.

(1) Contributions will, to the extent allocable thereto be allowed as a cost of renegotiable business if such contributions are estimated to be deductible in the fiscal year under review for Federal income tax purposes under section 23 (o) and (q) of the Internal Revenue Code.

(2) The primary consideration in determining the extent to which such contributions are allocable to renegotiable business is whether they are reasonably necessary for the conduct of such business. In this connection weight will be given to the practice of the contractor before July 1, 1950, with respect to charitable contributions.

Recipients Operating Abroad

Many companies with international interests desire to make contributions to welfare agencies abroad, or American agencies operating in foreign countries.

With respect to tax deductibility, the case is relatively clear. The contribution must be made "to or for the use of a corporation, trust, or community chest, fund, or foundation, created or organized" in the United States or its possessions. Moreover, since the close of 1948 (this special provision was not in effect for the war period) contributions to "a trust, chest, fund, or foundation" are deductible "only if such contributions or gifts are to be used within the United States or any of its possessions exclusively for such purposes."[2] But this is not the broad exclusion of gifts for foreign operations that a hasty reading suggests. The second listing of covered agencies significantly omits "corporation," included in the first listing. The Bureau of Internal Revenue has ruled that the limitation does not apply to contributions to a domestic *corporation* which uses part or all of its

---

[1] 32 CFR, 1950 Supp., Sec. 414.205(f).

[2] Internal Revenue Code, Sec. 23(q) Charitable and other contributions by corporations.

funds for charitable purposes in foreign countries.[1] Most of the agencies to which corporations are likely to make contributions for expenditure abroad are domestic corporations.

The only income-tax decision involving a donation for foreign use was that of a manufacturer of matzos to a theological school in Palestine.[2] The Tax Court allowed the deduction because of the historical background of the corporation and the business involved.

As to corporate power to make contributions for foreign use, the same general principles apply as for other contributions, with added limitations. Some of the state statutes restrict the authority to local beneficiaries; others, to furthering the corporate interest; in still others, the authority is unrestricted. Where direct corporate benefit must be shown, whether under the common law or a particular statute, the burden of establishing such benefit is vastly greater in the case of a contribution for foreign use.

[1] I.T. 3048, 1937-1 C.B. 85.
[2] *The B. Manischewitz Co.*, 10 T.C. 1139 (1948).

CHAPTER 14

Taxation Factors

OPINIONS differ on how much corporate contributions have been influenced by tax considerations. The first year contributions became deductible, in 1936, community chests in nine cities reported on their efforts to increase corporate contributions as a result of the new Revenue Act; six chests failed to find any tangible increases, and the remaining three felt it had helped, but "to no great extent."[1] Corporate taxes were then just beginning to rise. At the later very high wartime levels contributions vaulted to eight times their prewar amount. The savings due to deductibility had certainly a large influence, and need again to be examined in the present setting.

Conditions for Tax Deductibility

Since 1936 the federal government has encouraged gifts to charitable institutions and causes on the part of corporations by exempting from the corporation tax "contributions or gifts payment of which is made within the taxable year . . . to an amount which does not exceed 5 per centum of the taxpayer's net income as computed without the benefits of this subsection."[2] Corporations operating on an accrual basis may include gifts made before the fifteenth day of the third month following close of the taxable year if authorized by the board of directors within the year.

[1] *A 24-City Study of Corporation Giving to Community Chests.* Elizabeth (N. J.) Community Chest, 1936, p. 12. Multigraphed.

[2] Section 23(q) of the Internal Revenue Code is quoted in full in Appendix B, p. 274.

Organizations to which tax-exempt contributions can be made include those for "religious, charitable, scientific, veteran rehabilitation service, literary, or educational purposes, or for the prevention of cruelty to children," veterans' organizations under certain conditions, and contributions to the United States or any of its political subdivisions "for exclusively public purposes." If the gift is made to a trust, chest, fund, or foundation, it must be used within the United States or its possessions for the purposes noted[1]; this geographical limitation does not apply to gifts by individuals. The contribution may be made in money or property (not services), with the value of property gifts to be measured by fair market value at the time the contribution is made. If a manufacturing company's own product is given, the current wholesale price has sometimes been applied, but individual rulings should be sought. Dues or assessments for which the giver receives benefits cannot be deducted, nor can gifts to individuals.[2]

Numerous provisions and restrictions apply to the organizations to which deductible contributions may be made; among the more important are provisions that no part of their net earnings may benefit any private shareholder or individual, and no substantial part of their activities may consist in "carrying on propaganda, or otherwise attempting, to influence legislation." Charitable organizations are usually more than willing to inform contributors of their exempt status, and the Treasury Department has issued a series of rosters.[3]

Under current high taxation this deductibility is of great value to corporations in reducing the net cost of their gifts or in making possible much more substantial gifts at an agreed net profit outlay. Tax evasion is illegal; but to take full advantage of the provisions written into the tax laws to increase the size of gifts is perfectly proper. How great this advantage may be is made clear by an examination of the new Revenue Act.

[1] But this limitation does not apply if the tax-exempt organization is a domestic corporation. See p. 243.

[2] But gifts can be made to individuals through a corporation foundation or other nonprofit organization.

[3] *Cumulative List of Organizations . . . Revised to June 30, 1950* Government Printing Office, Washington, 1950.

The Revenue Act of 1951

The Revenue Act of 1951, fully effective on 1952 income, sets corporation taxes at 30 per cent on the first $25,000 of net income and 52 per cent on the rest, with excess profits taxed at an additional 30 per cent, totaling 82 per cent on this portion of income. No corporation averages 82 per cent on all its net income—the maximum is just less than 70 per cent for the largest corporations, 64.5 per cent for a corporation with profits of $100,000— but contributions and gifts may in nearly all cases be regarded as deductions from the highest applicable rate.[1]

Under these high rates corporations may make substantial gifts at relatively small cost in surrendered profits. Table 39 and Figure 10 show these costs for corporations in various tax brackets.

TABLE 39. NET COST OF CONTRIBUTIONS MADE BY CORPORA-
TIONS IN VARIOUS PROFIT BRACKETS, 1952

Taxed income[a]	Amount of gift	Tax saved	Net cost
$25,000 or less	$100	$ 30	$70
Over 25,000	100	52	48
Excess profits	100	82	18
$25,000 or less	142.86	42.86	100
Over 25,000	208.33	108.33	100
Excess profits	555.56	455.56	100

[a] The applicable rate is the highest bracket to which the amount of the gift can be applied.

As this table indicates, a corporation in the excess-profits bracket can contribute more than five and a half times the amount it could have retained for its own uses. This is radically different from the situation even so recently as 1949, when the maximum total tax for corporations was 38 per cent in place of the present possible maximum on a part of income of 82 per cent.

Some corporations see in this extraordinary situation a business opportunity. If corporate giving brings tangible benefits in terms of customer good will, aid to employees, or other corporate advantage, then these benefits are purchasable at 48 cents on the dollar, and in some situations at 18 cents on the dollar. Fund

[1] Note that under the carry forward-carry back tax rule, the effective rate may sometimes be changed by later developments.

collectors have not been slow to point out this bargain to business executives. "How to Give *almost twice as much* at the SAME NET COST!" screams the envelope stuffer of one hopeful agency.

Corporations are being urged to increase their contributions at once to the deductible 5 per cent so as to take full advantage of this charitable bargain. A possible total contribution of $2.2 billion for 1951, based on the estimated net profits of that year, was suggested. No such increase took place or is in present prospect,

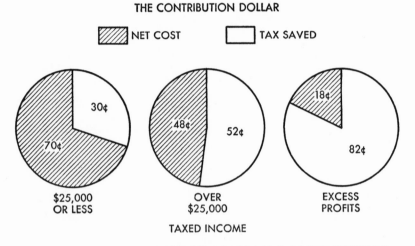

THE CONTRIBUTION DOLLAR

FIGURE 10. THE NET COST OF CORPORATE CONTRIBUTIONS

and until corporations have had more experience in wise giving, sudden increases of such dimensions might, indeed, be dangerous. But taxation at present levels does add a new perspective to business giving.

Corporate vs. Individual Gifts

Some recent increase in corporate giving may represent a mere shift from individual giving. It has become highly advantageous for individuals controlling closely held corporations to make their gifts through their companies rather than personally:

John Brown, who owns or controls all the stock in the John Brown Company, has been asked to contribute to a building fund for Alma

Mater College. Recent profits having been good, he decides to give $1,000. He can—

a. Vote himself an additional $1,000 in dividends and pay by personal check. His contribution credit on personal income is now exactly balanced by his added income, so there is no saving here. Meanwhile, the John Brown Company had to make $2,083 so that Mr. Brown could take out $1,000 net profit, after the 52 per cent tax.

b. Set aside the same $2,083. Pay $1,000 by company check. Pay the 52 per cent tax on the remaining $1,083 and pocket the balance of about $520 as profit for his sagacity.

c. Set aside the same $2,083, and pay the whole amount to the College by company check. He more than doubles the contribution at the same cost as a $1,000 personal contribution.

Company contributions in discharge of personal obligations may be part of the explanation for the notably higher contribution rate of the smaller companies. One chain store reports that its contribution budget has to be unusually large to meet "the heavy competition in contributions from local merchants who are able to make personal gifts through their stores and thereby deduct the corporation tax."

Giving Appreciated Assets or Products

Tax advantages can sometimes be achieved through giving appreciated assets or products. If securities, real estate, or other property has increased in value while in the company's possession, it can be given to a welfare agency with tax credit at the present fair market value without any payment of capital gains tax on its increase in value.

Corporation A purchased two acres of land for $5,000 for possible plant expansion. That expansion is no longer desirable, but the land is now worth $20,000. It can—

a. Sell the land for $20,000, paying a 26 per cent capital gains tax on $15,000, or $3,900. After deducting cost of land, the net profit is $11,100.

b. Present the land to Local College without restriction on use or sale. The tax credit on a contribution of $20,000 at the 82 per cent excess profits rate prevailing for this company amounts to $16,400. The company has made a contribution of $20,000 to the college and a net profit for itself of $11,400.

In this case, where an extreme increase in value had occurred and tax liability was at the highest rate, it was possible to make more money by giving the asset away than by selling it. Such an extreme will not often occur, but the principle is valid.

Similarly, it will sometimes be advantageous to give a company product rather than cash. Credit has sometimes been allowed on the basis of wholesale selling price. If the product is genuinely needed by the benefiting agency, and a cooperative arrangement can be worked out so as to avoid difficulties with the local supplier, quite remarkable gifts can sometimes be made at small cost, but Treasury approval must be secured for the wholesale valuation.

> Assume a Widget manufactured for $20, wholesaling at $50, retailing at $100. No advertising or promotion overhead is charged to the gift Widgets, since they are themselves useful promotion and good-will pieces. Each Widget given away costs the manufacturer $20, but he receives (not being in the excess profits bracket) a tax credit of 52 per cent of $50, or $26. The charitable agency gets a $100 Widget free, and the manufacturer makes a net $6 added profit on each Widget given away—up to the 5 per cent limit of deductibility.

These remarkable bargains are primarily due, not to any special characteristic of a charitable contribution, but to the tax structure. Corporations can also spend 48-cent dollars (and in some cases 18-cent dollars) hiring symphony orchestras as advertising or buying scooters for all the office boys as a business expense.

The dangers in this situation are well recognized. Senator Walter F. George, in presenting the 1951 tax bill, warned that we were close to the limit of taxation, which would be reached, he asserted, "when we destroy the incentives of the people to earn income, when we cause taxpayers to evade their taxes, and when we lead corporations to indulge in wasteful practices."[1] The serious abuses in giving that could arise under these emergency rates are obvious; in such a time what is legal must be tempered by what is wise.

[1] *New York Times*, September 20, 1951.

Deductions for Business Expense

As has been indicated, corporations sometimes deduct as a business expense contributions to agencies in the health, welfare, or educational fields which by many standards would seem to be philanthropy. Such contributions escape the 5 per cent limitation, though this is seldom an important factor, for most companies give less than 1 per cent. The decision whether to allocate an expenditure to trade or business expense under 23(a) or to charitable contributions under 23(q) is often made by the company lawyer, on the basis of the particular item. Properly to be chargeable under 23(a) the gift must be for a purpose quite closely related to corporate interest and advantage. The Internal Revenue Code further provides:

> 23(a) (B) Corporate Charitable Contributions—No deduction shall be allowable under subparagraph (A) to a corporation for any contribution or gift which would be allowable as a deduction under subsection (q) were it not for the 5 per centum limitation therein contained and for the requirement therein that payment must be made within the taxable year.

The government tabulations give no hint as to the amount of contributions corporations may be making under 23(a). Our Survey, therefore, asked for not only tabulation of contributions and gifts treated as charitable deductions and so reported on the income-tax form, but:

> 6. If additional sums were given to agencies for health, welfare, education, or religion in 1950 as a business expense, indicate the approximate amount here. $. . . . .

According to this sample, reported contributions should be increased by somewhat less than 8 per cent to include those of a charitable nature concealed in 23(a). Smaller corporations use 23(a) more frequently than the giants. Corporation 1292 reported no contributions under 23(q), all under 23(a); but the total was only $182, of which $100 went for "various police and fireman fund drives." Four other corporations in the random sample, two of which are utilities, classified all their contributions as business expenses. But this classification is employed less widely

TABLE 40. CONTRIBUTIONS TREATED AS A CHARITABLE DEDUC-
TION AND AS A BUSINESS EXPENSE IN 326 SURVEYED
CORPORATIONS, BY AMOUNT OF CORPORATION AS-
SETS, 1950[a]

Dollar figures in thousands

Asset classes (millions)	Corporations	Gifts reported as business expense (a)	Gifts reported as contributions (q)	Per cent (a) is of (q)
Under $1	101	$ 13	$ 91	14.9
1 under 50	166	190	1,544	12.3
50 and over	59	276	4,675	5.9
Total	326	$479	$6,310	7.6

[a] Russell Sage Foundation Survey.

than has often been assumed, and its use specifically as a device
to avoid the 5 per cent limitation is illegal.

State Income Taxes

Thirty-two states and the District of Columbia tax corporations
on their net income. The highest rate in 1951 was 8 per cent, and
in many states net income was determined after deduction of
federal income tax. Where charitable deductions are allowed,
these may be limited to contributions made to agencies within the
state. The provisions of the Oregon law may be cited:

> Sec. 110–1508 * * * In computing "net income" the following
> deductions shall be allowed * * *
> (h) Contributions or gifts made on or after January 1, 1947,
> within the tax year by the taxpayer to the United States, the State
> of Oregon or any political subdivision thereof for use exclusively for
> public purposes within the State of Oregon, or to corporations or
> associations operated exclusively for religious, charitable, scientific,
> or educational purposes, or for the prevention of cruelty to children
> or animals, no part of the net earnings of which inures to the benefit
> of any private shareholder or individual, which deductions for such
> purposes shall not exceed 5 per cent of the taxpayer's net income as
> computed without the benefit of this subdivision. * * *

In these states charitable contributions have an added taxation
advantage, but it is not considerable in comparison with the
present value of deductibility under federal taxation. The two in
concert under maximum conditions, however, may reduce the

cost of a gift to about 16.6 cents[1] on the dollar if the corporation is in the excess-profits bracket (82 per cent) and is in a state with the maximum 8 per cent rate based on net profit without deduction of federal income tax, as in Oregon.

Tax Aspects of Corporation Foundations

The general nature of the corporation foundation and certain of its administrative advantages have been discussed in Chapter 6. A closer examination of taxation factors may be desirable, particularly in view of the Revenue Act of 1950.

Before passage of that Act many private foundations, universities, churches, and other philanthropic organizations received invitations to take over the real-estate holdings or all the assets of business enterprises, and some did so. In a few cases the business enterprise itself was reorganized as a foundation, with income irrevocably assigned to a charitable use. It was assumed that in either case the income of the business operation would escape the federal income tax, since an early decision of the Supreme Court had made the question of tax exemption hinge upon ultimate use of funds, not their source.

Although this apparent transfer of business profit to charitable purposes (including the taxable portion of such profit) seemed within the law, and often was so, it was capable of severe abuse. The favored tax-free enterprise could rapidly accumulate a large surplus which its creator was sometimes able to "borrow" on convenient terms for the expansion of his profit-making ventures. No provision required payments to the ultimate beneficiary at any given time. Complicated leasebacks on real property were made through exempt corporations. Special salary arrangements might be possible because of the tax-free status of the favored corporation. In any event ordinary business, subject to heavy taxation, looked aghast at competition from tax-free units, and the government began to be concerned over the loss of revenue.

The Revenue Act of 1950 endeavored to cure these inequities and abuses. Its provisions need to be taken into account in the

[1] State taxes are deductible for federal tax purposes; therefore the combined effect is not the simple sum of the two rates.

organization and operation of corporation foundations, even when set up solely to facilitate corporate giving. The Act's pertinent provisions, including a minor amendment in 1951, are included in excerpts from the present Code in Appendix B.

In general, tax exemption is denied on income in excess of $1,000 of a business enterprise not "substantially related" to the organization's tax-free activities, and the regular corporate income tax (individual rates apply on trusts) is levied on certain previously exempt organizations which are in the nature of business corporations but devote their income to a philanthropic purpose. New regulations apply to long-term leases, taxing the income from such leases as "unrelated business income" under certain conditions. Tax exemption is forfeited if the organization engages in certain "prohibited transactions," including transactions in which it

(1) lends any part of its income or corpus, without the receipt of adequate security and a reasonable rate of interest, to;

(2) pays any compensation, in excess of a reasonable allowance for salaries or other compensation for personal services actually rendered, to;

(3) makes any part of its services available on a preferential basis to;

(4) makes any substantial purchase of securities or any other property, for more than adequate consideration in money or money's worth, from;

(5) sells any substantial part of its securities or other property, for less than an adequate consideration in money or money's worth, to; or

(6) engages in any other transaction which results in a substantial diversion of its income or corpus to;

the creator of such organization (if a trust); a person who has made a substantial contribution to such organization; a member of the family of an individual who is the creator of such trust or who has made a substantial contribution to such organization; or a corporation controlled by such creator or person through the ownership, directly or indirectly, of 50 per centum or more of the total combined voting power of all classes of stock entitled to vote or 50 per centum or more of the total value of shares of all classes of stock of the corporation.[1]

[1] Internal Revenue Code, Sec. 3813(b).

Tax exemption is also lost if the income accumulated in current and prior years is found to be "unreasonably" large, or held for an unreasonable period of time, in view of the exempt purposes for which the funds are intended; or used to a substantial degree for purposes other than the organization's exempt purpose; or invested in such a manner as to entail risk that the funds will be lost. Information form 990a must be filed annually, and pages three and four are open to public inspection; it covers income, expenses, charitable disbursements, accumulations of income, and a balance sheet. The Code continues the previous prohibition against devoting any substantial part of activities to "carrying on propaganda, or otherwise attempting, to influence legislation."

Some of the provisions of this law are vague, perhaps intentionally, and Treasury rulings have not yet been made, giving specific interpretations. They offer little danger, however, to the corporation foundation organized solely to facilitate wise giving.

For example, the corporation may wish to use its foundation to accumulate capital for giving in lean years, or to accomplish some major project. Gifts for such purposes are not income for the foundation, but constitute additions to capital, and will scarcely be questioned unless that capital is used in some of the prohibited ways.

A foundation, corporation or private, may be a useful and legitimate device for retaining control of a business, where retention of all the profits is not essential and a contribution to charity is desired. The Ford Foundation is the most notable example. Upon the deaths of Edsel and Henry Ford it was supposed that Ford Motor Company stock would have to come upon the market in order to discharge the heavy estate and inheritance taxes. But the stock had been divided into 10 per cent voting stock and 90 per cent nonvoting, and all of the latter was presented to the previously existing Ford Foundation, which also paid the death taxes on the heirs' estates. The family retained complete voting control, and the Foundation the right to about 90 per cent of future profits.

It should be noted that the Motor Company does pay usual corporate income taxes on all its dividends, even though 90 per cent of them go to the Ford Foundation. But, like other companies, it may deduct as a contribution up to 5 per cent of net income if it contributes that amount directly or through the Ford Motor Company Fund, its own corporation foundation, which is quite separate and distinct from its colossal brother, the Ford Foundation.

Corporation Giving and Federal Revenue

No consideration of corporation giving is complete which stops with a totaling of the contributions of corporations, their savings in taxes, and the receipts of the benefiting agencies. The other side of the coin is the effect on federal revenue.

Thus far, that effect has been negligible. If we assume that 1951 contributions may have been as high as $300 million and that enough of the contributors were in the excess-profits tax bracket to bring the average rate to 60 per cent, revenue lost through contribution deductions was no more than $180 million.

But the National Planning Association's Business Committee looks hopefully toward a full 5 per cent contribution from many companies, and points out that 5 per cent of the probable $45 billion profit before taxes in 1951 would amount to about $2.2 billion.[1] If the tax rate on the exempted income averaged 60 per cent, this could amount to an apparent tax loss of $1.3 billion.

On the surface, several adjustments seem obvious. The tax deficit, whatever the amount, might have to be made up by additional taxation. If this was directed chiefly against corporations, the tax deduction would be mere illusion, taking corporate net income as a whole. If the increased taxes fell on some other group, then that new group would in effect be paying a substantial part of the cost of corporate philanthropy, without any word in its direction.

Again, the Congress might regard the reduction in revenue so seriously, in the present emergency, that it would rescind the 5 per cent provision. Such action becomes probable if corpora-

[1] Ruml, Beardsley, and Theodore Geiger, *The Five Percent*. National Planning Association, Washington, 1951, rev. ed., p. 8.

tions, attracted by the present charitable bargain, should be in such a rush to take advantage of it that they indulge in many foolish, wasteful, or obviously selfish enterprises. Sudden abolition of this tax provision would be most unfortunate, and a catastrophe for agencies which have grown largely dependent on corporate giving over some fifteen years.

Another view is tenable, especially if corporation giving increases in wisdom as it increases in dimensions. Intelligent philanthropy is not a pit into which money sinks, and is lost. It may be an investment, yielding dividends as large and sometimes as tangible as business enterprise itself.

The money a life insurance company invests in health research or safety promotion may come back to that very company in delayed death payments for its own policyholders, and in a larger social dividend of longer productive lives. The money a company in a small community spends on the local college it expects to receive back in trained workers, and it suspects that if such voluntary support is not forthcoming, government will step in and the corporation will still pay, this time through taxes. Viewed nationally, the situation is more complicated, but many of the philanthropic expenditures of corporations are for purposes which, directly or indirectly, reduce government expenditure.

The case of the Joseph Bulova School of Watchmaking[1] may be examined from the tax viewpoint. The Company received a tax deduction for its expenditures in setting up and operating the School. But in the absence of such special training, nearly all the disabled veterans now graduates of the School would have had to be supported by government subsidy the rest of their lives. Though they continue to receive disability pensions, most of them are performing useful work and many are making such substantial incomes that they pay substantial personal income taxes.

In Conclusion

Private initiative has been the key to American progress. Only a portion of that initiative has directed itself toward making profits. It has also been expressed in political inventions, medical

[1] See p. 111.

discoveries, voluntary associations of a thousand kinds, educational experiments, and basic research into the ultimate facts of the physical universe and of man and his relationships.

In the present money economy some of this private initiative is finding survival difficult. Certain proved institutions and services that must be provided for all the people have come within the orbit of government, and it is probably desirable that they should be paid for equitably out of taxation. But governmental institutions are seldom the climate in which fundamental discoveries are made, or new ventures begun.

Business statesmanship needs to consider what its share should be in supporting existing free enterprises in health, welfare, education, and research, and possibly in initiating fresh ventures in these areas. Such support is not a necessity. Private individuals can and do bear much of this burden, and government will take over any essential services which fail of private support, and add them to the tax bill. Corporate giving is chiefly an opportunity.

The amount given matters, of course. In 1948, the latest year for which tax returns are available, corporate contributions amounted to $239 million. This is a great increase over prewar giving, and already an important part of the budgets of many health and welfare agencies. It is not a large part of total philanthropic giving (about $4 billion) nor a big item in the corporate budget. In that same year deductions for bad debts were three times as much—$711 million. Advertising (and corporate giving also has substantial advertising values) cost nearly fifteen times as much—$3.5 billion. The amount could be greatly increased without becoming a major budget consideration.

Of greater importance is the method. Ill-considered giving, particularly if it should become large, will do little good and some harm, and may rouse public reaction against wastefulness of what is now more the taxpayers' than the corporation's money. But a sound program, informed by intimate knowledge of the needs of the local community and powered by each company's unique interests and resources, can strongly undergird America's free institutions, including the institution of free business enterprise itself.

APPENDICES

APPENDIX A

METHOD OF THE STUDY

This study of corporation giving grew directly out of the writer's earlier general survey, *Philanthropic Giving*,[1] in the course of which he had become impressed with the great recent growth of corporate philanthropy and the urgent need for more information in the field. Preliminary explorations in the fall of 1950 confirmed widespread interest in such a study and an outline was prepared; upon approval by the Trustees of Russell Sage Foundation, intensive work was begun early in 1951.

Factual content of the survey has been derived from three main sources: fragmentary published information in books, pamphlets, magazine articles, newspaper clippings; statistical data from the Bureau of Internal Revenue's corporation income-tax returns; and a special survey conducted by the writer.

Published Information

The only earlier extensive survey of this subject was conducted by the National Bureau of Economic Research[2] and published in 1930. This report reflected data now more than two decades old and was based largely upon information from community chests. More recently, useful information on various aspects of the subject has been collected by several private organizations, but usually for their own clients or memberships. The writer has been permitted access to most of these data, and where he has requested permission to quote, in all cases it has been granted.

Among the more noteworthy efforts in this field are the following: the National Industrial Conference Board's studies of the giving of large companies and general contribution policies; a special survey of the attitudes on corporation giving on the part of the general public, community leaders, and stockholders made by Public Opinion Index for Industry, Opinion Research Corporation, Princeton, New Jersey; a collection of corporation policy statements on giving prepared by the American Society of Corporate Secretaries; data now annually col-

---

[1] Andrews, F. Emerson, *Philanthropic Giving*. Russell Sage Foundation, New York, 1950.

[2] Williams, Pierce, and Frederick E. Croxton, *Corporation Contributions to Organized Community Welfare Services*. The Bureau, New York, 1930.

lected by Community Chests and Councils of America on corporate contributions to the chests; information compiled at various times by the Controllers Institute of America; recent pamphlets of the National Planning Association, and its new *Manual of Corporate Giving*, which appeared after this volume was in type; and several surveys conducted by private corporations for the guidance of their own directors.

Information has also been gleaned from books in the welfare field; from magazine articles and newspaper clippings; from reports of corporations to their stockholders; from the records of recipient organizations and interviews with their officers. But a careful study of all these sources has served chiefly to emphasize the fact that corporate philanthropy has grown faster than the efforts to record it, and no comprehensive appraisal of its present status has existed.

Bureau of Internal Revenue Data

For statistics on the dimensions of corporate giving main reliance must be placed on data of the Bureau of Internal Revenue compiled from income-tax returns of corporations. Only the government has both the power to compel returns from all corporations and the facilities for collecting information on so vast a scale, involving now more than 600,000 corporations. We have used both the published information in *Statistics of Income* and unpublished material, available in the manuscript *Source Book* in the offices of the Bureau; grateful acknowledgment is here made for the helpfulness of Bureau personnel with respect to these sources.

Information on "gifts and contributions" of corporations began to appear on corporate income-tax returns for the year 1936, the first year in which such contributions were deductible. Currently, returns have been tabulated only through 1948, and the figures for 1947 and 1948 are tentative. For general purposes these figures are the most nearly complete and reliable that can be obtained. For the statistician certain reservations need to be made, and we should clarify some of the details of our handling of them.

The "gifts and contributions" item on some returns may be inflated, either through deliberate falsification—probably rare, in view of the customary audits both within the corporation and within the Bureau— or through inclusion of items such as memberships in business organizations, which in many corporations are handled with the contributions budget but for tax purposes should be reported as a business expense. We doubt whether many corporations have erred in either of these respects.

The "gifts and contributions" item may be too low in some corporate reports, and entirely lacking in others. Such gifts are deductible only up to "5 per centum of the taxpayer's net income as computed without the benefits of this subsection." A very few corporations contribute as a matter of policy the full 5 per cent and sometimes more; numerous corporations experience bad years in which they have no net income against which any contributions can legally be deducted. The fact is that the "no net" corporations as a group do report substantial contributions, many of them apparently being ignorant of the law or mistakenly hopeful that they can thereby build up a larger loss carryover; but no way exists of determining what unreported contributions may have been actually made by other corporations.

In addition, life insurance companies, mutual savings banks, and a few other types of corporations report on different forms on which provision is not made for a net income item against which contributions could be deducted. On these reports "gifts and contributions" do not appear in any identifiable form.

Finally, some contributions, which by most tests would fall in the field of philanthropy, are so closely related to the business welfare of the company or its employees that they are deducted as a business expense, where there is no 5 per cent limitation. In our Survey we found that even the person in charge of contributions sometimes did not know where the company lawyers and tax experts had finally allocated certain items of his expenditures. No correction has been possible for this source of error, but its dimensions are later examined.

In comparing rates of giving we used as our divisor "compiled net profit," which is the result of deducting from total compiled receipts the total compiled deductions, including contributions. A desirable refinement would have been to remove the contributions item from the deductions before calculating the percentage, as the individual corporation must do in determining the 5 per cent limitation; but in the group summaries the microscopic difference did not justify this labor. To have made this adjustment for the 1948 contributions, for example, would have decreased the general rate as shown in Table 4 a mere 5/1000 of 1 per cent—from 0.692 per cent to 0.687. Another desirable refinement, determination of median gifts and rates, could not be undertaken since the government does not itself compute rates of giving nor permit access to individual returns.

We have uniformly computed giving rates on "compiled net profit" in the government data in preference to "net income," which others have sometimes used. The difference is slight; in most years "net income" is less merely by the deduction of receipts from interest on wholly tax-exempt government obligations. It was our opinion that such receipts belonged in the base against which contributions were calculated.

For persons not familiar with corporate income-tax returns it may need to be stated that "net profit," which appears in many tables in this book, is not the final amount available for distribution to stockholders; the corporation tax, now at a rate of 30 per cent up to $25,000 and 52 per cent thereafter, must first be deducted. In many returns the still higher excess-profits levy also applies.

Finally, except where otherwise noted, we have used "all returns" in our summaries rather than returns merely of those corporations which had net income. Although, as noted above, it is probable that the "no net income" group did not fully report contributions, it seemed desirable to include as far as known the gifts made in spite of a loss position. Their inclusion results, of course, in a higher giving rate for "all returns" than would have prevailed for the "net income" returns alone. The "no nets" both add to the total contribution and, with their losses, reduce the base on which the rate is computed.

In a few special cases, the "no net income" group is relatively so large that rate figures become meaningless, or must be handled with caution. For example, in 1948 almost half the corporations with assets under $50,000 (109,000 out of 235,000) were in the "no net income" category. Their losses of $361 million nearly wiped out the actual net profit of $414 million of the "net income" group. The contribution rate for "all returns" became 7.48 per cent—although 5 per cent is the deductible limit, and it is probable that not one of the corporations in this class which had a substantial profit that year contributed at this "average" rate. Such distortions, fortunately, are infrequent. Tables 8 and 42,[1] presenting data separately for corporations with net income, those with no net income, and all returns, illustrate the effect of this factor.

The Survey Questionnaire

The Russell Sage Foundation Survey was based principally upon the confidential questionnaire reproduced on pages 265–266. To encourage full and frank returns, the questionnaires carried only a code identification and their information was kept confidential, to be used only in nonidentifiable summaries.

Question 1, type of business, offered no difficulties except where a company operated in several fields. All companies were classified into the eight major industrial categories used by the Bureau of Internal Revenue, so that comparisons could be made.

Question 2, on assets, also offered no problems.

Question 3, number of employees, was asked since with respect to corporation giving the number of persons employed is often a more significant factor than asset class. No problems were encountered.

[1] See pp. 52, 347.

CORPORATION QUESTIONNAIRE

PHILANTHROPY

Note. All information in this questionnaire is for the confidential use of Russell Sage Foundation, to be used only in non-identifiable summaries, unless released by specific arrangement.

1. Please indicate type of business _____

2. What were your approximate assets, as of close of 1950 or fiscal year ending in 1950? $_____

3. About how many employes did you have on January 1, 1951? _____

4. Net income (or net loss)   1950[1]
   Line 32 of 1950 corporate income tax form _____ $_____

5. Contributions and gifts treated as charitable deductions
   Line 23 of 1950 corporate income tax form _____ $_____

6. If additional sums were given to agencies for health, welfare, education, or religion in 1950 as a business expense, indicate the approximate amount here _____ $_____

7. *Analysis of Contributions, 1950*

8. **Welfare agencies**
   a. Community chest _____ $_____
   b. Other welfare agencies _____ _____

9. **Health agencies**
   a. Hospitals _____ _____
   b. National health agencies (polio, cancer, Red Cross, etc.) _____ _____
   c. Other health agencies _____ _____

10. **Education**
    a. Scholarships and fellowships _____ _____
    b. Research in colleges _____ _____
    c. Institutional aid, schools and colleges _____ _____
    d. Agencies supporting "the American way" _____ _____

11. **Religious agencies** (include churches, Salvation Army, YMCA, etc.) _____ _____

---

[1]Calendar year 1950, or fiscal year ending in 1950.

Procedures

12. Requests for contributions are referred to (title or titles) ....

    ....

13. Contributions of $............................ or more require special action by ....

    ....

14. We $_{do\ not}^{do}$ have a written policy on contributions. If YES, please attach, indicating whether it is confidential.

15. We $_{do\ not}^{do}$ contribute to capital-fund drives (buildings or endowment). If YES, such contributions in 1950 represented about ....% of our total gifts.

16. About ....% of our gifts go to annually recurring drives.

17. We $_{do\ not}^{do}$ include an item for contributions at the beginning of our budget year.

18. We $_{have\ not}^{have}$ set up a corporation foundation to handle our contributions.

19. We $_{are\ not}^{are}$ considering changes in our present policies and procedures on philanthropic contributions.

20. For checking on charitable appeals we use ....
    name of organization(s)

For corporations with local branches

21. We distribute our contributions approximately ....% from the national office, ...% from local offices or plants.

22. Within the local budgets, decision of the local management is final for
    ☐ all amounts; ☐ amounts not exceeding $................................ .

23. The size of the local contribution budget is determined primarily by
    ☐ relative business; ☐ number of employes; ☐ ....(specify)

Purposes of Gifts

24. Please name the factors you give most weight in deciding on a contribution. (A confidential down-to-earth statement would be most helpful—benefit to the company, stockholder pressure, keeping government out of the area, public reaction if we do not contribute, or other.)

    1. ....

    2. ....

    3. ....

Employe Solicitation

25. We $_{do\ not}^{do}$ permit plant solicitation of employes. If YES, we limit such drives to .... per year.

26. We $_{do\ not}^{do}$ make payroll deductions for charitable contributions. If YES, we limit them to ....
    smallest amount
    per ....
    week, month, etc.

RUSSELL SAGE FOUNDATION
505 Park Avenue
New York 22, N. Y.

Question 4, net income, was necessary for computation of rates of giving. It caused more hesitation, correspondence, and final refusals than any other question. Numerous corporations filled out every item but this. We sent urgent letters, pointing out that the figure was needed, and would be kept in complete confidence. A considerable proportion finally supplied it, but others did not, and their questionnaires had to be thrown out. Corporation 1842 reported "Mutual life insurance accounting is not done on the basis of net income" and this and two other similar corporations, contributing a total of $55,379, had to be assigned zero income.

Question 5 asked that contributions and gifts be reported at precisely the amounts given on Line 23 of the 1950 corporate income-tax return. It was explicit, and created few problems. In several cases attempts to stretch the facts into a more favorable report had to be resisted. Said Corporation 1103: "Wishing to cooperate, we have done so but have used 1949 contributions. For tax reasons we deferred some payments during 1950, hence the actual outlay for that year was nominal."

Question 6 called for additional sums "given to agencies for health, welfare, education, or religion in 1950 as a business expense." This question was designed to give us some measure of the additional charitable giving which is not represented in the Bureau of Internal Revenue's summaries. Several corporations with net losses reported all their contributions on this line. Sums given as a business expense amounted to $479,088, or an addition of 7.6 per cent to the total reported under 5.

Questions 7 through 11 asked for an analysis of the contributions reported in 5 and 6. The four major and nine subcategories were not intended as an ideal or fully coordinate division of the field of philanthropy; they were pragmatic. Community chests, for example, often include hospitals and other health agencies, but we could not ask the corporation to go back into the budget of the chest itself and apportion its contribution.

Under Question 9, health agencies, several companies attempted to include payments in behalf of employees to "blue shield and blue cross" but this was disallowed. Some questions arose as to the proper classification of the Red Cross.

A special category, "agencies supporting 'the American way'" was inserted at the request of a number of corporation executives, who believed a measure of expenditures in this field was currently important. It appears under education, for want of a more suitable place.

No "miscellaneous" category was listed, for fear it would become a catch-all, discouraging the desired effort to classify expenditures. Of course, in the final tabulations it had to be added to care for items that fitted in no category and for the several corporations that could not or did not classify. Items that Corporation 1434 could not classify included contributions "to various local clubs and civic enterprises, such as the Lions Club, Navy League, Good Fellers, R——— Symphony Orchestra, Downtown Businessmen's Association, Etc." Corporation 1809 added as miscellaneous $50 in "contributions" to "policemen, firemen, postal clerks for tickets to balls." One corporation that maintains a foundation reported a large miscellaneous item, which presumably represented funds accumulated in the foundation for later distribution.

Questions 12 through 20 were directed at discovering administrative practices and policies with respect to contributions. No special problems were encountered. The answers were coded and machine-punched, and are reported in the appropriate sections of the book.

Questions 21 through 23 applied only to corporations with multiple plants or branches. Replies to this section of the questionnaire numbered 68.

Question 24 probed into the motives for giving. Frankness was urged, but we doubt whether the resulting answers may in all cases be taken at face value. This subject was emphasized in most of the personal interviews which supplemented the questionnaire and the information developed by that method proved most enlightening.

Questions 25 and 26 deal with employee solicitation, a subject marginal to this particular study. But since it does have a direct bearing on corporation giving and in many companies has become a management concern, some indication of the present situation was sought and is presented.

The Survey Sample

This questionnaire, obviously, could not be circulated to the 600,000 existing corporations under any reasonable budget, and even if that had been possible, Russell Sage Foundation possessed no compulsory powers for obtaining replies. The most hopeful procedure seemed to be to find a sample of manageable size of corporations of all types and asset classifications, and invite their cooperation.

A completely satisfactory roster of corporations, from which to create this sample, was not found. After extensive comparison of the various listings available, we finally selected as probably the list most nearly meeting our needs Poor's *Register of Directors and Executives*,[1] which includes a directory of some 19,000 corporations. From this list we took 1,200 names by a method of random sampling, first eliminating partnerships and Canadian addresses.

[1] Standard and Poor's Corporation, New York, 1951.

To the presidents or the general managers of these 1,200 corporations a personal letter was sent in March, 1951, enclosing the questionnaire and explaining our Survey. A number of corporations answered promptly, usually with complete information and often with a commendatory word on the desirability of the Survey and expressing interest in learning of its findings. A few expressed their inability, or unwillingness, to cooperate. Said Corporation 1037:

> Information of this kind merely gives a lot of fund-raising organizations an opportunity to further harass corporations for contributions.

And Corporation 1979 echoed a difficulty that must have been felt by many businessmen in a year when plants were working overtime on war-related production and desks were piled high with report forms and restricted-material requisitions:

> I regret to say that our Statistical Department is so busy now making out reports for the Federal Government that it takes about all of their time to do this. Under these circumstances, I am sorry we cannot complete your corporation questionnaire at the present time.

A few corporations proved defunct, and one had just been burned out, with all records lost; in these cases substitutions were made. Some expressed unwillingness to comply, but in terms that suggested further explanation might alter the decision; some replied, but incompletely. One, a savings bank, submitted figures that did not check in addition. Extensive correspondence grew up around these problems. By May, 240 questionnaires in complete detail had been received and tabulated.

In June, 916 additional letters were sent to nonrespondents and those with incomplete replies in the hope of enlarging the sample. Eighty-six more complete returns resulted from this mailing and further correspondence. The record finally stood:

Original mailing	1,200
Complete returns	326
Incomplete returns	43
Refusals	44
No replies	787

Among the nonrespondents was a prominent newspaper that later asked for early release of the findings, which would be of much interest to its readers.

The final return of 27 per cent in completely usable replies is regarded as good for a voluntary study asking intimate questions in a difficult year. These 326 complete replies are the basis for the statistical tables in the book based on the Survey. Our sincere appreciation goes to the many executives who cooperated with us so fully.

A number of corporations known to have interesting or unusual contribution programs did not fall within the random sample. In these cases personal interviews were usually arranged, and customarily the questionnaire was also filled out. But their data are not included in the basic tables unless noted.

Bias in the Sample

Although an attempt was made to study a group of corporations that would be representative, no illusions are entertained that the 326 corporations here studied are a sample which can safely be "blown up" to represent all corporations. The sample is biased in at least two respects.

First, Poor's list from which the sample was obtained is itself, for our purposes, inadequate. It is heavily weighted toward large as against small corporations, and toward manufacturing corporations and utilities as against trade, service, or finance. This is due partly to the special purposes of the directory, partly to the practice of including many firms on simple request rather than by fixed standards. As a result, our sampling group shows 56 per cent manufacturing corporations as against the 20 per cent of the 1948 government figures, and only 13 per cent in finance as compared with the governmental tabulation of 27 per cent. By asset classes, 18 per cent of the sample are in the $50 million or above class while actually fewer than 1 per cent of corporations were in this high category in 1948.

The second difficulty lies in the considerable proportion of nonrespondents. A random sample is accurate for its universe only if substantially all the persons in the sample respond. If many do not respond, the chance is strong that they are of a different type from the respondents or have special reasons for failure to reply; the absence of their data may bias the sample. Therefore our 326 corporations cannot safely be called an adequate sample of even the 19,000 corporations in Poor's directory.

In what ways have the nonrespondents biased the sample? It is sometimes possible to determine at least the direction of bias by comparing the replies of those who respond at once without pressure with replies made after repeated requests. Presumably the latter more nearly approach the nonrespondents.

With this in mind we carefully segregated the first 240 replies and the additional 86. The outstanding difference was the anticipated one—the slow respondents were the poorer givers. The contribution rate of the early replies was 0.60 per cent of net income; the second wave had a rate of only 0.39, which leveled the combined rate to 0.51. It therefore seems likely that our sample overstates the giving rate for the 19,000 corporations in Poor's. Whether it overstates the rate for all corporations in 1950, however, is another question; the directory group is itself biased toward the large corporations, which usually give at a lower rate than smaller corporations.

Little other pronounced bias was discovered. The proportion of corporations which set up a contributions budget dropped in the second group of respondents. But they were remarkably like the early respondents in types of industry, asset classes, and in answers to substantially all the other questions.

The sample in our Survey, it may be concluded, does contain corporations of all types and asset groups, but not in the proportions which prevail in the whole corporate universe. Within each group some bias toward the more liberal givers seems probable. It is a broader sampling than has previously been available, but it cannot safely be equated with all corporations.

The Legal Sections

Ray Garrett, of the Chicago firm of Sidley, Austin, Burgess and Smith, was retained as legal consultant for the study. Mr. Garrett has for some years been chairman of the Committee on Corporate Laws of the American Bar Association, which has devised a standard permissive clause on corporation donations suggested for adoption in state legislation. He has therefore a special familiarity with legislation and court decisions in this field. Mr. Garrett has supplied the legal appendices, has reviewed the whole volume with respect to legal and tax aspects, and the writer has leaned heavily upon him in drafting the several chapters of Part III, Legal and Taxation Factors.

APPENDIX B

SELECTIONS FROM THE INTERNAL REVENUE CODE

as amended to January 7, 1952

SECTION 23. DEDUCTIONS FROM GROSS INCOME.

In computing net income there shall be allowed as deductions:

(a) EXPENSES.—

(1) TRADE OR BUSINESS EXPENSES.—

(A) IN GENERAL.—All the ordinary and necessary expenses paid or incurred during the taxable year in carrying on any trade or business, including a reasonable allowance for salaries or other compensation for personal services actually rendered; traveling expenses (including the entire amount expended for meals and lodging) while away from home in the pursuit of a trade or business; and rentals or other payments required to be made as a condition to the continued use or possession, for purposes of the trade or business, of property to which the taxpayer has not taken or is not taking title or in which he has no equity.

(B) CORPORATE CHARITABLE CONTRIBUTIONS.—No deduction shall be allowable under subparagraph (A) to a corporation for any contribution or gift which would be allowable as a deduction under subsection (q) were it not for the 5 per centum limitation therein contained and for the requirement therein that payment must be made within the taxable year.

(C) EXPENDITURES FOR ADVERTISING AND GOOD WILL.—If a corporation has, for the purpose of computing its excess profits tax credit under Chapter 2E, or subchapter D of this Chapter, claimed the benefits of the election provided in section 733 or section 451, as the case may be, no deduction shall be allowed under subparagraph (A) to such corporation for expenditures for advertising or the promotion of good will which, under the rules and regulations prescribed under section 733 or section 451, as the case may be, may be regarded as capital investments.

(2) NON-TRADE OR NON-BUSINESS EXPENSES.—In the case of an individual, all the ordinary and necessary expenses paid or incurred during the taxable year for the production or collection of income,

or for the management, conservation, or maintenance of property held for the production of income.

* * * * *

(o) CHARITABLE AND OTHER CONTRIBUTIONS.—In the case of an individual, contributions or gifts payment of which is made within the taxable year to or for the use of:

(1) The United States, any State, Territory, or any political subdivision thereof or the District of Columbia, or any possession of the United States, for exclusively public purposes;

(2) A corporation, trust, or community chest, fund, or foundation, created or organized in the United States or in any possession thereof or under the law of the United States or of any State or Territory or of any possession of the United States, organized and operated exclusively for religious, charitable, scientific, literary, or educational purposes, or for the prevention of cruelty to children or animals, no part of the net earnings of which inures to the benefit of any private shareholder or individual, and no substantial part of the activities of which is carrying on propaganda, or otherwise attempting, to influence legislation. For disallowance of certain charitable, etc., deductions otherwise allowable under this paragraph, see sections 3813 and 162(g) (2);

(3) the special fund for vocational rehabilitation authorized by section 12 of the World War Veterans' Act, 1924, 43 Stat. 611 (U.S.C., Title 38 §440);

(4) posts or organizations of war veterans, or auxiliary units or societies of any such posts or organizations, if such posts, organizations, units, or societies are organized in the United States or any of its possessions, and if no part of their net earnings inures to the benefit of any private shareholder or individual;

(5) a domestic fraternal society, order, or association, operating under the lodge system, but only if such contributions or gifts are to be used exclusively for religious, charitable, scientific, literary, or educational purposes, or for the prevention of cruelty to children or animals; or

(6) the United Nations, but only if such contributions or gifts (A) are to be used exclusively for the acquisition of a site in the city of New York for its headquarters, and (B) are made after December 1, 1946, and before December 2, 1947;

to an amount which in all the above cases combined does not exceed 15 per centum of the taxpayer's adjusted gross income. Such contributions or gifts shall be allowable as deductions only if verified under rules and regulations prescribed by the Commissioner, with the approval of the Secretary.

For unlimited deduction if contributions and gifts exceed 90 per centum of the net income, see section 120.

* * * * *

(q) CHARITABLE AND OTHER CONTRIBUTIONS BY CORPORATIONS.— In the case of a corporation, contributions or gifts payment of which is made within the taxable year to or for the use of:

(1) The United States, any State, Territory, or any political subdivision thereof or the District of Columbia, or any possession of the United States, for exclusively public purposes; or

(2) A corporation, trust, or community chest, fund, or foundation, created or organized in the United States or in any possession thereof or under the law of the United States, or of any State or Territory, or of the District of Columbia, or of any possession of the United States, organized and operated exclusively for religious, charitable, scientific, veteran rehabilitation service, literary, or educational purposes or for the prevention of cruelty to children (but in the case of contributions or gifts to a trust, chest, fund, or foundation, payment of which is made within a taxable year beginning after December 31, 1948, only if such contributions or gifts are to be used within the United States or any of its possessions exclusively for such purposes), no part of the net earnings of which inures to the benefit of any private shareholder or individual, and no substantial part of the activities of which is carrying on propaganda, or otherwise attempting, to influence legislation. For disallowance of certain charitable, etc., deductions otherwise allowable under this paragraph, see sections 3813 and 162(g) (2); or

(3) Posts or organizations of war veterans, or auxiliary units of, or trusts or foundations for, any such posts or organizations, if such posts, organizations, units, trusts, or foundations are organized in the United States or any of its possessions, and if no part of their net earnings inure to the benefit of any private shareholder or individual; or

(4) the United Nations, but only if such contributions or gifts (A) are to be used exclusively for the acquisition of a site in the city of New York for its headquarters, and (B) are made after December 1, 1946, and before December 2, 1947;

to an amount which does not exceed 5 per centum of the taxpayer's net income as computed without the benefits of this subsection. Such contributions or gifts shall be allowable as deductions only if verified under rules and regulations prescribed by the Commissioner, with the approval of the Secretary.

In the case of a corporation reporting its net income on the accrual basis, at the election of the taxpayer any contribution or gift payment of which is made after the close of the taxable year and on or before the 15th day of the third month following the close of such year shall, for the purposes of this subsection, be considered as paid during such taxable year if, during such year, the board of directors authorized such contribution or gift. Such election shall be made only at the time of the filing of the return for the taxable year, and shall be signified in such manner as the Commissioner, with the approval of the Secretary, shall by regulations prescribe.

* * * * *

SECTION 101. EXEMPTIONS FROM TAX ON CORPORATIONS.

Except as provided in paragraph (12) (B) and in supplement U, the following organizations shall be exempt from taxation under this chapter—

(1) Labor, agricultural, or horticultural organizations;

(2) [Mutual savings banks not having a capital stock represented by shares. Repealed by the 1951 Revenue Act.]

(3) Fraternal beneficiary societies, orders, or associations, (A) operating under the lodge system or for the exclusive benefit of the members of a fraternity itself operating under the lodge system; and (B) providing for the payment of life, sick, accident or other benefits to the members of such society, order, or association or their dependents;

(4) Credit unions without capital stock organized and operated for mutual purposes and without profit; and corporations or associations without capital stock organized prior to September 1, 1951, and operated for mutual purposes and without profit for the purpose of providing reserve funds for, and insurance of, shares or deposits in—

(A) domestic building and loan associations,

(B) cooperative banks without capital stock organized and operated for mutual purposes and without profit, or

(C) mutual savings banks not having capital stock represented by shares;

(5) Cemetery companies owned and operated exclusively for the benefit of their members or which are not operated for profit; and

any corporation chartered solely for burial purposes as a cemetery corporation and not permitted by its charter to engage in any business not necessarily incident to that purpose, no part of the net earnings of which inures to the benefit of any private shareholder or individual;

(6) Corporations, and any community chest, fund, or foundation, organized and operated exclusively for religious, charitable, scientific, literary, or educational purposes, or for the prevention of cruelty to children or animals, no part of the net earnings of which inures to the benefit of any private shareholder or individual, and no substantial part of the activities of which is carrying on propaganda, or otherwise attempting, to influence legislation. For loss of exemption under certain circumstances, see sections 3813 and 3814;

(7) Business leagues, chambers of commerce, real-estate boards, or boards of trade, not organized for profit and no part of the net earnings of which inures to the benefit of any private shareholder or individual;

(8) Civic leagues or organizations not organized for profit but operated exclusively for the promotion of social welfare, or local associations of employees, the membership of which is limited to the employees of a designated person or persons in a particular municipality, and the net earnings of which are devoted exclusively to charitable, educational, or recreational purposes;

(9) Clubs organized and operated exclusively for pleasure, recreation, and other nonprofitable purposes, no part of the net earnings of which inures to the benefit of any private shareholder;

(10) Benevolent life insurance associations of a purely local character, mutual ditch or irrigation companies, mutual or cooperative telephone companies, or like organizations; but only if 85 per centum or more of the income consists of amounts collected from members for the sole purpose of meeting losses and expenses;

(11) Mutual insurance companies or associations other than life or marine (including interinsurers and reciprocal underwriters) if the gross amount received during the taxable year from interest, dividends, rents, and premiums (including deposits and assessments) does not exceed $75,000;

(12) (A) Farmers', fruit growers', or like associations organized and operated on a cooperative basis (a) for the purpose of marketing the products of members or other producers, and turning back to them the proceeds of sales, less the necessary marketing expenses, on the basis of either the quantity or the value of the products furnished

by them, or (b) for the purpose of purchasing supplies and equipment for the use of members or other persons, and turning over such supplies and equipment to them at actual cost, plus necessary expenses. Exemption shall not be denied any such association because it has capital stock, if the dividend rate of such stock is fixed at not to exceed the legal rate of interest in the State of incorporation or 8 per centum per annum, whichever is greater, on the value of the consideration for which the stock was issued, and if substantially all such stock (other than nonvoting preferred stock, the owners of which are not entitled or permitted to participate, directly or indirectly, in the profits of the association, upon dissolution or otherwise, beyond the fixed dividends) is owned by producers who market their products or purchase their supplies and equipment through the association; nor shall exemption be denied any such association because there is accumulated and maintained by it a reserve required by State law or a reasonable reserve for any necessary purpose. Such an association may market the products of nonmembers in an amount the value of which does not exceed the value of the products marketed for members, and may purchase supplies and equipment for nonmembers in an amount the value of which does not exceed the value of the supplies and equipment purchased for members, provided the value of the purchases made for persons who are neither members nor producers does not exceed 15 per centum of the value of all its purchases. Business done for the United States or any of its agencies shall be disregarded in determining the right to exemption under this paragraph;

(B) An organization exempt from taxation under the provisions of subparagraph (A) shall be subject to the taxes imposed by sections 13 and 15, or section 117(c) (1), except that in computing the net income of such an organization there shall be allowed as deductions from gross income (in addition to other deductions allowable under section 23)—

(i) amounts paid as dividends during the taxable year upon its capital stock, and

(ii) amounts allocated during the taxable year to patrons with respect to its income not derived from patronage (whether or not such income was derived during such taxable year) whether paid in cash, merchandise, capital stock, revolving fund certificates, retain certificates, certificates of indebtedness, letters of advice, or in some other manner that discloses to each patron the dollar amount allocated to him. Allocations made after the close of the taxable year and on or before the fifteenth day of the ninth month following the close of such year shall be considered as made on the last day of such taxable year to the extent the allocations are attributable to income derived before the close of such year.

Patronage dividends, refunds, and rebates to patrons with respect to their patronage in the same or preceding years (whether paid in cash, merchandise, capital stock, revolving fund certificates, retain certificates, certificates of indebtedness, letters of advice, or in some other manner that discloses to each patron the dollar amount of such dividend, refund, or rebate) shall be taken into account in computing net income in the same manner as in the case of a cooperative organization not exempt under subparagraph (A). Such dividends, refunds, and rebates made after the close of the taxable year and on or before the 15th day of the ninth month following the close of such year shall be considered as made on the last day of such taxable year to the extent the dividends, refunds, or rebates, are attributable to patronage occurring before the close of such year.

(13) Corporations organized by an association exempt under the provisions of paragraph (12), or members thereof, for the purpose of financing the ordinary crop operations of such members or other producers, and operated in conjunction with such association. Exemption shall not be denied any such corporation because it has capital stock, if the dividend rate of such stock is fixed at not to exceed the legal rate of interest in the State of incorporation or 8 per centum per annum, whichever is greater, on the value of the consideration for which the stock was issued, and if substantially all such stock (other than nonvoting preferred stock, the owners of which are not entitled or permitted to participate, directly or indirectly, in the profits of the corporation, upon dissolution or otherwise, beyond the fixed dividends) is owned by such association, or members thereof; nor shall exemption be denied any such corporation because there is accumulated and maintained by it a reserve required by State law or a reasonable reserve for any necessary purpose;

(14) Corporations organized for the exclusive purpose of holding title to property, collecting income therefrom, and turning over the entire amount thereof, less expenses, to an organization which itself is exempt from the tax imposed by this chapter;

(15) Corporations organized under Act of Congress, if such corporations are instrumentalities of the United States and if, under such Act, as amended and supplemented, such corporations are exempt from Federal income taxes;

(16) Voluntary employees' beneficiary associations providing for the payment of life, sick, accident, or other benefits to the members

of such association or their dependents, if (A) no part of their net earnings inures (other than through such payments) to the benefit of any private shareholder or individual, and (B) 85 per centum or more of the income consists of amounts collected from members and amounts contributed to the association by the employer of the members for the sole purpose of making such payments and meeting expenses;

(17) Teachers' retirement fund associations of a purely local character, if (A) no part of their net earnings inures (other than through payment of retirement benefits) to the benefit of any private shareholder or individual, and (B) the income consists solely of amounts received from public taxation, amounts received from assessments upon the teaching salaries of members, and income in respect of investments;

(18) Religious or apostolic associations or corporations, if such associations or corporations have a common treasury or community treasury, even if such associations or corporations engage in business for the common benefit of the members, but only if the members thereof include (at the time of filing their returns) in their gross income their entire pro-rata shares, whether distributed or not, of the net income of the association or corporation for such year. Any amount so included in the gross income of a member shall be treated as a dividend received.

(19) Voluntary employees' beneficiary associations providing for the payment of life, sick, accident, or other benefits to the members of such association or their dependents or their designated beneficiaries, if (A) admission to membership in such association is limited to individuals who are officers or employees of the United States Government, and (B) no part of the net earnings of such association inures (other than through such payments) to the benefit of any private shareholder or individual.

An organization operated for the primary purpose of carrying on a trade or business for profit shall not be exempt under any paragraph of this section on the ground that all of its profits are payable to one or more organizations exempt under this section from taxation. For the purposes of this paragraph the term "trade or business" shall not include the rental by an organization of its real property (including personal property leased with the real property).

Notwithstanding paragraph (12) (B) and supplement U, an organization described in this section (other than in the preceding paragraph) shall be considered an organization exempt from income taxes for the purpose of any law which refers to organizations exempt from income taxes.

* * * * *

SECTION 153. INFORMATION REQUIRED FROM CERTAIN TAX-EXEMPT ORGANIZATIONS AND CERTAIN TRUSTS.

(a) CERTAIN TAX-EXEMPT ORGANIZATIONS.—Every organization described in section 101(6) which is subject to the requirements of section 54(f) shall furnish annually information, at such time and in such manner as the Secretary may by regulations prescribe, setting forth—

(1) its gross income for the year,

(2) its expenses attributable to such income and incurred within the year,

(3) its disbursements out of income within the year for the purposes for which it is exempt,

(4) its accumulation of income within the year,

(5) its aggregate accumulations of income at the beginning of the year,

(6) its disbursements out of principal in the current and prior years for the purposes for which it is exempt, and

(7) a balance sheet showing its assets, liabilities and net worth as of the beginning of such year.

(b) TRUSTS CLAIMING CHARITABLE, ETC., DEDUCTIONS UNDER SECTION 162(a).—Every trust claiming a charitable, etc., deduction under section 162(a) for the taxable year shall furnish information with respect to such taxable year, at such time and in such manner as the Secretary may by regulations prescribe, setting forth—

(1) the amount of the charitable, etc., deduction taken under section 162(a) within such year (showing separately the amount of such deduction which was paid out and the amount which was permanently set aside for charitable, etc., purposes during such year),

(2) the amount paid out within such year which represents amounts for which charitable, etc., deductions under section 162(a) have been taken in prior years,

(3) the amount for which charitable, etc., deductions have been taken in prior years but which has not been paid out at the beginning of such year,

(4) the amount paid out of principal in the current and prior years for charitable, etc., purposes,

(5) the total income of the trust within such year and the expenses attributable thereto, and

(6) a balance sheet showing the assets, liabilities, and net worth of the trust as of the beginning of such year.

This subsection shall not apply in the case of a taxable year if all the net income for such year, determined under the applicable principles of the law of trusts, is required to be distributed currently to the beneficiaries.

(c) INFORMATION AVAILABLE TO THE PUBLIC.—The information required to be furnished by subsections (a) and (b), together with the names and addresses of such organizations and trusts, shall be made available to the public at such times and in such places as the Secretary may prescribe.

(d) PENALTIES.—In the case of a willful failure to furnish the information required under this section, the penalties provided in section 145(a) shall be applicable.

* * * * *

SECTION 162. NET INCOME.

The net income of the estate or trust shall be computed in the same manner and on the same basis as in the case of an individual, except that—

(a) Subject to the provisions of subsection (g), there shall be allowed as a deduction (in lieu of the deduction for charitable, etc., contributions authorized by section 23 (o)) any part of the gross income, without limitation, which pursuant to the terms of the will or deed creating the trust, is during the taxable year paid or permanently set aside for the purposes and in the manner specified in section 23(o), or is to be used exclusively for religious, charitable, scientific, literary, or educational purposes, or for the prevention of cruelty to children or animals, or for the establishment, acquisition, maintenance or operation of a public cemetery not operated for profit. Where any amount of the income so paid or set aside is attributable to gain from the sale or exchange of capital assets held for more than six months, proper adjustment of the deduction otherwise allowable under this subsection shall be made for any deduction allowable to the trust under section 23(ee);

* * * * *

(g) RULES FOR APPLICATION OF SUBSECTION (a) IN THE CASE OF TRUSTS.—

(1) TRADE OR BUSINESS INCOME.—In computing the deduction allowable under subsection (a) to a trust for any taxable year beginning after December 31, 1950, no amount otherwise allowable under subsection (a) as a deduction shall be allowed as a deduction with respect to income of the taxable year which is allocable to its supplement U business income for such year. As used in this paragraph the

term "supplement U business income" means an amount equal to the amount which, if such trust were exempt under section 101(6) from taxation, would be computed as its unrelated business net income under section 422 (relating to income derived from certain business activities and from certain leases).

(2) OPERATIONS OF TRUSTS.—

(A) LIMITATION ON CHARITABLE, ETC., DEDUCTION.—The amount otherwise allowable under subsection (a) as a deduction shall not exceed 15 per centum of the net income of the trust (computed without the benefit of subsection (a)) if the trust has engaged in a prohibited transaction, as defined in subparagraph (B) of this paragraph.

(B) PROHIBITED TRANSACTIONS.—For the purposes of this paragraph the term "prohibited transaction" means any transaction after July 1, 1950, in which any trust while holding income or corpus which has been permanently set aside or is to be used exclusively for charitable or other purposes described in subsection (a)—

(i) lends any part of such income or corpus, without receipt of adequate security and a reasonable rate of interest, to;

(ii) pays any compensation from such income or corpus, in excess of a reasonable allowance for salaries or other compensation for personal services actually rendered, to;

(iii) makes any part of its services available on a preferential basis to;

(iv) uses such income or corpus to make any substantial purchase of securities or any other property, for more than an adequate consideration in money or money's worth, from;

(v) sells any substantial part of the securities or other property comprising such income or corpus, for less than an adequate consideration in money or money's worth, to; or

(vi) engages in any other transaction which results in a substantial diversion of such income or corpus to;

the creator of such trust; any person who has made a substantial contribution to such trust; a member of the family (as defined in section 24(b) (2) (D)) of an individual who is the creator of the trust or who has made a substantial contribution to the trust; or a corporation controlled by any such creator or person through the ownership, directly or indirectly, of 50 per centum or more of the total combined voting power of all classes of stock entitled to vote or 50 per centum or more of the total value of shares of all classes of stock of the corporation.

(C) Taxable Years Affected.—The amount otherwise allowable under subsection (a) as a deduction shall be limited as provided in subparagraph (A) only for taxable years subsequent to the taxable year during which the trust is notified by the Secretary that it has engaged in such transaction, unless such trust entered into such prohibited transaction with the purpose of diverting such corpus or income from the purposes described in subsection (a), and such transaction involved a substantial part of such corpus or income.

(D) Future Charitable, Etc., Deductions of Trusts Denied Deduction Under Subparagraph (C).—If the deduction of any trust under subsection (a) has been limited as provided in this paragraph, such trust, with respect to any taxable year following the taxable year in which notice is received of limitation of deduction under subsection (a), may, under regulations prescribed by the Secretary, file claim for the allowance of the unlimited deduction under subsection (a), and if the Secretary, pursuant to such regulations, is satisfied that such trust will not knowingly again engage in a prohibited transaction, the limitation provided in subparagraph (A) shall not be applicable with respect to taxable years subsequent to the year in which such claim is filed.

(E) Disallowance of Certain Charitable, Etc., Deductions.—No gift or bequest for religious, charitable, scientific, literary, or educational purposes (including the encouragement of art and the prevention of cruelty to children or animals), otherwise allowable as a deduction under section 23(o) (2), 23(q) (2), 162(a), 505(a) (2), 812(d), 861(a) (3), 1004(a) (2) (B), or 1004(b) (2) or (3), shall be allowed as a deduction if made in trust and, in the taxable year of the trust in which the gift or bequest is made, the deduction allowed the trust under subsection (a) is limited by subparagraph (A). With respect to any taxable year of a trust in which such deduction has been so limited by reason of entering into a prohibited transaction with the purpose of diverting such corpus or income from the purposes described in subsection (a), and such transaction involved a substantial part of such income or corpus, and which taxable year is the same, or prior to the, taxable year of the trust in which such prohibited transaction occurred, such deduction shall be disallowed the donor only if such donor or (if such donor is an individual) any member of his family (as defined in section 24(b) (2) (D)) was a party to such prohibited transaction.

(F) DEFINITION.—For the purposes of this paragraph the term "gift or bequest" means any gift, contribution, bequest, devise, legacy, or transfer.

(3) CROSS REFERENCE.—For disallowance of certain charitable, etc., deductions otherwise allowable under subsection (a), see section 3813.

(4) ACCUMULATED INCOME.—If the amounts permanently set aside, or to be used exclusively, for the charitable and other purposes described in subsection (a) during the taxable year or any prior taxable year and not actually paid out by the end of the taxable year—

(A) are unreasonable in amount or duration in order to carry out such purposes of the trust; or

(B) are used to a substantial degree for purposes other than those described in subsection (a); or

(C) are invested in such a manner as to jeopardize the interests of the religious, charitable, scientific, etc., beneficiaries,

the amount otherwise allowable under subsection (a) as a deduction shall be limited to the amount actually paid out during the taxable year and shall not exceed 15 per centum of the net income of the trust (computed without the benefit of subsection (a)).

* * * * *

SECTION 421. IMPOSITION OF TAX.

(a) IN GENERAL.—There shall be levied, collected, and paid for each taxable year beginning after December 31, 1950.—

(1) upon the supplement U net income (as defined in subsection (c)) of every organization described in subsection (b) (1), a normal tax of 25 per centum of the supplement U net income, and a surtax of 22 per centum of the amount of the supplement U net income in excess of $25,000; except that (A) in the case of taxable years beginning before April 1, 1951, and ending after March 31, 1951, the normal tax shall be 28¾ per centum of the Supplement U net income, and (B) in the case of taxable years beginning after March 31, 1951, and before April 1, 1954, the normal tax shall be 30 per centum of the Supplement U net income.

(2) Upon the supplement U net income of every trust described in subsection (b) (2), a normal tax computed at the rate and in the manner provided in section 11 and a surtax computed at the rates and in the manner provided in section 12(b). In making such computations for the purposes of this section, the term "the amount of the net income in excess of the credits against net income provided in section 25" as used in section 11 shall be read as "the amount of the supplement U net income" and the term "surtax net income" as used in section 12(b) shall be read as "supplement U net income."

(b) ORGANIZATIONS SUBJECT TO TAX.—

(1) ORGANIZATIONS TAXABLE AS CORPORATIONS.—

(A) Organizations Exempt Under Section 101(1), (6), (7) and (14).—The taxes imposed by subsection (a) (1) shall apply in the case of any organization (other than a church, a convention or association of churches, or a trust described in paragraph (2)) which is exempt, except as provided in this supplement, from taxation under this chapter by reason of paragraph (1), (6), or (7) of section 101. Such taxes shall also apply in the case of a corporation described in section 101(14) if the income is payable to an organization which itself is subject to the tax imposed by subsection (a) or to a church or to a convention or association of churches.

(B) State Colleges and Universities.—The taxes imposed by subsection (a) (1) shall apply in the case of any college or university which is an agency or instrumentality of any government or any political subdivision thereof, or which is owned or operated by a government or any political subdivision thereof or by any agency or instrumentality of any one or more governments or political subdivisions. Such taxes shall also apply in the case of any corporation wholly owned by one or more such colleges or universities.

(2) TRUSTS TAXABLE AT INDIVIDUAL RATES.—The taxes imposed by subsection (a) (2) shall apply in the case of any trust which is exempt, except as provided in this supplement, from taxation under this chapter by reason of paragraph (6) of section 101 and which, if it were not for such exemption, would be subject to the provisions of supplement E.

(c) DEFINITION OF SUPPLEMENT U NET INCOME.—The term "supplement U net income" of an organization means the amount by which its unrelated business net income (as defined in section 422) exceeds $1,000.

(d) FOREIGN ORGANIZATIONS.—The supplement U net income of an organization described in subsection (b) (1) or (2) which is a foreign organization shall be its supplement U net income derived from sources within the United States determined in accordance with the rules of section 119 and sections 212, 213(a), 231(c) and (d), and 232(a).

* * * * *

SECTION 422. UNRELATED BUSINESS NET INCOME.

(a) DEFINITION.—The term "unrelated business net income" means the gross income derived by any organization from any unrelated trade or business (as defined in subsection (b)) regularly carried on by it, less the deductions allowed by section 23 which are directly connected with the carrying on of such trade or business, subject to the following exceptions, additions, and limitations:

(1) There shall be excluded all dividends, interest, and annuities, and all deductions directly connected with such income.

(2) There shall be excluded all royalties (including overriding royalties) whether measured by production or by gross or net income from the property, and all deductions directly connected with such income.

(3) There shall be excluded all rents from real property (including personal property leased with the real property) and all deductions directly connected with such rents.

(4) Notwithstanding paragraph (3), in the case of a supplement U lease (as defined in section 423(a)) there shall be included, as an item of gross income derived from an unrelated trade or business, the amount ascertained under section 423(d) (1) and there shall be allowed, as a deduction, the amount ascertained under section 423 (d) (2).

(5) There shall be excluded all gains or losses from the sale, exchange, or other disposition of property other than (A) stock in trade or other property of a kind which would properly be includible in inventory if on hand at the close of the taxable year, or (B) property held primarily for sale to customers in the ordinary course of the trade or business. This paragraph shall not apply with respect to the cutting of timber which is considered, upon the application of section 117(k) (1), as a sale or exchange of such timber.

(6) The net operating loss deduction provided in section 23(s) shall be allowed, except that—

(A) the net operating loss for any taxable year, the amount of the net operating loss carry-back or carry-over to any taxable year, and the net operating loss deduction for any taxable year shall be determined under section 122 without taking into account any amount of income or deduction which is excluded under this supplement in computing the unrelated business net income; and

(B) the terms "preceding taxable year" and "preceding taxable years" as used in section 122 shall not include any taxable year for which the organization was not subject to the provisions of this supplement.

(7) There shall be excluded all income derived from research for (A) the United States, or any of its agencies or instrumentalities, or (B) any State or political subdivision thereof; and there shall be excluded all deductions directly connected with such income.

(8) (A) In the case of a college, university, or hospital, there shall be excluded all income derived from research performed for any person, and all deductions directly connected with such income.

(B) In the case of an organization operated primarily for the purposes of carrying on fundamental research the results of which are freely available to the general public, there shall be excluded all income derived from research performed for any person, and all deductions directly connected with such income.

(9) (A) In the case of any organization described in section 421(b) (1), the so-called "charitable contribution" deduction allowed by section 23(q) shall be allowed (whether or not directly connected with the carrying on of the trade or business), but shall not exceed 5 per centum of the unrelated business net income computed without the benefit of this subparagraph.

(B) In the case of any trust described in section 421(b) (2), the so-called "charitable contribution" deduction allowed by section 23(o) shall be allowed (whether or not directly connected with the carrying on of the trade or business), and for such purpose a distribution made by the trust to a beneficiary described in section 23(o) shall be considered as a gift or contribution. The deduction allowed by this subparagraph shall not exceed 15 per centum of the unrelated business net income computed without the benefit of this subparagraph.

If a trade or business regularly carried on by a partnership of which an organization is a member is an unrelated trade or business with respect to such organization, such organization in computing its unrelated business net income shall, subject to the exceptions, additions, and limitations contained in paragraphs (1) through (9) above, include its share (whether or not distributed) of the gross income of the partnership from such unrelated trade or business and its share of the partnership deductions directly connected with such gross income. If the taxable year of the organization is different from that of the partnership, the amounts to be so included or deducted in computing the unrelated business net income shall be based upon the income and deductions of the partnership for any taxable year of the partnership (whether beginning on, before, or after January 1, 1951) ending within or with the taxable year of the organization. In the case of an organization described in section 3813(a) (2) which is a member of a partnership all of whose members are organizations described in section 3813(a) (2), if a trade or business regularly carried on by such partnership is an unrelated trade or business with respect to such organization, such organization shall, for taxable years beginning before January 1, 1954, be allowed a deduction in an amount equal to the portion of the gross income of such partnership from such unrelated trade or business which such organization is required (by a provision of a written contract executed by such organization prior to January 1, 1950, which provision expressly deals with the disposition of the gross income of the partnership) to pay within the taxable year in discharge of indebtedness incurred by such organization in acquiring its share of such trade or business, or to irrevocably set aside within the taxable year for the discharge of such indebtedness (to the extent that such amount has been so paid or set aside) if (i) such partnership was formed prior to January 1, 1950, for the purpose of carrying on such trade or business, and (ii) substantially all the assets used in carrying on such trade or business were acquired by it or by its members prior to such date. As used in the preceding sentence, the word "indebtedness" does not include indebtedness incurred after January 1, 1950.

(b) UNRELATED TRADE OR BUSINESS.—The term "unrelated trade or business" means, in the case of any organization subject to the tax imposed by section 421(a), any trade or business the conduct of which is not substantially related (aside from the need of such organization for income or funds or the use it makes of the profits derived) to the exercise or performance by such organization of its charitable, educational, or other purpose or function constituting the basis for its exemption under section 101 (or, in the case of an organization described in section 421(b) (1) (B), to the exercise or performance of any purpose or function described in section 101(6)), except that such term shall not include any trade or business—

(1) in which substantially all the work in carrying on such trade or business is performed for the organization without compensation; or

(2) which is carried on, in the case of an organization described in section 101(6) or in the case of a college or university described in section 421(b) (1) (B), by the organization primarily for the convenience of its members, students, patients, officers, or employees; or

(3) which is the selling of merchandise, substantially all of which has been received by the organization as gifts or contributions.

The term "unrelated trade or business" means, in the case of a trust computing its unrelated business net income under this section for the purpose of section 162(g) (1), any trade or business regularly carried on by such trust or by a partnership of which it is a member. If a publishing business carried on by an organization during a taxable year beginning before January 1, 1953, is, without regard to this sentence, an unrelated trade or business, but before the beginning of the third succeeding taxable year the business is carried on by it (or by a successor who acquired such business in a liquidation which would constitute a tax-free exchange under section 112(b) (6)) in such manner that the conduct thereof is substantially related to the exercise or performance by such organization (or such successor) of its educational or other purpose or function described in section 101(6), such publishing business shall not be considered, for the taxable year, as an unrelated trade or business.

* * * * *

SECTION 3813. REQUIREMENTS FOR EXEMPTION OF CERTAIN ORGANIZATIONS UNDER SECTION 101(6) AND FOR DEDUCTIBILITY OF CONTRIBUTIONS MADE TO SUCH ORGANIZATIONS.

(a) ORGANIZATIONS TO WHICH SECTION APPLIES.—This section shall apply to any organization described in section 101(6) except—

(1) a religious organization (other than a trust);

(2) an educational organization which normally maintains a regular faculty and curriculum and normally has a regularly enrolled body of pupils or students in attendance at the place where its educational activities are regularly carried on;

(3) an organization which normally receives a substantial part of its support (exclusive of income received in the exercise or performance by such organization of its charitable, educational, or other purpose or function constituting the basis for its exemption under section 101(6)) from the United States or any State or political subdivision thereof or from direct or indirect contributions from the general public;

(4) an organization which is operated, supervised, controlled, or principally supported by a religious organization (other than a trust) which is itself not subject to the provisions of this section; and

(5) an organization the principal purposes or functions of which are the providing of medical or hospital care or medical education or medical research.

(b) PROHIBITED TRANSACTIONS.—For the purposes of this section, the term "prohibited transaction" means any transaction in which an organization subject to the provisions of this section—

(1) lends any part of its income or corpus, without the receipt of adequate security and a reasonable rate of interest, to;

(2) pays any compensation, in excess of a reasonable allowance for salaries or other compensation for personal services actually rendered, to;

(3) makes any part of its services available on a preferential basis to;

(4) makes any substantial purchase of securities or any other property, for more than adequate consideration in money or money's worth, from;

(5) sells any substantial part of its securities or other property, for less than an adequate consideration in money or money's worth, to; or

(6) engages in any other transaction which results in a substantial diversion of its income or corpus to;

the creator of such organization (if a trust); a person who has made a substantial contribution to such organization; a member of the family (as defined in section 24(b) (2) (D)) of an individual who is the creator of such trust or who has made a substantial contribution to such organization; or a corporation controlled by such creator or person through the ownership, directly or indirectly, of 50 per centum or more of the total combined voting power of all classes of stock entitled to vote or 50 per centum or more of the total value of shares of all classes of stock of the corporation.

(c) DENIAL OF EXEMPTION TO ORGANIZATIONS ENGAGED IN PROHIBITED TRANSACTIONS. —

(1) GENERAL RULE.—No organization subject to the provisions of this section which has engaged in a prohibited transaction after July 1, 1950 shall be exempt from taxation under section 101(6).

(2) TAXABLE YEARS AFFECTED.—An organization shall be denied exemption from taxation under section 101(6) by reason of paragraph (1) only for taxable years subsequent to the taxable year during which it is notified by the Secretary that it has engaged in a prohibited transaction, unless such organization entered into such prohibited transaction with the purpose of diverting corpus or income of the organization from its exempt purposes, and such transaction involved a substantial part of the corpus or income of such organization.

(d) FUTURE STATUS OF ORGANIZATION DENIED EXEMPTION.—Any organization denied exemption under section 101(6) by reason of the provisions of subsection (c), with respect to any taxable year following the taxable year in which notice of denial of exemption was received, may, under regulations prescribed by the Secretary, file claim for exemption, and if the Secretary, pursuant to such regulations, is satisfied that such organization will not knowingly again engage in a prohibited transaction, such organization shall be exempt with respect to taxable years subsequent to the year in which such claim is filed.

(e) DISALLOWANCE OF CERTAIN CHARITABLE, ETC., DEDUCTIONS.—No gift or bequest for religious, charitable, scientific, literary, or educational purposes (including the encouragement of art and the prevention of cruelty to children or animals), otherwise allowable as a deduction under section 23(o) (2), 23(q) (2), 162(a), 505(a) (2), 812(d), 861(a) (3), 1004(a) (2) (B), or 1004(b) (2) or (3), shall be allowed as a deduction if made to an organization which, in the taxable year of the organization in which the gift or bequest is made, is not exempt under section 101(6) by reason of the provisions of this section. With respect to any taxable year of the organization for which the organization is not exempt pursuant to the provisions of subsection (c) by reason of having engaged in a prohibited transaction with the purpose of diverting the corpus or income of such organization from its exempt purposes and such transaction involved a substantial part of such corpus or income, and which taxable year is the same, or prior to the, taxable year of the organization in which such transaction occurred, such deduction shall be disallowed the donor only if such donor or (if such donor is an individual) any member of his family (as defined in section 24(b) (2) (D)) was a party to such prohibited transaction.

(f) DEFINITION.—For the purposes of this section, the term "gift or bequest" means any gift, contribution, bequest, devise, legacy, or transfer.

* * * * *

SECTION 3814. DENIAL OF EXEMPTION UNDER SECTION 101(6) IN THE CASE OF CERTAIN ORGANIZATIONS ACCUMULATING INCOME.

In the case of any organization described in section 101(6) to which section 3813 is applicable, if the amounts accumulated out of income during the taxable year or any prior taxable year and not actually paid out by the end of the taxable year—

(1) are unreasonable in amount or duration in order to carry out the charitable, educational, or other purpose or function constituting the basis for such organization's exemption under section 101(6); or

(2) are used to a substantial degree for purposes or functions other than those constituting the basis for such organization's exemption under section 101(6); or

(3) are invested in such a manner as to jeopardize the carrying out of the charitable, educational, or other purpose or function constituting the basis for such organization's exemption under section 101(6),

exemption under section 101(6) shall be denied for the taxable year.

APPENDIX C

PERMISSIVE LEGISLATION IN THE STATES AND TERRITORIES

[*State and territorial permissive legislation with respect to charitable contributions is presented as of January 1, 1952, with notations on applicability and, where pertinent, a historical résumé. A section of the National Banking Act is appended. No pertinent legislation was found for Alaska and 22 states: Alabama, Arizona, Florida, Georgia, Idaho, Iowa, Kentucky,[1] Louisiana, Mississippi,[1] Montana, Nebraska, Nevada, New Hampshire, North Dakota, Oregon, Rhode Island,[1] South Carolina, South Dakota, Utah, Vermont, Washington, and Wyoming.*]

ARKANSAS

Sec. 1. From and after the passage of this Act, all business corporations, railroad corporations, banking corporations, insurance corporations, building and loan corporations, benevolent corporations and cooperative associations, shall have the power to make donations for the public welfare or for charitable, scientific or educational purposes, subject to such limitations, if any, as may be contained in its articles of incorporation, or any amendment thereto.

[Acts of 1951, No. 69, approved February 9, 1951; Sec. 64–112 Arkansas Statutes 1947 Annotated; applicable to all corporations of the classes stated therein.]

CALIFORNIA

Sec. 802. Every corporation may also: * * *

(g) Make donations for the public welfare or for charitable, scientific, or educational purposes.

[Subsection (g) added to Section 802, General Corporations Code, by Laws of 1949, Chapter 997, effective October 1, 1949; applicable to all profit corporations.]

COLORADO

Sec. 1. It is hereby declared to be the public policy of the State of Colorado that contributions to community funds and to charitable, philanthropic, benevolent, religious, scientific or educational instru-

[1] Legislation passed in 1952, as this book went to press.

293

mentalities, are valid and constitute a proper use of corporate funds. It is further declared that the making of such contributions by corporations is within their powers and inures to the benefit of such corporations.

Sec. 2. It shall be lawful for any corporation created or existing under the laws of this state to contribute to community funds or to charitable, philanthropic, benevolent, religious, scientific or educational instrumentalities such sums as its Board of Directors or Trustees may deem proper.

Sec. 3. The provisions of the next preceding Section 2 shall not be construed as invalidating any such contribution heretofore made by any corporation of this state, and all such contributions made by corporations of this state prior to the enactment hereof shall be valid as if made after the effective date hereof.

[Session Laws of 1947, Chapter 161, approved February 26, 1947; Section 26(1), Chapter 41, Colorado Statutes Annotated; applicable to all corporations.]

CONNECTICUT

Each corporation, except as herein otherwise provided, in addition to all other powers specially granted to it by law, shall have power, subject to such provisions and limitations as may be contained in its charter or certificate of incorporation or in any statute affecting it: * * * (10) to make donations for the public welfare or for charitable, scientific or educational purposes.

[Public Acts of 1951, Act No. 115, effective October 1, 1951, amending Section 5136, General Statutes; Section 1049b, 1951 Supplement to General Statutes; applicable to all corporations with capital stock.]

DELAWARE

Sec. 2. Powers:—Every corporation created under the provisions of this Chapter shall have power: * * *

9. To make donations for the public welfare or for charitable, scientific, or educational purposes.

[Subsection 9 added to Section 2 of General Corporation Law by Laws of 1941, Chapter 132; amended by Laws of 1951, Senate Bill 397, approved June 15, 1951; Section 2034, Revised Code of Delaware; applicable to all corporations organized under General Corporation Law, which excludes banks, savings societies, and trust companies.]

The earliest permissive legislation was enacted in 1941, when the following subsection 9 was added to Section 2 of the General Corporation Law (Laws of 1941, Chapter 132):

9. To cooperate with other corporations and with natural persons in the creation and maintenance of community funds or of charitable, philanthropic, benevolent or patriotic instrumentalities conducive to the public welfare, and its directors may appropriate and expend for these purposes such sum or sums as they may deem expedient and as in their judgment will benefit or contribute to the protection of the corporate interests.

The 1951 amendment substituted the language of the Model Business Corporation Act for the 1941 subsection 9.

ILLINOIS

Sec. 5. General Powers. Each corporation shall have power: * * *

(m) To make donations for the public welfare or for charitable, scientific, religious or educational purposes; and in time of war to * * * make donations to associations and organizations aiding in war activities.

[Second clause of subsection (m) originally enacted as subsection (12) of Section 6 of The General Corporation Act by Laws of 1919, page 312, and reenacted as part of Section 5 of The Business Corporation Act by Laws of 1933, page 310. First clause of subsection (m) added to Section 5 of The Business Corporation Act by Laws of 1949, page 605, effective July 11, 1949; Chapter 32, Smith-Hurd Annotated Statutes; applicable to all corporations subject to The Business Corporation Act, which excludes corporations organized for purpose of banking, insurance, or operation of railroads, cooperative associations that have not accepted the Act, and nonprofit corporations.]

The General Corporation Act, approved June 28, 1919, was a complete revision of the prior law enacted in 1872, which it repealed. The 1919 Act contained the following provision:

Section 6. Every corporation organized under this Act shall, subject to the conditions and limitations prescribed by this Act, have the following powers, rights and privileges: * * *

(12) In time of war to transact any lawful business in aid of the United States in the prosecution of war, to make donations to associations and organizations aiding in war activities, and to loan money to the State or Federal government for war purposes.

The Business Corporation Act, effective July 13, 1933, repealed the 1919 Act and completely revised the law of business corporations. It contained the following provision:

Section 5. General Powers. In order to carry out the purposes for which it is organized, each corporation shall have power: * * *

(m) In time of war * * * [Same as subsection (12) above, except "loan" changed to "lend" in the last clause].

By amendment, approved June 30, 1945, the words "In order to carry out the purposes for which it is organized," were deleted from Section 5, and the Section now opens with "Each corporation shall have power:".

By further amendment in 1949, the following clause was inserted in subsection (m) preceding the "in time of war" provision: "To make donations for public welfare or for charitable, scientific, religious or educational purposes:".

The first permissive legislation in Illinois was the 1919 Act if authority to aid in war activities in time of war is considered.

INDIANA

Sec. 12b. Contributions. The board of directors of every corporation shall have power, subject to any restrictions contained in the articles of incorporation, to make contributions out of gross income of the corporation to such entities, and for any one or more of such purposes, as such board may reasonably believe will constitute such contributions deductions from such gross income in computing the net income of the corporation subject to tax, pursuant to the provisions of the Internal Revenue Code as amended from time to time.

[Section 12b added to The Indiana General Corporation Act by Acts of 1949, Chapter 194, effective September 10, 1949; Section 25–211b, Burns' Annotated Indiana Statutes; applicable to all business corporations subject to The Indiana General Corporation Act, which excludes banking, railroad, insurance, surety, trust, safe deposit, mortgage guarantee, building and loan, credit union, and rural loan and savings corporations, and business corporations organized prior to adoption of Act in 1929 that have not accepted the Act.]

KANSAS

Sec. 1. It shall be lawful for any corporation created or existing under the laws of this state to contribute to community funds or to charitable, philanthropic, benevolent, religious, scientific or educational instrumentalities, such sums as its board of directors or trustees may deem proper.

[Laws of 1951, Chapter 214, effective March 23, 1951; applicable to all corporations.]

MAINE

Sec. 15. General Powers. Corporations may * * * make donations for the public welfare or for charitable, scientific or educational purposes.

[Public Laws of 1951, Chapter 4, effective August 20, 1951; amending Section 13, Chapter 49, Revised Statutes; applicable to all corporations.]

MARYLAND

9. (Powers).—(a) Every corporation of this State shall have the following general powers, except where special provisions of law relating to corporations of that particular class are inconsistent herewith: * * *

(10) To make reasonable gifts or contributions out of profits, when authorized by its board of directors so to do, to or for the use of (i) this State, its institutions and agencies, or any political subdivision of this State, and (ii) any corporation, trust, community chest or fund, foundation, society or other organization for religious, charitable, scientific, civic, literary or educational purposes. * * *

[Subsection (6) added to Section 8 of General Corporation Law by Laws of 1945, Chapter 1018; amended and revised as Subsection (10) of Section 9 by Laws of 1951, Chapter 135, effective June 1, 1951; revised Article 23, Annotated Code of Maryland; applicable to all corporations, except banks.]

HISTORICAL

The first permissive legislation in Maryland was enacted in 1945 (Laws of 1945, Chapter 1018), when the following Act was passed:

Whereas, it has been the legislative intent and understanding that corporations incorporated under the provisions of Article 23 of the Annotated Code of Maryland (1939 Edition) have and have had the power to make gifts and contributions, unless otherwise restricted in their charters or by-laws for religious, charitable, scientific, civic, literary, educational and public purposes; and

Whereas, it is the desire of the General Assembly of Maryland to clarify and declare the existing law with respect thereto; therefore,

Section 1. Be it enacted by the General Assembly of Maryland, That Sub-section (6) of Section 8 of Article 23 of the Annotated Code of Maryland (1939 Edition), title "Corporations," sub-title "Provisions for Formation of Corporations—Powers," be and it is hereby repealed and re-enacted, with amendments, to read as follows:

Section 8. Every corporation which is subject to the provisions of this Article shall have the following general powers, except where the special provisions relating to any particular classes of corporations are inconsistent herewith: * * *

(6) Subject to the provisions of Article 38 of the Declaration of Rights, to acquire by purchase or in any other manner, and to take, receive, hold, use and employ, sell, mortgage, lease, dispose of and otherwise deal with any property, real or personal, situated in or out of this State, including shares in, and bonds, notes and other obligations of other corporations, incorpo-

rated under the laws of this State or of any other State or otherwise, which may be appropriate to enable it to carry on the operations or fulfill the purposes named in the charter, and, unless otherwise provided in its charter or by-laws, to make reasonable gifts or contributions out of profits, when authorized by its board of directors so to do, to or for the use of (1) this State, its institutions and agencies, or any political subdivision of this State, or (2) any corporation, or trust, or community fund, or foundation, or society, or organization for religious, charitable, scientific, civic, literary, or educational purposes; but nothing herein shall authorize the sale, mortgage, lease, or other disposition by a public service corporation of any part of its property or franchises in any case in which the approval or consent of The Public Service Commission of Maryland is now or may hereafter be required by law, unless and until such approval or consent shall have been obtained.

Article 23 of the Code was completely revised in 1951, and the authority for donations now appears as Section 9(a) (10) as above quoted.

MASSACHUSETTS

Sec. 12A. Every corporation may, by vote of its directors, or of its officers having the powers of directors, contribute such sum or sums of money as said directors or officers may determine to be reasonable to any fund being raised by a relief committee or agency approved by the commissioner of public welfare, as evidenced by a writing filed in his office, and formed for the purpose of raising money to be used for the betterment of social and economic conditions in any community in which such corporation is doing business. Nothing in this section shall be construed as directly or indirectly restricting or otherwise affecting, except as herein provided, the rights and powers of any corporation with reference to payments of the nature above specified.

[Section 12A added to General Corporation Law by Acts of 1938, Chapter 164; amended by Acts of 1946, Chapter 278, approved May 8, 1946; Chapter 155, Annotated Laws of Massachusetts; applicable to all corporations.]

HISTORICAL

The earliest permissive legislation in Massachusetts was enacted in 1933 (Acts of 1933, Chapter 8), when the following act was passed:

Section 1. Every corporation organized under the laws of this commonwealth and doing business or operating therein may, by vote of its directors, or of its officers having the powers of directors, contribute such sum or sums of money as said directors or officers may determine to be reasonable to any general fund being raised by a relief committee or agency approved by the commissioner of public welfare, as evidenced by a writing filed in his office, and formed for the purpose of raising money to be used for the betterment of social and economic conditions and in any community in which such corporation is doing business.

Section 2. Nothing in this Act shall be construed as directly or indirectly restricting or otherwise affecting, except as herein provided, the rights and powers of any corporation with reference to payments of the nature above specified.

Section 3. This Act shall become inoperative at the expiration of one year from its effective date.

In 1934, the limitation in Section 3 was amended to two years. (Acts of 1934, Chapter 9)

In 1935, the limitation in Section 3 was again amended to three years. (Acts of 1935, Chapter 4)

In 1936, the limitation in Section 3 was again amended to six years. (Acts of 1936, Chapter 20)

In 1938, this statute was made permanent and added to the General Corporation Law as Section 12A. (Acts of 1938, Chapter 164)

In 1946, Section 12A was amended by striking out the word "general" before "fund" in Section 3 (Acts of 1946, Chapter 278).

MICHIGAN

Sec. 10. Every corporation, unless otherwise provided, or inconsistent with the act under which a particular corporation is or shall have been formed shall have power: * * *

(k) to make contributions for public welfare.

[Subsection (k) added as subsection (1) to Section 10 of General Corporation Act by Public Acts of 1935, No. 194; reenacted as subsection (k) by Public Acts of 1947, No. 209, approved June 16, 1947; Section 450.10, Compiled Laws of Michigan; applicable to all corporations organized under General Corporation Act, which excludes insurance, railroad, bridge, tunnel, and union depot companies.]

MINNESOTA

Sec. 1. Contributions by Corporations.—Subdivision 1. Any corporation heretofore or hereafter organized under the laws of this state or any corporation authorized to do business in this state may contribute to or for the uses enumerated in the following subdivisions of this section such sums as its board of directors or trustees may deem proper.

Subd. 2. It may contribute to the United States, any state, territory or any political subdivision thereof or the District of Columbia, or any possession of the United States, for exclusively public purposes.

Subd. 3. It may contribute to any community chest, corporation, organization, trust, fund, association or foundation, organized and operating for religious, charitable, philanthropic, benevolent, scientific, veteran rehabilitation service, literary, artistic, educational, civic or patriotic purposes or for the prevention of cruelty to children or animals.

Subd. 4. It may contribute to a fraternal society, order or association, operating under the lodge system if such contributions or gifts are to be used for the purposes specified in Subd. 3 of this section, or posts or organizations of war veterans or any auxiliary unit or society of such posts or organizations if no part of their net income inures to the benefit of any private shareholder or individual.

Sec. 2. It is hereby declared to be the public policy of the state of Minnesota that any contributions made in accordance with the provisions of Section 1 shall constitute a valid and proper use of corporate funds, and in the absence of an express provision in its charter to the contrary, the making of such contributions or gifts by any corporation is within its powers and inures to the benefit of such corporation.

Sec. 3. This act shall not be construed as invalidating any such contributions or gifts heretofore made by any such corporation and all such contributions or gifts made by such corporations prior to the enactment hereof shall be as valid as if made after the effective date hereof.

[Laws of 1949, Chapter 156, approved March 21, 1949; Sections 300.66–68, Minnesota Statutes Annotated; applicable to all corporations.]

MISSOURI

Sec. 4. In order to carry out the purposes for which it is organized, each corporation shall have power: * * *

(15) To make contributions to any corporation organized for civic, charitable or benevolent purposes, or to any incorporated or unincorporated association, community chest or community fund, not operated or used for profit to its members but operated for the purposes of raising funds for and of distributing funds to other civic, charitable or benevolent organizations or agencies.

[Laws of 1937, page 204; superseded by Section 4(15) of The General and Business Corporation Act of Missouri, Laws of 1943, page 410, as amended by Laws of 1945, page 696; Section 351.385, Missouri Revised Statutes; applicable to all corporations for profit formed under The General and Business Corporation Law of Missouri, which excludes banking, insurance, railroad corporations, building and loan associations, savings banks and safe deposit companies, credit unions, mortgage loan companies, union stations, trust companies, and exposition companies.]

HISTORICAL

The first permissive legislation in Missouri was enacted in 1937 (Laws of 1937, page 204, approved March 25, 1937), when the following act was passed:

Section 1. Corporations shall have right to make contributions, when.—That any corporation for profit organized under the laws of this State shall have the right by vote of a majority of the members of its board of directors, to make contributions to any corporation organized under the laws of Missouri for civic, charitable or benevolent purposes, or to any incorporated or unincorporated association, community chest or community fund, not operated or used for profit to its members but operated for the purposes of raising funds for and of distributing funds to other civic, charitable or benevolent organizations or agencies.

This statute was superseded by Section 4(15) of The General and Business Corporation Act of Missouri, enacted in 1943 and reenacted in 1945.

NEW JERSEY

Any corporation, organized under any laws of this state whatsoever, may co-operate with other corporations and with natural persons in the creation and maintenance of community funds or of charitable, philanthropic or benevolent instrumentalities conducive to public welfare, and its directors or trustees may appropriate and expend for those purposes such sum or sums as they deem expedient and as in their judgment will contribute to the protection of the corporate interests.

When, however, in case of a corporation having capital stock, the expenditures for those purposes in any calendar year shall in the aggregate amount to one per centum (1%) of the capital and surplus as of the end of the preceding year, then before any further expenditure is made during the year for those purposes by the corporation, ten days' notice shall be given to the stockholders in the manner the directors or trustees direct, of the intention to make the further expenditure, specifying the amount thereof, and if written objections be made by the stockholders holding twenty-five per centum (25%) or more of the stock of the corporation the further expenditure shall not be made until it has been authorized at a stockholders' meeting.

[Laws of 1930, Chapter 105, as amended by Laws of 1931, Chapter 190, and reenacted by Laws of 1949, Chapter 171, approved May 20, 1949; Section 14:3–13, New Jersey Statutes Annotated; applicable to all corporations, except savings banks, building and loan associations, insurance or surety companies, railroads, telephone and telegraph companies operating in state, canal and turnpike companies, and institutions for finance and insurance.]

1. The Legislature declares that it shall be the public policy of this State that encouragement shall be given to the creation and mainte-

nance of institutions or organizations engaged in community fund, hospital, charitable, philanthropic, educational, scientific or benevolent activities or patriotic or civic activities conducive to the betterment of social and economic conditions; that such a policy will be in the public interest in that the public welfare will be thereby promoted; and that to the end that the public policy herein declared may be supported and furthered, corporations organized under the laws of this State should be specifically empowered to appropriate, spend or contribute such sum or sums as in the judgment of their respective governing boards will conduce to the betterment of social and economic conditions, thereby permitting such corporations, as creatures of this State, to discharge their obligations to society while, at the same time, reaping the benefits which essentially accrue to them through public recognition of their existence within the economic and social, as well as within the legal, structure of society.

2. Every domestic corporation organized under the laws of this State, unless otherwise provided in its certificate of incorporation or other certificate filed pursuant to law or its by-laws, shall have power to aid, singly or in cooperation with other corporations and with natural persons, in the creation or maintenance of institutions or organizations engaged in community fund, hospital, charitable, philanthropic, educational, scientific or benevolent activities or patriotic or civic activities conducive to the betterment of social and economic conditions, and the members of the board of trustees or directors or other governing board of such corporation may appropriate, spend or contribute for such purposes such reasonable sum or sums as they may determine; provided, that a contribution shall not be authorized hereunder if at the time of the contribution or immediately thereafter the donee institution shall own more than ten per centum (10%) of the voting stock of the donor corporation or one of its subsidiaries; and provided further, that in the case of a corporation having capital stock, contributions in any fiscal year shall not in the aggregate exceed one per centum (1%) of the capital and surplus as of the end of the preceding fiscal year, unless any contribution or contributions in excess of one per centum (1%) of such capital and surplus shall be authorized by the stockholders of the corporation at a regular or special meeting.

3. The provisions of this act shall not be construed as directly or indirectly minimizing or interpreting the rights and powers of corporations, as heretofore existing, with reference to appropriations, expenditures or contributions of the nature above specified.

4. Nothing in this act shall affect the power of any foreign corporation doing business or operating in this State, unless otherwise provided in its certificate of incorporation or other certificate filed pursuant to

law or its by-laws, to appropriate, spend or contribute for the purposes above set forth such sum or sums as its trustees or directors or other governing board may determine.

[Laws of 1950, Chapter 220, approved June 13, 1950, adding Sections 14:3–13.1, 14:3–13.2, 14:3–13.3, and 14:3–13.4 to Section 14:3–13, New Jersey Statutes Annotated; applicable to all corporations, except savings banks, building and loan associations, insurance or surety companies, railroads, telephone and telegraph companies operating in state, canal and turnpike companies, and institutions for finance and insurance.]

HISTORICAL

History of Section 14:3-13

The first permissive legislation in New Jersey was enacted in 1930 (Laws of 1930, Chapter 105), when the following act was passed:

14:3–13 Philanthropic Contributions:—Any corporation organized under the laws of this state may cooperate with other corporations and with natural persons in the creation and maintenance of community funds or of charitable, philanthropic or benevolent instrumentalities conducive to public welfare, and its directors or trustees may appropriate and expend for such purposes such sum or sums as they deem expedient and as in their judgment will contribute to the protection of the corporate interests.

Whenever, however, the expenditures for such purposes in any calendar year shall in the aggregate amount to one per centum of the capital stock outstanding then, before any further expenditure is made during the year for such purposes by the corporation, ten days' notice shall be given to the stockholders in such manner as the directors or trustees may direct, of the intention to make such further expenditure, specifying the amount thereof, and if written objection be made by the stockholders holding twenty-five per centum or more of the stock of the corporation, such further expenditure shall not be made until it shall have been authorized at a stockholders' meeting.

This statute was amended by Laws of 1931, Chapter 190, with minor textual changes.

It was reenacted in 1949 in the form first above quoted.

NEW MEXICO

Sec. 54–202. Corporate Powers Enumerated. Every corporation heretofore or hereafter organized shall have power: * * *

VIII. To make donations or contributions for the public welfare, or for charitable, scientific or educational purposes.

[Subsection VIII added to Sec. 54–202, New Mexico Statutes 1941 Annotated, by Laws of 1951, Chapter 105, approved March 13, 1951; applicable to all corporations authorized by any general incorporation law of State, except corporations for construction and operation of railroads, telegraph lines, express companies, savings banks, commercial banks, trust companies, building and loan associations, insurance, surety, and irrigation companies, unless organized for operation outside the State.]

NEW YORK

Sec. 34. Corporations authorized to contribute for betterment of social and economic conditions.—Every domestic corporation organized under the laws of this state, unless otherwise provided in its certificate of incorporation or other certificate filed pursuant to law or its by-laws, shall have power to cooperate with other corporations and with natural persons in the creation and maintenance of institutions or organizations which are engaged in community fund, hospital, charitable, educational, scientific or civic activities in the state or states in which such corporation is operating, or which are engaged within or without such state or states in similar activities which in the judgment of the trustees or directors of the corporation may be beneficial to the business activities of the corporation or the well being of its employees, and its trustees or directors may appropriate, spend or contribute for such purposes such reasonable sum or sums as they may determine; provided that a contribution shall not be authorized hereunder if at the time of the contribution or immediately thereafter the donee institution shall own more than ten per centum of the voting stock of the donor corporation or one of its subsidiaries (which term for the purposes of this section shall be deemed to mean any corporation in which the donor corporation owns fifty-one per centum or more of the securities having voting power for the election of directors, either at all times or only so long as no class of stock having preference or priority in the payment of dividends or in the distribution of assets upon any dissolution, liquidation or winding up of the corporation has such voting power because of default in dividends or some other default as set forth in the terms and provisions thereof); provided, however, that the provisions of this section shall not be construed as directly or indirectly minimizing or interpreting the rights and powers of corporations, as heretofore existing, with reference to subscriptions and payments of the nature above specified. However, no part of any funds hereafter subscribed or paid by any public utility company subject to the jurisdiction of the department of service for any of the purposes of or pursuant to the authorization of this section shall be deemed a part of the expenses of the operation of the business of such company or properly chargeable to such expense and no such company shall charge any such funds to or credit the same against its operating expense account or any other account which is directly or indirectly considered for rate-making purposes.

Nothing in this section shall affect the power of any foreign corporation doing business or operating in this state, unless otherwise provided in its certificate of incorporation or other certificate filed pursuant to law or its by-laws, to appropriate, spend or contribute for the purposes above set forth such sum or sums as its trustees or directors may determine.

[Section 34 added to General Corporation Law by Laws of 1941, Chapter 343; amended by Laws of 1951, Chapters 7 and 388; Article 2, Book 22, McKinney's Consolidated Laws of New York Annotated; applicable to all domestic corporations.]

Sec. 35. Corporations authorized to contribute to The American National Red Cross. Every corporation organized under the laws of this state, and doing business or operating in this state shall have power to make contributions to The American National Red Cross, a corporation organized under an act of congress, as a proper part of the expense of its business to the end that such corporations may, in their discretion, expend such reasonable sums as they may deem expedient, provided, however, that the provisions of this section shall not be construed as directly or indirectly minimizing or interpreting the rights and powers of corporations, as heretofore existing, with reference to subscriptions and payments of the nature above specified. However, no part of any funds hereafter subscribed or paid by any public utility company subject to the jurisdiction of the department of public service for any of the purposes of or pursuant to the authorization of this section shall be deemed a part of the expenses of the operation of the business of such company or properly chargeable to such expense and no such company shall charge any such funds to or credit the same against its operating expense account or any other account which is directly or indirectly considered for rate-making purposes.

[Section 35 added to General Corporation Law by Laws of 1946, Chapter 448; Article 2, Book 22, McKinney's Consolidated Laws of New York Annotated; applicable to all corporations.]

HISTORICAL

History of Section 34

The first permissive legislation in New York appears to have been enacted in 1918 (Laws of 1918, Chapter 240), when the following emergency act was passed:

Section 1. That during the continuance of the war any corporation organized under the laws of this State may cooperate with other corporations and with natural persons in the creation and maintenance of instrumentalities conducive to the winning of the war, and its directors or trustees may appropriate and expend for such purposes such sum or sums as they may deem expedient and as, in their judgment, will contribute to the protection of the corporate interests, provided that whenever the expenditures for such purposes in any calendar year shall in the aggregate amount to one per centum on the capital stock outstanding, then, before any further expenditure is made during such year for such purposes by the corporation, ten days' notice shall be given to the stockholders in such manner as the directors or trustees may direct of the intention to make such other expenditure, specifying the amount thereof, and if written objection be made by stockholders holding twenty-five per centum or more of the stock of the corporation, such further expenditure shall not be made until it shall have been authorized at a stockholders' meeting.

This act was approved April 16, 1918, and by its terms was effective immediately. It seems to have been the source of the donation statutes in New Jersey and Ohio.

In 1923 (Laws of 1923, Chapter 190), the following new section was added to Chapter 28 of the Laws of 1909 (General Corporation Law):

§ 45. *Expenditures for social and economic benefit.* Nothing contained in this chapter or in any other law shall be deemed to make it unlawful for any corporation or joint stock association to cooperate with other corporations and with natural persons in the creation and maintenance of instrumentalities conducive to the betterment of the social and economic conditions under which such corporation or joint stock association is operating, and its directors or trustees may appropriate and expend for such purposes such reasonable sum or sums as they may deem expedient and as in their judgment will contribute to the protection of the corporate property and tend to promote the interests of the corporation and its stockholders.

Section 45 was reenacted in 1924 (Laws of 1924, Chapter 127) in the same form, except that before the words "to cooperate" there was inserted, "other than a mutual corporation engaged in the business of receiving deposits,".

In 1929 (Laws of 1929, Chapter 650), the General Corporation Law of 1909 was amended and revised, and apparently Section 45 was repealed.

In 1931 (Laws of 1931, Chapter 76), Section 33 was added to Chapter 28 of the Laws of 1909, as amended in 1929 (General Corporation Law), as follows:

§ 33. Every corporation organized under the laws of this State and doing business or operating in this State, other than public utility corporations, shall have power to cooperate with other corporations and with natural persons in the creation and maintenance of instrumentalities conducive to, or to subscribe or make payments to funds for, the betterment of the social and economic conditions in any community or communities in which such corporation is operating, and to that end such corporations may in their discretion expend such reasonable sums as they may deem expedient, provided, however, that this act shall not be construed, either by reason of the limited period fixed herein or otherwise, as directly or indirectly minimizing or interpreting the rights and powers of corporations, as heretofore existing, with reference to subscriptions and payments of the nature above specified.

This Section was to continue in effect for one year only, but was reenacted for one year in 1932 (Laws of 1932, Chapter 188).

In 1933 (Laws of 1933, Chapter 104), Section 33 was again reenacted for another year, but with the following changes: the phrase "other than public utility corporations" was deleted, and after the words "make payments" there was inserted "as a proper part of the expense of its business."

Section 33, as amended in 1933, was reenacted by Laws of 1934, Chapter 129, effective to March 31, 1935; by Laws of 1935, Chapter 306, effective for one year; and by Laws of 1936, Chapter 101, effective for one year, but amended by adding the following:

> However, no part of any funds hereafter subscribed or paid by any public utility company subject to the jurisdiction of the Department of Public Service for any of the purposes of or pursuant to this section shall be deemed a part of the expenses of the operation of the business of such company or properly chargeable to such expense, and no such company shall charge any such funds to or credit the same against its operating expense account or any other account which is directly or indirectly considered for rate making purposes.

As thus amended, Section 33 was reenacted by Laws of 1937, Chapter 187, for one year; by Laws of 1938, Chapter 544, for one year; by Laws of 1939, Chapter 56, for one year from April 12, 1939; and by Laws of 1940, Chapter 235, for one year.

In 1941 (Laws of 1941, Chapter 343), a new Section 34 was added to the General Corporation Law, substantially in the same form as Section 33 but without limitation as to the period of its effectiveness.

Section 34 was amended in 1950 (Laws of 1950, Chapter 297) effective July 1, 1950, by adding the following paragraphs:

> 2. A domestic corporation which submits an annual report to its stockholders and which, pursuant to the authority of this section, appropriates, spends or contributes a sum or sums aggregating in excess of five hundred dollars to or on behalf of any one donee, during the period covered by such report, shall include in such report the identity of each such donee together with the total amount appropriated, spent or contributed to it or on its behalf during such period. If such corporation does not submit such an annual report to its stockholders it shall send to each one a statement of the total amount of all such appropriations, expenditures and contributions made during each fiscal year and any stockholder, upon written request, shall be entitled to an itemized list of such donees and amounts. The corporation need not comply with such a request regarding any year more than five years prior to that in which such request is made.

> 3. Nothing in this section shall affect the power of any foreign corporation doing business or operating in this state, unless otherwise provided in its certificate of incorporation or other certificate filed pursuant to law or its by-laws, to appropriate, spend or contribute for the purposes above set forth such sum or sums as its trustees or directors may determine.

Paragraph 2 was repealed in a 1951 amendment (Laws of 1951, Chapters 7 and 388), and Section 34 now appears as first above quoted.

History of Section 35

In 1942 (Laws of 1942, Chapter 3), a special statute was enacted authorizing contributions by corporations to the American National Red Cross, substantially in the form of Section 33 as amended in 1936.

In 1946, that statute was repealed and reenacted as Section 35 of the General Corporation Law (Laws of 1946, Chapter 448), as above quoted.

Other Acts

A series of special acts authorizing corporate contributions to specified organizations have been enacted from time to time, as follows:

Navy Relief Society:

Laws of 1942, Chapter 507, effective to July 1, 1943.

American Overseas Aid, Inc.:

Laws of 1948, Chapter 539, effective to July 1, 1949.

U.S.O.:

Laws of 1942, Chapter 29, effective to July 1, 1943;
Laws of 1943, Chapter 96, effective to July 1, 1944;
Laws of 1944, Chapter 36, effective to July 1, 1945;
Laws of 1945, Chapter 256, effective to July 1, 1946;
Laws of 1946, Chapter 482, effective to July 1, 1947;
Laws of 1947, Chapter 172, effective to July 1, 1948;
Laws of 1948, Chapter 295, repealed act of 1942 as amended, effective March 21, 1948;
Laws of 1949, Chapter 380, reenacted law in favor of U.S.O. until July 1, 1950.

National War Fund:

Laws of 1943, Chapter 48, effective to July 1, 1944;
Laws of 1944, Chapter 37, effective to July 1, 1945;
Laws of 1945, Chapter 144, effective to July 1, 1946;
Laws of 1946, Chapter 425, effective to July 1, 1947;
Laws of 1947, Chapter 445, repealed act of 1943 and extensions, effective July 1, 1947.

Each of these statutes was substantially the same as the present Section 35, except as to the beneficiary.

Apparently some statutory authority to make corporate donations to the Army Emergency Relief Fund has been given (McKinney's Unconsolidated Laws, Section 2532).

NORTH CAROLINA

Sec. 55–26. Every corporation has power— * * *

12. To make contributions or gifts to corporations, trusts, community chests, funds, foundations, or associations organized and operated exclusively for religious, charitable, literary, scientific, or educational

purposes or for the prevention of cruelty to children or animals, no part of the net earnings of which inures to the benefit of any private stockholder or individual, when such contributions or gifts are authorized or approved by its board of directors: Provided, that such contributions or gifts during any income year of the corporation do not exceed five per centum (5%) of its net income as computed under Article four, Schedule D, of Chapter one hundred five, of the General statutes, disregarding for such purpose the aggregate amount of such contributions or gifts: Provided, further, that the assets of the corporation exceed its liabilities immediately after any such contribution or gift is made.

[Subsection 12 added to Section 55–26, General Statutes, by Session Laws of 1945, Chapter 775, effective March 19, 1945; Article 4, Chapter 55, General Statutes of North Carolina; applicable to all corporations, except certain nonprofit and cooperative organizations exempt from state income taxation.]

OHIO

Sec. 8623–119. Any corporation may cooperate with other corporations and with natural persons in the creation and maintenance of funds or credits for aiding community growth or development or for aiding charitable, philanthropic or benevolent instrumentalities, conducive to public welfare, and its directors may appropriate and expend or obligate the corporation to pay or pledge its credit for such purpose or purposes, such sum or sums as they may deem expedient and as, in their judgment, will contribute to the protection or advancement of the corporate interests, provided that whenever the expenditures for such purposes in any calendar year shall be equal in aggregate amount to one per centum of the capital and surplus of the corporation, then, before any further expenditure is made or obligation is incurred during such year for such purposes by the corporation, ten days' notice shall be given to the shareholders in such manner as the directors may specify of the intention to make such further expenditure or to incur such further obligation, specifying the amount thereof, and if written objection be made by shareholders holding twenty-five per centum or more of the total number of voting shares of the corporation, such further expenditure shall not be made nor shall such further obligation be incurred until it shall have been authorized at a shareholders' meeting.

[108 Ohio Laws, page 1245, approved February 19, 1920; amended and revised as Section 119 of General Corporation Act by 112 Ohio Laws, page 52, approved June 6, 1927; amended by 121 Ohio Laws, page 70, approved April 20, 1945; Section 8623–119, Page's Ohio General Code Annotated; applicable to banks and all corporations subject to General Corporation Act.]

HISTORICAL

The first permissive legislation in Ohio was enacted in 1920 (108 Ohio Laws, Part 2, page 1245, approved February 19, 1920), which provided as follows:

Section 1. That any corporation organized under the laws of this State may cooperate with other corporations and with natural persons in the creation and maintenance of community funds or of charitable, philanthropic or benevolent instrumentalities conducive to the public welfare, and its directors and officers may appropriate and expend for such purposes such sum or sums as they may deem expedient and as, in their judgment, will contribute to the protection of the corporate interests, provided that whenever the expenditures for such purposes in any current year shall in the aggregate amount to one per centum of the capital stock outstanding, then, before any further expenditure is made during such year for such purposes by the corporation, ten days' notice shall be given to the stockholders in such manner as the directors or trustees may direct of the intention to make such expenditure, specifying the amount thereof, and if written objection be made by stockholders holding twenty-five per centum or more of the stock of the corporation, such further expenditure shall not be made until it shall have been authorized at a stockholders' meeting.

All such corporations making appropriations and expenditures under the provisions of this Act shall report annually to the Secretary of State the sums so appropriated or expended and the name or names of the community funds or philanthropic, charitable or benevolent instrumentalities in whose behalf such sums were appropriated or expended.

Upon the enactment of the new General Corporation Act in 1927, the above provision, with some alterations and without the second paragraph, became Section 119 of the new Act.

Section 119 was amended in 1945 to read as above quoted.

OKLAHOMA

Sec. 19. Every domestic corporation shall, in so far as incidental to the transaction of its business or expedient for the attainment of the purposes stated in its articles of incorporation, have and possess the following general powers: * * *

(11) And, notwithstanding any other provisions of this Act, to cooperate with other corporations and organizations and with natural persons in the creation and maintenance of community funds or of charitable, philanthropic, benevolent, educational, patriotic or civic instrumentalities conducive to public welfare; or of boards of trade, Chambers of Commerce, and commercial clubs; and of employee credit unions, company pension, annuity and bonus plans, and its directors or trustees may appropriate and expend for any of these purposes such sum or sums as they deem expedient, and as in their judgment will benefit or contribute to the corporate or public interest.

[Subsection (11) added to Business Corporation Act by Laws of 1949, page 114, effective May 31, 1949; Section 1.19, Title 18, Oklahoma Statutes Annotated; applicable to all corporations, except land companies and agencies.]

PENNSYLVANIA

Sec. 302. General Powers. Subject to the limitations and restrictions contained in this act or in its articles, every business corporation shall have power: * * *

(16) To make contributions to or for the use or benefit of—

(a) The United States, any state, territory, or any political subdivision thereof, or the District of Columbia or any possession of the United States for exclusively public purposes, or

(b) A corporation, trust or community chest fund, or foundation created or organized in the United States or in any possession thereof, or under the laws of the United States or of any state or territory, or of the District of Columbia, or of any possession of the United States and organized and operated exclusively for religious, charitable, scientific, veteran rehabilitation service, literary or educational purposes, or for the prevention of cruelty to children, no part of the net earnings of which inures to the benefit of any private shareholder or individual, and no substantial part of the activities of which is carrying on propaganda or otherwise attempting to influence legislation to the extent authorized, approved or ratified by action of the board of directors of the corporation, except as otherwise specifically provided or limited by its articles of incorporation, or its by-laws or by resolution duly adopted by its shareholders. All contributions made heretofore by authority of the board of directors of the corporation for the purposes prescribed by this act are hereby ratified and confirmed.

[Subsection (16) added to Section 302 of Business Corporation Law by Laws of 1945, P.L. 605; amended by Laws of 1947, P.L. 290, approved May 23, 1947; 15 P.S. 2852–302; applicable to all corporations subject to the Business Corporation Law, which excludes cooperative associations, corporations formed under Non-Profit Corporation Law, and corporations subject to supervision by Department of Banking, Insurance Department, Public Utility Commission, or Water and Power Resources Board.]

Sec. 716. Any corporation for profit, and any Mutual Insurance Company, Mutual Savings Bank, or other corporation on a mutual plan heretofore or hereafter organized under any general or special law of this Commonwealth, be and hereby it is authorized and empowered by action of its board of directors to make contributions to or for the use or benefit of:

(a) the United States, any state, territory or any political subdivision thereof, or the District of Columbia, or any possession of the United States, for exclusively public purposes, or

(b) a corporation, trust or community chest fund or foundation created or organized in the United States, or in any possession thereof, or under the laws of the United States, or of any state, or territory, or of the District of Columbia, or of any possession of the United States and organized and operated exclusively for religious, charitable, scientific, veteran rehabilitation service, literary or educational purposes; or for the prevention of cruelty to children, no part of the net earnings of which inures to the benefit of any private shareholder or individual, and no substantial part of the activities of which is carrying on propaganda or otherwise attempting to influence legislation to the extent authorized, approved or ratified by action of the board of directors of the corporation, except as otherwise specifically provided or limited by its articles of incorporation or its by-laws, or by resolution duly adopted by its shareholders or members.

All contributions made heretofore by authority of the board of directors of the corporation, for the purposes prescribed by this act are hereby ratified and confirmed.

[Laws of 1945, P.L. 594; amended by Laws of 1947, P.L. 288, approved May 23, 1947; 15 P.S. 716; applicable to all corporations for profit organized under any general or special law, including Banking Laws, Insurance Laws, and General Corporation Law of 1874, P.L. 73.]

HISTORICAL

The first permissive legislation in Pennsylvania was enacted in 1945, when two separate acts were passed. One act added a new subsection to Section 302 of the Business Corporation Law (Laws of 1945, P.L. 605, approved May 16, 1945). The other act added Section 716 to the general corporation laws (Laws of 1945, P.L. 594, also approved May 16, 1945). These acts were almost identical with the present laws but will be quoted in full.

History of Section 302

The following subsection was added to Section 302. General Powers—

(16) To make contributions out of its income in any taxable year to or for the use of—

(a) The United States, any state, territory, or any political subdivision thereof, or the District of Columbia or any possession of the United States for exclusively public purposes, or

(b) A corporation, trust or community fund, or foundation created or organized in the United States or in any possession thereof, or under the laws of the United States or of any state or territory, or of the District of Columbia, or of any possession of the United States, organized and operated exclusively for religious, charitable, scientific, literary or educational purposes, or for the prevention of cruelty to children (in the case of contributions to a trust, chest fund or foundation, payment of which is made within the taxable year of such business corporation beginning after the date of the cessation of hostilities in the present war, as proclaimed by the President of the United States, only if such contributions are to be used within the United States or any of its possessions exclusively for such purposes) no part of the net earnings of which enures to the benefit of any private shareholder or individual, and no substantial part of the activities of which is carrying on propaganda or otherwise attempting to influence legislation to the extent in the aggregate authorized, approved or ratified by the by-laws of the corporation or by resolution of its shareholders. All such contributions made heretofore or at any time prior to the next annual meeting of the shareholders held after the passage of this act by authority of the board of directors of the corporation for the purposes prescribed by this act are hereby ratified and confirmed.

This subsection was amended in 1947 (Laws of 1947, P.L. 290, approved May 23, 1947), and now appears as first above quoted.

History of Section 716

Section 716 was enacted in 1945 (Laws of 1947, P.L. 594, approved May 16, 1945) in almost the exact form of subsection (16) except the first paragraph which read as follows:

Any corporation for profit, heretofore or hereafter organized under any general or special law of this Commonwealth, be and hereby it is authorized and empowered by action of its board of directors to make contributions out of its income in any taxable year to or for the use of: * * *

In 1947 the first paragraph of Section 716 was amended (Laws of 1947, P.L. 288, approved May 23, 1947) by inserting: "and any mutual insurance company, mutual savings bank, or other corporation on a mutual plan" after "profit"; deleting "out of its income in any taxable year"; and inserting "or benefit" after "use."

The remainder of Section 716 was amended in 1947 in accordance with the 1947 amendments to Section 302 (16) (b).

TENNESSEE

Sec. 4085. Corporations may make contributions for Charitable Purposes.—Any corporation organized or created under the laws of this State is empowered in the discretion of its board of directors to make gifts, donations or contributions for charitable purposes or to charitable enterprises and undertakings; provided, however, that such gifts or contributions shall be made out of the earnings of such corporations, and shall be charged to operating expenses. This Section shall apply to corporations chartered by special legislative action prior to the Constitution of 1870 except in the case of a corporation with special legislative charter which contains provisions forbidding or limiting the exercise of power hereby granted.

[Public Acts of 1925, Chapter 59, as amended by Public Acts of 1943, Chapter 88, approved February 10, 1943; Section 4085, Tennessee Code; applicable to all profit corporations, except as stated.]

HISTORICAL

The first sentence of Section 4085 as quoted was enacted in 1925. The second sentence was added in 1943.

TEXAS

Art. 1349. Acts Prohibited.—No corporation, domestic or foreign, doing business in this State, shall employ or use its stock, means, assets or other property, directly or indirectly, for any purpose whatever other than to accomplish the legitimate business of its creation, or those purposes otherwise permitted by law; provided that nothing in this Article shall be held to inhibit corporations from contributing to any bona fide association, incorporated or unincorporated, organized for purely religious, charitable or eleemosynary activities, or to commercial or industrial clubs or associations or other civic enterprises or organizations not in any manner nor to any extent directly or indirectly engaged in furthering the cause of any political party, or aiding in the election or defeat of any candidate for office, or aiding in defraying the expenses of any candidate for office, or defraying or aiding in defraying the expenses of any political campaign, or political headquarters, or aiding or assisting the success or defeat of any question to be voted upon by the qualified voters of this State or any subdivision thereof.

[Acts of 1917, page 25, as amended by Acts of 1943, Chapter 202, effective April 30, 1943; Article 1349, Revised Civil Statutes; applicable to all corporations doing business in Texas.]

HISTORICAL

As originally enacted in 1917, Article 1349 contained the phrase "and actively engaged for one year prior to such contribution in" before "purely religious"; and the words "local, district or statewide" before "commercial."

VIRGINIA

Sec. 3903(I). Certain public service corporations may make donations to charities or charitable institutions. Every railroad, electric railway, or steamboat corporation and every transportation corporation, telegraph or telephone company or other public service corporation subject to regulation by the State Corporation Commission which is chartered or created under the laws of the State shall have and possess the power through its board of directors to make donations and gifts to war funds, community funds, and other charities or charitable institutions.

[Laws of 1945, Chapter 27, effective March 29, 1945; Section 3903(I), Virginia Code; applicable to corporations of classes stated therein.]

WEST VIRGINIA

Sec. 3. Powers; Provision for Compromises and Reorganizations.—* * *

Any corporation created or existing under the laws of the state is hereby authorized by action of its board of directors to make contributions to or for the use or benefit of: The United States, any state, territory, or any political subdivision thereof or the District of Columbia, or any possession of the United States, for exclusively public purposes; or a corporation, trust, or community chest, fund, or foundation, created or organized in the United States, or in any possession thereof, or under the laws of the United States, or of any state or territory or of the District of Columbia or of any possession of the United States, organized and operated exclusively for religious, charitable, scientific, veterans rehabilitation service, literary or educational purposes, or for the prevention of cruelty to children, no part of the earnings of which inures to the benefit of any private shareholders or individuals, and no substantial part of the activities of which is carrying on propaganda, or otherwise attempting to influence legislation; or posts or organizations of war veterans, or auxiliary units of, or trusts or foundations for, any such posts or organizations, if such posts, organizations, units, trusts, or foundations are organized in the United States or any of its possessions, and if no part of their net earnings inures to the benefit of any private shareholder or individual. All contributions made heretofore by authority of the board of directors of the corporation for the purposes prescribed by this act are hereby ratified and confirmed. * * *

[Laws of 1949, H.B. 209, effective June 9, 1949; Section 3015(3), West Virginia Code of 1949 Annotated; applicable to all corporations.]

WISCONSIN

Sec. 180.04. Each corporation, when no inconsistent provision is made by law or by its articles of incorporation, shall have power to: * * *

(12) To make donations for the public welfare or for charitable, scientific, educational or religious purposes.

[Laws of 1951, Chapter 731, approved August 3, 1951, published August 18, 1951; applicable to all existing stock corporations electing to become subject to Wisconsin Business Corporation Law prior to July 1, 1953, and to all stock corporations thereafter.]

HAWAII

At any duly called meeting of the stockholders of a corporation or joint stock company organized under the laws of the Territory of Hawaii, donations for charitable purposes or to eleemosynary institutions * * * may be authorized by the affirmative vote of the holders of a majority of the stock of any such corporation, present in person or by proxy at such meeting, whether such corporation is continuing in business or is being dissolved. Nothing contained in this Act shall affect the validity of any such action heretofore taken by any corporation.

[Laws of 1947, Act 104, Series C-138, approved May 14, 1947; applicable to all corporations and joint stock companies.]

THE NATIONAL BANKING ACT

Upon duly making and filing articles of association and an organization certificate, a national banking association shall become, as from the date of the execution of its organization certificate, a body corporate, and as such, and in the name designated in the organization certificate, it shall have power— * * *

EIGHTH. To contribute to community funds, or to charitable, philanthropic, or benevolent instrumentalities conducive to public welfare, such sums as its board of directors may deem expedient and in the interests of the association, if it is located in a state the laws of which do not expressly prohibit state banking institutions from contributing to such funds or instrumentalities.

[Subsection Eighth added to Section 24 of The National Banking Act by Act of June 11, 1940, Chapter 301, 54 Stat. 261; Section 24, Title 12, United States Code Annotated.]

APPENDIX D

AN ANNOTATED LIST OF SIGNIFICANT LAW AND TAX CASES

[*This Appendix attempts to summarize all cases in the United States that bear significantly on corporation giving. The 106 law and tax cases are classified by purpose of the contribution. Included in the tax category are cases tried before the federal courts, the Board of Tax Appeals, and the Tax Court. The selections and annotations were made by Ray Garrett, legal consultant for the study.*]

AMUSEMENT PROJECTS

Law Cases	*Valid*
Guaranty by railroad of deficit in music festival (Massachusetts). Davis et al. v. Old Colony Railroad Co., 131 Mass. 258 (1881)	No
Subscription by railroad to capital stock of public amusement park (Georgia). Military Interstate Assn. etc. v. Savannah, etc., Ry. Co., 105 Ga. 420, 31 S.E. 200 (1898)	No

Income-Tax Cases	*Deduction allowed*
Donation by cotton mill to village baseball team where some players are employed by mill. Climax Spinning Co., 8 B.T.A. 970 (1927)	No
Same facts. National Yarn Mills, 10 B.T.A. 1102 (1928)	No
Same facts. Majestic Mfg. Co., 11 B.T.A. 37 (1928)	No
Donation by hotel to Fleet Entertainment Committee where business increase was shown. Ranier Grand Co., 11 B.T.A. 520 (1928)	Yes
Donation by warehouse and transfer business to Shriners' convention in expectation of increased business. Merchants Transfer & Storage Co., 17 B.T.A. 290 (1929)	Yes

BUILDING PROJECTS

Law Cases	*Valid*
Subscription by hardware company to site for post office adjacent to business location (Illinois). B.S. Green Co. v. Blodgett, 159 Ill. 169, 42 N.E. 176 (1895)	Yes

Subscription by land company to stock exchange building (Illinois). Merchants Bldg. Impr. Co. v. Chicago Exchange Bldg. Co., 210 Ill. 26, 71 N.E. 22 (1904)	Yes
Note given by railroad to raise funds for public school and town development (Georgia). Brinson Ry. Co. v. Exchange Bank, etc., 16 Ga. App. 425, 85 S.E. 634 (1915)	No
Subscription by brokerage company to building theater in another neighborhood (Missouri). Orpheum Theatre & Realty Co. v. Brokerage Co., 197 Mo. App. 661, 199 S.W. 257 (1917)	No
Subscription by wholesale grocery company to hotel building (held to be "civic enterprise" under Texas statute of 1917). McCord Co. v. Citizens' Hotel Co., 287 S.W. 906 (1926)	Yes
Donation by town site company of profits from sale of lots to building state capitol (Oklahoma). Colcord, et al. v. Granzow, et al., 137 Okla. 194, 278 Pac. 654 (1928)	Yes

CHARITY

Law Cases	*Valid*
Announced policy of Ford Motor Company to put all profits over 5 per cent per month on $2,000,000 capital stock back into the business to increase employment, thereby spreading benefits of this industrial system to the greatest possible number. Dodge v. Ford Motor Co., 204 Mich. 459, 170 N.W. 668 (1919)	No
Free passes and reduced railroad fares to ministers and charity workers (Nebraska). State ex rel. Sorensen v. C.B. & Q.R. Co., 112 Neb. 248, 199 N.W. 534 (1924)	Yes

COMMUNITY FUNDS

Income-Tax Cases	*Deduction allowed*
Donation by steel mill to civic fund for local American Legion, etc., for welfare of employees and to make city more desirable. Forbes Lithograph Mfg. Co. v. White, 42 Fed. (2d) 287 (D. C. Mass.) (1930)	Yes
Donation by fur importer to Charity Chest of Fur Industry in New York. Eitingon-Schild Co., Inc., 21 B.T.A. 1163 (1931)	No

Donation by traction company to local Community Chest. The Capital Traction Co., 27 B.T.A. 926 (1933)   No

Donation by cement company to San Francisco Community Chest, for good will and increased business, but no evidence of direct benefit to business or employees. Old Mission Portland Cement Co. v. Helvering, 293 U.S. 289 (1934)[1]   No

Donation by newspaper to local community chest for advertising value and good will. Helvering v. Evening Star Newspaper Co., 78 Fed. (2d) 604 (C.C.A. 4th), Cert. Den. 296 U.S. 628 (1935)   No

Donation by bank to local community chest. Merchants National Bank of Mobile v. Commissioner, 90 Fed. (2d) 223 (C.C.A. 5th) (1937)[2]   No

Donation by construction company to local welfare federation, representing 32 charities. Morgan Construction Co. v. U.S., 18 Fed. Sup. 892 (D.C. Mass.) (1937)[2]   No

EDUCATIONAL PROJECTS

Law Cases   *Valid*

Donation of city lots by town site company to university to enable it to complete certain buildings outside of town (Kansas). Whetstone v. Ottawa University, 13 Kan. 240, originally 320 (1874)   Yes

Donation by officer of corporate funds of pump manufacturer to Columbia University for hydraulic engineering laboratory (New York). Worthington v. Worthington, 91 N.Y. Sup. 443 (1905)   No

Subscriptions by manufacturing company to endowment funds of local colleges for establishment of business schools (New York). Armstrong Cork Co. v. H. A. Meldrum Co., 285 Fed. 58 (1922)   Yes

Income-Tax Cases   *Deduction allowed*

Donation by factory to building for grade school, where 80–90 per cent of students are children of employees. Holt-Granite Mills Co., 1 B.T.A. 1246 (1925)   Yes

[1] Leading case, cited by most court decisions after 1934.

[2] Dates are the years of decision. This deduction was disallowed as a business expense in a tax year before contributions were authorized.

Donation by book store in New Orleans to Tulane University. J. A. Majors Co., 5 B.T.A. 260 (1926)   No

Donation by electric utility to Pacific College endowment fund to enable customer to survive. Yamhill Electric Co., 20 B.T.A. 1232 (1930)   Yes

Donation by newspaper to Tulane University to establish school of journalism as source of trained reporters. Times-Picayune Publishing Co., 27 B.T.A. 277 (1932)   Yes

Donation by newspaper to local college to retain it as advertising customer. Walter R. Willcuts, et al. v. Minnesota Tribune Co., 103 Fed. (2d) 947 (C.C.A. 8th) (1939)   Yes

Donation by manufacturer of matzos to theological school in Palestine. The B. Manischewitz Co., 10 T.C. 1139 (1948)   Yes

EMPLOYEES' WELFARE

Law Cases   *Valid*

Contributions by musical instrument company to construction of housing, church, schools, library, and free bath for employees (New York). Steinway v. Steinway & Sons, et al., 17 Misc. Rep. 43, 40 N.Y. Supp. 718 (1896)   Yes

Contributions by railroad to benefit society for employees (Iowa). Main v. C.B. & Q.R. Co., 109 Iowa 260, 70 N.W. 630, 80 N.W. 315 (1899)   Yes

Purchase of real estate by insurance company to be used as hospital for employees suffering from tuberculosis (New York). People ex rel. Metropolitan Life Ins. Co. v. Hotchkiss, 136 App. Div. 150, 120 N.Y. Supp. 649 (1909)   Yes

Donations by textile company to trust (later foundation) for care of employees and dependents (North Carolina). Wachovia Bank & Trust Co. v. Steele's Mills, et al., 34 S.E. (2d) 425 (1945)   Yes

                                                            Deduction
Income-Tax Cases   *allowed*

Donation by cotton manufacturer to benefit association formed for welfare of employees. Elm City Cotton Mills, 5 B.T.A. 309 (1926)   Yes

Donations by cotton manufacturer to churches near mill village (25–35 per cent employees), school clinic, school library, Boy Scouts and Red Cross, in the interest of employee relations. E. M. Holt Plaid Mills, Inc., 9 B.T.A. 1360 (1928) — No

Donation by manufacturer to Forbes Foundation established for benefit of employees and dependents. American Rolling Mill Co. v. Commissioner, 41 Fed. (2d) 314 (C.C.A. 6th) (1930) — Yes

GOOD WILL

Income-Tax Cases

Deduction allowed

Donations by fuel company to various charitable and similar organizations to satisfy customers. Stephens Fuel Co., Inc., 13 B.T.A. 666 (1928) — No

Donations by retail store for theater tickets and advertising for hospitals, etc., to please customers. Bonwit Teller & Co. v. Commissioner, 53 Fed. (2d) 381 (C.C.A. 2d), Cert. Den. 284 U.S. 690 (1931) — No

Donations by department store to various charitable and educational organizations in Buffalo to satisfy customers. Adam, Meldrum and Anderson Co., Inc., 29 B.T.A. 419 (1933) — No

Donation by railroad to American Legion, for good will. Atlantic Coast Line Railroad Co., 31 B.T.A. 730 (1934) — No

GOVERNMENT PROJECTS

Income-Tax Cases

Deduction allowed

Donation by shoe manufacturer to fund for purchase of land for Naval Ordnance Plant. Thomas Shoe Co., 1 B.T.A. 124 (1924) — No

Donation by wholesale and retail concern to fund for purchase of land for government picric acid plant. Coney & Parker Co., 2 B.T.A. 400 (1925) — No

Donation by land company to fund for purchase of adjacent land for Army post. Anniston City Land Co., 2 B.T.A. 526 (1925) — Yes

Donation by bank to County Farm Bureau for prizes and field work, where bank officers actively participated in contests and awards. Citizens Trust Co. of Utica, 2 B.T.A. 1239 (1925) — Yes

Donation by fruit and produce wholesaler to local chamber
of commerce to purchase site for Camp McClellan. (Held
controlled by Thomas Shoe Co., cited above.) Bell-Rogers &
Zemurray Brothers Co., 4 B.T.A. 687 (1926)   No

Donation by retail automobile and repair company for
same purpose. (Compare with Anniston City Land Co.,
above.) Anniston Auto Co., 4 B.T.A. 689 (1926)   No

Donation by sugar company to Hawaiian Bureau of Governmental Research. Bishop Trust Co., Ltd., 36 B.T.A. 1173
(1937)   No

HOSPITALS

Income-Tax Cases   *Deduction allowed*

Donation by paper manufacturer to establish hospital in city
where principal plant was located. Carso Paper Co. Inc., 3
B.T.A. 28 (1925)   No

Donation by cotton mill to local Salvation Army hospital
to serve employees at lower price. Franklin Mills, 7 B.T.A.
1290 (1927)   Yes

Donation by glass manufacturer to local hospital building
fund in lieu of enlarging plant dispensary, where employees
and dependents comprised two-thirds of population. Corning
Glass Works v. Lucas, 37 Fed. (2d) 798 (C.C.A. D.C.), Cert.
Den. 281 U.S. 742 (1929)   Yes

Donation by office building to nearby hospital treating
tenants of building. Fire Companies Building Corp., 18
B.T.A. 1258 (1930)   No

Donation by thread manufacturer to local hospitals for free
service to employees. Clark Thread Co., 28 B.T.A. 1128
(1933)   Yes

Donation by railroad to fund to provide hospitalization for
employees. Union Pacific Railroad Co., 32 B.T.A. 383 (1935) Yes

INDUSTRIAL PROJECTS

Law Cases   *Valid*

Donation by real estate company to railroad for increasing
width of road and frequency of service and for reducing fares
to development site (California). Vandall v. South San
Francisco Dock Co., 40 Cal. 83 (1870)   Yes

Subscription by bank to building of creamery. Holt v. Winfield Bank, 25 Fed. 812 (1885)   No

Donation by town site company for relocation of bank, barn, and restaurant in the town (Kansas). Sherman Center Town Co. v. Russell, 46 Kan. 382, 26 Pac. 715 (1891)   Yes

Subscription by religious society for construction of railroad and to induce location of depot near buildings of society (Kentucky). L. & N. Ry. Co. v. Literary Society, etc., 91 Ky. 395, 15 S.W. 1065 (1891)   Yes

Subscription by hotel company to fund to establish military encampment (Illinois). Richelieu Hotel Co. v. International Military Encampment Co., 140 Ill. 248, 29 N.E. 1044 (1892)   Yes

Donation by bank to induce manufacturing company to remain in town where bank is located (Illinois). McCrory, et al. v. Chambers, et al., 48 Ill. App. 445 (1892)   No

Contract by land company to pay part of cost of bridge to afford access to real estate development (Texas). Ft. Worth City Co. v. Smith Bridge Co., 151 U.S. 294 (1894)   Yes

Subscription by bank for erection of paper mill (Nebraska). Robertson v. Buffalo County National Bank, 40 Neb. 235, 58 N.W. 715 (1894)   No

Donation by street railway to manager of baseball park to relocate on railway line and pay 10 per cent of gross receipts to street railway (California). Temple St. Cable Ry. Co. v. Hellman et al., 37 Pac. 530 (1894)   Yes

Note given by bank to railroad, payable on completion of railroad (Oklahoma). Arkansas Valley & W. Ry. Co. v. Farmers & Merchants Bank, 21 Okla. 322, 96 Pac. 765 (1908)   No

Note given by brewing company to promote commercial and industrial interests of city (Indiana). Huntington Brewing Co. v. McGrew, 64 Ind. App. 273, 112 N.E. 534 (1916)   Yes

Note given by railroad to induce relocation of rod and wire mill (Alabama). Alabama, etc., Ry. Co. v. Kyle, et al., 202 Ala. 552, 81 So. 54 (1918)   Yes

Note given by live stock company for construction of railroad to its land (Texas). Richardson, et al. v. Bermuda Land & Live Stock Co., 231 S.W. 337 (1921)   Yes

Income-Tax Cases   *Deduction allowed*

Donation by wholesale millinery company to highway fund to repair roads used by salesmen and employees. David Baird & Son, Inc., 2 B.T.A. 901 (1925)   No

Donation by cotton warehouse to fund for railroad extension to provide better shipping connection. Planters Warehouse Co., 8 B.T.A. 1103 (1927)   No

Donation by ferry company to highway association for new direct highway and recommended travel by ferry. The Rodeo-Vallejo Ferry Co., 24 B.T.A. 936 (1931)   Yes

RELIGIOUS PROJECTS

Income-Tax Cases   *Deduction allowed*

Donation by textile mill to repair church in village owned by mill, where employees comprised 90 per cent of congregation. Poinsett Mills, 1 B.T.A. 6 (1924)   Yes

Donation by coal mining company to building fund for parsonage in nearby town, where employees lived and comprised 25–30 per cent of membership. Boucher-Cortright Coal Co., 7 B.T.A. 1 (1927)   No

Donation by coal mining company to rebuild church, where employees comprised 75–90 per cent of congregation. Superior Pocahontas Coal Co., 7 B.T.A. 380 (1927)   Yes

Donation by Hawaiian sugar plantation to organizations conducting church services on plantation and welfare work among employees. Kekaha Sugar Co., Ltd., 13 B.T.A. 690 (1928)   Yes

TRADE ASSOCIATIONS

Income-Tax Cases   *Deduction allowed*

Donation by local brewers association to state association. California Brewing Assn., 5 B.T.A. 347 (1926)   Yes

Donations by hosiery manufacturer to American Protective Tariff League and League of Industrial Rights. Richmond Hosiery Mills, 6 B.T.A. 1247 (1927)   Yes

Donation by beer manufacturer to Lager Beer Board of Trade and United States Brewers Association. George Ringler & Co., 10 B.T.A. 1134 (1928)   Yes

Donation by oil company to Oil Industry Association.
North American Oil Consolidated, 12 B.T.A. 68 (1928)   No

Donations by brick and tile company to associations promoting industrial peace and encouraging location of industries and residents;   Yes
But donation to citizens' committee to exercise surveillance
over public works. Simons Brick Co., 14 B.T.A. 878 (1928)   No

Donation by bank to Clearing House Association for expenses of conventions and civic organizations. First National
Bank of Omaha, 17 B.T.A. 1358 (1929)   Yes

Donation by bank to industrial club to finance industrial
development and public activities. First National Bank in St.
Louis, 23 B.T.A. 1125 (1931)   Yes

Donation by cotton dealer to fund for eradication of boll
weevil and advertising in labor and trade magazines. Alexander Sprunt & Son, Inc., 24 B.T.A. 599 (1931)   Yes

YMCA

Income-Tax Cases   *Deduction allowed*

Donation by Hawaiian sugar plantation to YMCA to
maintain welfare workers for employees. Lihue Plantation
Co., Ltd., 2 B.T.A. 740 (1925)   Yes

Donation by railroad to YMCA maintained for benefit of
employees. Indiana Harbor Belt Railroad Co., 16 B.T.A. 279
(1929)   Yes

Donation by railroad to YMCA railroad branch serving
employees. Terminal Railroad Assn. of St. Louis, 17 B.T.A.
1135 (1929)   Yes

Donation by railroad to YMCAs at division points, used by
Company and employees but not exclusively. Gulf, Mobile &
Northern Railroad Co., 22 B.T.A. 233 (1931)   Yes

COMBINATIONS

Income-Tax Cases   *Deduction allowed*

Donations by wholesale grocery to Red Cross and Army
and Navy YMCA at direction of U.S. Food Administration to
retain license. Huff, Andrews & Thomas, 1 B.T.A. 542 (1925)   Yes

Donation by bank to various local civic organizations. Joplin
National Bank, 1 B.T.A. 586 (1925)   No

Donations by retail clothier to various war funds, hospitals, etc. Woolf & Reynolds, Inc., 1 B.T.A. 1092 (1925)   No

Donations by manufacturer to various civic projects and funds. Oliver Finnie Co., 2 B.T.A. 134 (1925)   No

Donation by public utility to Baltimore Fund, Red Cross, YMCA and war work campaign. Consolidated Gas Electric Light & Power Co. of Baltimore v. U.S., 65 Ct. Cls. 252, Cert. Den. 272 U.S. 612 (1928)   No

Donation by shoe manufacturer to local YMCA, YWCA, and hospital, for improved labor relations. Alfred J. Sweet, Inc., v. U.S., 66 Ct. Cls. 654 (1929)   No

Donation by machine tool manufacturer to Red Cross and others. Niles Bement Pond Co. v. U.S., 67 Ct. Cls. 693 (1929)   No

Donations by roofing material manufacturer to various organizations:

To hospital, press club, colored YMCA, and Craig Colony in Denver;   Yes

To church, theological school, YMCA, Festival Association and Denver University   No

Western Elaterite Roofing Co., 19 B.T.A., 467 (1930)

Donations by printing concern to various customer organizations:

To State Fair, hospitals, college, chamber of commerce;   Yes
To Citizens' League   No

S. C. Toof & Co., 21 B.T.A. 916 (1930)

Donation by railroad to railroad YMCA's and to hospital for care of injured employees in lieu of providing its own. Missouri Pacific Railroad Co., 22 B.T.A. 267 (1931)   Yes

Donations by insurance agency to local college, church, and civic funds. The Harry A. Koch Co., 23 B.T.A. 161 (1931)   No

Donations by lumber company:

To fund for welfare and betterment work among employees;   Yes

To Community Fund and numerous charitable, religious, and educational organizations   No

W. M. Ritter Lumber Co., 30 B.T.A. 231 (1934)

Donations by newspapers to various charitable, religious, educational, and social welfare agencies, such as community funds, hospitals, Red Cross, churches, Boy Scouts, YMCA, American Legion, Salvation Army, etc. The Brush-Moore Newspapers, Inc., 33 B.T.A. 362 (1935)   No

Donations by railroad to policemen's and firemen's ball and to National Guard of Missouri. Kansas City Southern Railway Co. v. Commissioner, 75 Fed. (2d) 786 (C.C.A. 8th) (1935)   No

Donation by creamery to local YMCA and Catholic College to retain their business. Fairmount Creamery Corp. v. Helvering, 89 Fed. (2d) 810 (C.C.A. D.C.) (1937)   Yes

Donations by department store to local Community Fund, Salvation Army, and White Cross Hospital. Commissioner v. F. & R. Lazarus & Co., 101 Fed. (2d) 728 (C.C.A. 6th) (1939)[1]   No

Donation by mercantile concern to YMCA and Chamber of Commerce as customers. A. L. Killian Co., 44 B.T.A. 169 (1941)   Yes

Donations by sewing machine company to various local charities in 13 cities where business was carried on. Singer Sewing Machine Co. v. Commissioner, 158 Fed. (2d) 982 (C.C.A. 3d), Cert. Den. 331 U.S. 837 (1947)   Yes

Donations by exporting concern to dependents of deceased employees and to maintain Bureau of Governmental Research in Hawaii. (See last case under Government Projects, where donation to latter was denied.) American Factors, Ltd. v. Kanne, 76 Fed. Supp. 133 (D.C. Hawaii) (1947)   Yes

[1] Dates are the years of decision. This deduction was disallowed as a business expense in a tax year before contributions were authorized.

APPENDIX E

SAMPLE FOUNDATION CHARTER[1]

*   *   *   *   *

CERTIFICATE OF INCORPORATION
OF
THE X FOUNDATION

(Pursuant to Membership Corporation Law)

We, the undersigned, desiring to form a membership corporation pursuant to the Membership Corporation Law of the State of New York, do hereby make, sign and acknowledge this certificate as follows:

FIRST: The name of the corporation is THE X FOUNDATION.

SECOND: The purposes for which it is formed are as follows:

The corporation is organized and shall be operated exclusively for religious, charitable, scientific, literary, or educational purposes. In furtherance of such purposes it may promote, establish, conduct, and maintain activities on its own behalf or it may contribute to or otherwise assist other corporations, organizations, and institutions carrying on such activities or any thereof; and for such purposes it may solicit and receive funds and other property, real, personal, and mixed, and interests therein, by gift, transfer, devise, or bequest, and invest, reinvest, hold, manage, administer, expend, and apply such funds and property, subject to such conditions and limitations, if any, as may be expressed in any instrument evidencing such gift, transfer, devise, or bequest.

No part of the income or principal of the corporation shall inure to the benefit of or be distributed to any member, director, or officer of the corporation or any other private individual, but reimbursement for expenditures or the payment of reasonable compensation for services rendered shall not be deemed to be a distribution of income or principal. The corporation shall not carry on propaganda, or otherwise attempt, to influence legislation.

[1] Suitable as a channel for giving either by individuals or a corporation. The New York locus is simply by way of example.

THIRD: The territory in which its operations are principally to be conducted is the United States of America.

FOURTH: Its principal office is to be located at ....
.... Street, in the Borough of Manhattan, City, County, and State of New York.

FIFTH: The number of its directors shall be no fewer than three (3) nore more than nine (9), as shall be provided from time to time in its by-laws.

SIXTH: The names and places of residence of its directors until the first annual meeting are as follows:

Name	*Address*
....	....
....	....
....	....
....	....

SEVENTH: All of the subscribers of this Certificate are of full age, at least two-thirds of them are citizens of the United States of America, and at least one of them is a resident of the State of New York. Of the persons named as directors, at least one is a citizen of the United States of America and a resident of the State of New York.

IN WITNESS WHEREOF, we have hereunto set our hands and seals this .... day of ...., 195.....

APPENDIX F

SELECTED CORPORATION POLICY
STATEMENTS

I. INTERNATIONAL HARVESTER CONTRIBUTIONS[1]

For many years International Harvester Company has contributed from its corporate funds to many worthy undertakings. It has not been alone in this policy, by any means. Most corporations today, large and small, give of their funds to many different kinds of charitable, welfare and other types of organizations.

Because the Company is requested to contribute to so many organizations, it seems desirable to have a written statement of policy concerning our contributions, for the guidance of those people in the Company who receive these solicitations, and particularly for the organization in the field.

General Policy

Certain considerations of general policy apply to all contributions. The most important of these considerations are:

1. Any contribution to charitable, welfare or other organizations which our Company makes comes from funds that belong to the stockholders. The theory under which such contributions are made is that they bring direct or indirect benefits to our business, and that corporations have a generally recognized responsibility to support such organizations when there are direct or indirect benefits.

2. The nature of our business has an important bearing upon our contributions policy. Ours is a national, even an international business. Hence, there must be a general pattern that governs our contributions in all parts of the country. We have to consider precedents carefully. We cannot very well give to certain types of organizations in one part of the country and not give to them in another. So, while every contribution request should be considered on its individual merits, nation-wide consistency in our contribution policy is almost a necessity.

3. Because we must contribute in so many different communities, we sometimes cannot make local contributions as large as those made by the larger, purely local businesses.

[1] Reprinted by permission of International Harvester Company.

4. We regard our first contribution responsibility as being to those approximately 200 communities in which we have manufacturing plants, parts depots, district offices and other operations. We seldom make contributions, therefore, in other towns or cities. To try to do so would spread our efforts too thin, and the businesses with operations in these other localities have a responsibility there that we do not have.

5. Company executives should bear in mind that if they accept important working assignments in fund-raising campaigns, the Company is very likely to be asked for a corporate contribution because of that connection. Harvester executives should exercise discretion, therefore, as to the fund-raising campaigns in which they participate as workers. Key management people should limit such participation to organizations where support would fall within the policy of the Company.

Summing up general policy, it must be remembered that since any contribution made by any unit of our Company is stockholders' money, the responsibility of justifying it is great. The first test, therefore, that should be applied to all contribution requests is: Does it benefit the Company directly or indirectly? Unless it can be demonstrated that it does, the contribution should not be made.

Types of Contributions Made

The contributions our Company makes can be classified into five main categories, as follows:

1. *Relief and Health:* Contributions of this type are made to Community Chest funds, American Red Cross, hospital building funds, cancer, tuberculosis, infantile paralysis, heart and other similar health campaigns, etc. We follow a definite policy of not contributing to the operating expenses of agencies that are members of Community Chests in cities where we have operations, since such operating funds are provided in large part from Community Chest funds. Such agencies, however, are given permission by their Community Chest organizations from time to time to seek capital funds, and in such cases their requests to us are given consideration on their merits, and in the light of our contributions policy.

Because of the large expansion of hospital facilities in recent years, it seems advisable to state in some detail the Company's policy on contributions to hospitals.

Contributions to hospitals are restricted to building programs, equipment additions, or for unusual medical research in which the Company may have a strong interest. Contributions are not made for hospital operating expenses. Hospital contributions are restricted, also, to communities in which the Company has works, sales offices, parts depots, or other important operations.

The first consideration applied to hospitals is the direct benefit which the Company's employes receive from use of the hospital. In works cities, this takes the form of industrial usage. This is the most important factor in extending support to hospitals, and in works cities would limit our support to the one hospital which our works physicians use for Company employes.

The Company on occasion contributes to other hospitals in works cities, however, either to help relieve the patient load upon the hospital which we use for industrial purposes, or for public relations reasons. Sometimes the Company gains an advantage in the hospital we use because one or more other hospitals, by increasing their facilities, make more beds available for Company use in the hospital we use. In every case where the Company makes a contribution to a hospital, it must rank high as a medical institution, and must possess high-grade business administration.

In district office cities and towns contributions are made to hospitals on occasion where the situation makes it advisable from a public relations or customer relations standpoint. These cases usually occur in the smaller cities and towns where the Harvester district office is an important business unit in the community. Amounts in such cases are quite modest.

The recommendations of Company physicians, both locally and at the General Office, are given important consideration in all hospital requests for contributions.

2. *Public Welfare:* There are many organizations which we classify under this heading, including taxpayers' associations, Better Business Bureaus, civic federations, safety organizations, etc.

3. *Social Betterment:* Social betterment agencies include such organizations as the YMCA, YWCA, 4-H Clubs, Future Farmers of America, Junior Achievement, and many others.

4. *Educational Institutions:* Many educational institutions today seek corporation financial support. Such support to educational institutions, we think, can be looked upon as a proper expenditure of corporation funds where it brings direct or indirect benefit to the Company. We believe such support must be limited to assistance of specific research projects, scholarship and fellowship programs and loans of, or discounts on purchases of, machinery and equipment by these institutions, provided any crops that may be produced by the institution are not sold in competition with crops produced by our farmer customers.

We follow the policy of not making contributions to tax-supported public educational institutions, except in rare instances where public funds may not be available for some special project that is of great interest and potential direct benefit to the Company's business.

Consequently, such support as we give to educational institutions usually is to privately endowed schools, not supported by tax funds, and which are generally located in cities where we have large operations. We are in position to benefit from such support. Amounts of such contributions are related to the size of the Company operation in the community and the anticipated benefit.

5. *Business Organizations and Trade Associations:* These types of financial outlay are not strictly a contribution, but are in the nature of a business expense. They are included as a part of our contributions setup, however. Included in the list are such professional and trade associations as it seems desirable for the Company to support: Chambers of Commerce—local, state and national; service clubs in cities where we have operations; manufacturers' associations; etc.

Types of Contributions Not Made

The Company does *not* make certain types of contributions as a matter of policy:

1. Corporations are prohibited by law from making political contributions.

2. Because our stockholders, employes and customers represent all religious groups, the Company does not contribute to strictly sectarian or denominational religious organizations, such as churches, missionary groups, etc.

3. Generally, we do not contribute to war veterans' organizations, unless the undertakings for which they are seeking funds are for the welfare of all the people of a community.

4. Except in unusual circumstances, such as some clear evidence of Company benefit, we do not give Company support to so-called "courtesy advertising" in such media as fraternal programs, yearbooks, labor union papers, convention souvenirs, etc. Requests for advertising of this nature should first be screened at field operations, and if it is felt a request has some unusual merit, it should be referred to the Public Relations group in the General Office.

Many of these groups to which we do not contribute are very worthy. But worthiness alone cannot justify our contributing to them. There are too many worthy institutions for us to try to support all of them. Many of them should be supported by individuals. We can justify corporation support only through direct or indirect benefit to stockholders, employes or customers.

Contribution Procedure

Works managers hereafter are authorized to approve local contributions or business membership expenditures, if they conform to the general policies of the Company as stated in this document, in individual amounts up to $100, such expenditures to be charged against the local works operation.

District managers hereafter are authorized to approve local contributions or business membership expenditures, if they conform to the general policies of the Company as stated in this document, in individual amounts up to $50, such expenditures to be charged against the local district operation.

Since these locally authorized contributions are charged against local operations, they are subject to the controls of the annual budget.

Frequently, however, requests are received locally where the local management feels that the contribution should exceed the amounts authorized for local handling. In such cases the following procedure should be followed:

1. The works or district manager should first investigate the request and determine whether, in his opinion, the Company should or should not make a contribution, taking into consideration the same factors by which he would judge a request for an amount he is authorized to make above, and the factors applied by the General Office Contributions Committee as listed in the following section. If he is certain no contribution should be made, he should dispose of the matter finally.

2. If the works or district manager feels a contribution should be made in excess of the amount authorized for local handling, he should so advise the manager of manufacturing or regional manager as to the reasons why he feels it should be made. In all cases where he favors the contribution, he should state a recommended amount.

3. The contribution request is then considered by divisional or sales organizations in the General Office. The recommended contribution either is approved and passed on to the Contributions Committee for final action, or is referred back to the local operation for further study.

4. The Company contributes to many organizations with a single, national contribution, made at the Chicago office. Before local operations contribute any amount to any organization they should be certain no national contribution is being made in Chicago. If they have a ques-

tion about it they should write Frank W. Jenks, Chairman of the Contributions Committee.

5. Final approval is given by the Contributions Committee, except in cases of large amount or of an unusual nature, where approval must be had from the President or the Board of Directors.

Ordinarily, contributions and business membership expenditures are to be considered as a charge against the local or divisional organization. Exceptions will be made, however, in the case of larger contributions made for unusual reasons, where a charge back against the General Office is permitted with the approval of the Contributions Committee.

It will be the policy of the Contributions Committee, in deciding where the charge is to be made, to take into consideration the size of the contribution, the size of the Company unit recommending it, and whether it is reasonable to charge the contribution against the local operation.

Contributions Committee

Responsibility for the Company's contributions rests with the Company's Contributions Committee in the General Office. This committee is appointed by the President of the Company. Frank W. Jenks is chairman of the committee. Other members of the committee are: Forest D. Siefkin, Ivan L. Willis, William R. Odell, Jr., Gerard J. Eger and Dale Cox.

If a contribution request involves special policy questions, the request is taken to the President, with the recommendation of the committee. Contributions of more than $5,000 also are taken to the President, and if these larger contributions are approved by him, they are then taken to the Board of Directors for final approval.

In considering whether a contribution should be made, the committee takes into account these things:

1. Will the contribution benefit the Company, directly or indirectly?

2. Does the Company's present business position justify it?

3. Will the request likely lead to other similar requests in the future?

4. Is the purpose of the soliciting organization a good one, and does the organization have widespread acceptance and support?

5. Is the soliciting organization efficiently and honestly managed?

6. Does it aid all kinds of people, or is it restricted in its operations?

7. Is the request consistent with the Company's place in the community?

8. What will be the public reaction if we give or do not give?

9. Are some of our large customers interested in the solicitations?

10. Are some other companies in the community similar to ours supporting the soliciting organization, and if so, in what amounts?

11. Who are the people heading the organization asking our support? Are they first rate people?

12. Will the contribution advance the community and public relations of the Company?

If the committee decides the contribution should be made, it takes these factors into account, among others, in deciding what amounts should be given:

1. What is the best measurable extent of the Company's benefit? Is it great or small?

2. What is the total amount being asked for in the campaign? What seems to be a reasonable share for us to assume?

3. What amounts are other businesses in the community giving? What are other businesses most similar to our operation giving?

4. What is the size of the community from which the request came?

5. What is the size of the Company's operation in the community?

6. What is the relationship of the size of the Company's local operation to the total life of the community? Is Harvester a big or a little factor in the community?

7. How many employes do we have in the community? Is there any relationship between employes and the amount we should give?

8. As a matter of policy, we will not accept suggested formulas prepared by some organizations as a means of determining how much we should give. We do not believe any such formulas can work equitably for all types of businesses in the community. We will listen to suggested formulas, but all contribution solicitors should be frankly told the Company cannot follow them.

II. STATEMENT OF THE POLICY OF C.I.T. FINANCIAL CORPORATION AND SUBSIDIARIES WITH RESPECT TO CORPORATE PHILANTHROPIC CONTRIBUTIONS[1]

Introduction

By the law, the funds of C.I.T. Financial Corporation can be expended for charitable or membership purposes if the expenditure brings direct or indirect benefits to our business and the interests of our stockholders. We recognize the general obligation of corporations to support

[1] Reprinted by permission of C.I.T. Financial Corporation.

organizations which contribute such benefits. It is our intention, within the above limitation, that C.I.T. assume its equitable share of this support.

There are a great many causes which are very worthy and it is obviously impossible for C.I.T. to support all of these on the justification of their worth alone. Beyond the worth of the cause, we must look in each instance to the limitations of our established reserves and the degree of applicability to our interests in the cause in order to justify a contribution.

Charitable Donations

The above basic policy will govern our activities but we will observe the following standards with respect to specific types of charitable appeals.

1. We will make contributions on both a national and/or local level to the American Red Cross and local community chests or their equivalents, in communities where our offices are located.

Consideration will be given and favorable action may be taken *in cases of unusual merit*, in the following cases:

1. *Social Betterment Appeals*, meaning organizations established to improve the lot of individuals but which do not usually function in the relief and health fields. Such organizations might include national educational programs, the Boy or Girl Scouts, Salvation Army, Travelers' Aid, USO, etc., in time of war, organizations combating juvenile delinquency, and many others.

2. *Appeals for Construction Funds*, as distinguished from appeals for maintenance funds, for hospitals and similar necessary public institutions, in cases where there exists exceptional applicability to our interests or when the business concerns in a community have supported the cause so generally that, for institutional reasons, we should assume a proper share of the responsibility.

Only in exceptional cases will the following receive contributions, the nature of the exception being set forth:

1. *Sectarian or Denominational Appeals*, to which contributions will be made only in cases of unusual merit when made to institutions under sectarian sponsorship which offer their services to the general public on a broad basis without regard to sectarian considerations.

2. *Veterans' Appeals*, to which contributions will be made only in rare cases of unusual merit when the cause is under the sponsorship of a

veterans' organization but the purpose is to offer benefits to the general public as a whole.

3. *Specific Educational Institutions*, to which contributions will be made only when the institutions render direct service to C.I.T. through courses of instruction for our employees, specific research activities or other similar functions.

The corporation will not contribute to the following:

1. *Specialized Health Appeals*, such as campaigns to combat heart, cancer, tuberculosis, infantile paralysis, cerebral palsy, alcoholism, etc., etc. Because of long standing social custom, an exception will be made to permit nominal purchases of Christmas Seals on a local basis.

2. *The Miscellaneous Group of Appeals*, including political donations, contributions to labor organizations or gifts to fraternal organizations or any donations in the form of complimentary advertising in programs, yearbooks, etc.

It is not possible to establish a series of policies which will permit intelligent administration in all future cases which may arise in the complex field of corporate charity donations. Therefore, it is to be recognized that a particular appeal may receive favorable consideration, for special and extraordinary reasons, even though it does not conform in some or any particulars to the qualifications established here as necessary for favorable action. It is to be expected that such exceptions, while necessary on occasion, will be very rare.

The Committee will establish policies with respect to permissible solicitations for charitable purposes among employee groups. Generally speaking, these solicitations will be limited to not more than three per year and will be restricted to organizations which, on the local level, represent the functions of the Red Cross, the community chest and any general local hospital campaign.

Each such solicitation should be approved by the Committee in advance in order to protect the employee group against excessive soliciting by outside organizations.

The above policy and the annual reserve approved by the Board of Directors of C.I.T. Financial Corporation will be related to philanthropic contributions exclusively. Appeals for funds from organizations whose principal services are in the fields of safety, business development or economic matters will be administered by the Committee and applied against a separate operational budget.

A Procedure for Administering the Policy of C.I.T. Financial Corporation and Its Subsidiaries for Charitable Donations and Corporate Memberships

1. All requests except those authorized under Paragraph 7 below for charitable donations or corporate memberships will be routed to the secretary of the Contributions Committee. These should be accompanied by the comments or recommendations from the person in the organization who refers the request to the committee. If no comments or recommendations are made, it will be assumed that the sender does not favor the request.

2. The committee will consider and take positive action upon all requests submitted to it. The signatures of the four members of the committee will be required to authorize any contribution.

3. The committee will approve on its own authority charitable donations or membership contributions up to the amount of $500 and will report such action as it takes to the Policy Committee at its next meeting.

4. Charitable donations or membership contributions in excess of $500 which are proposed by the Contributions Committee will require the approval of the President or Executive Vice President and will usually be discussed in advance with the Policy Committee.

5. The secretary of the Contributions Committee will arrange for reply by letter to all appeals except those which are obviously not specifically directed to C.I.T., such as printed appeals unaccompanied by a letter, etc. If the proposal is rejected the pertinent portion of our contributions policy usually will be cited in the letter as explanation for our action. In most cases this reply will be made by the person within our organization who originally received the request. But, whenever it is desirable, the Secretary of the Committee will make the reply.

6. When a contribution is approved a check will be requested through the usual procedure by the secretary of the Contributions Committee or he will authorize the officers of the particular subsidiary to issue a check.

In many cases, it is expected that the maximum benefit to the corporation will be obtained if checks are transmitted by the particular person or subsidiary or office which originated the request for the donation. Whenever such benefits can be secured, the contribution check will be sent by the secretary of the Contributions Committee to the proper person within the organization who will then handle the transmittal of the gift.

7. All subsidiaries will be expected to refer to the Contributions Committee those appeals on which they wish to recommend favorable action. However, it will be permissible for subsidiaries to establish policies permitting nominal contribution, not exceeding $10 in each instance, to local causes which may or may not fall within the qualifications of the corporate policy as established. Such contributions have been notably limited in number in the past and it is not anticipated that their number should increase materially but it is also recognized that in certain cases nominal gifts necessarily must be made.

Each subsidiary will be expected to establish its own policy with respect to these nominal gifts and will supply all members of the committee with statements of its policy and any subsequent revisions of it.

8. An annual report of all major charitable donations and membership contributions, plus the accumulated amount of smaller or nominal expenditures which will not be detailed, will be made to the Board of Directors of C.I.T. Financial Corporation. This report will be prepared by the Contributions Committee and delivered to the President.

9. A summary of the policy and procedure set forth here will be generally distributed to principal executives of each subsidiary. It will be their responsibility to disseminate information as to this procedure and policy to their organizations but all such announcements or statements of procedure shall be approved in advance by the Contributions Committee.

10. In its consideration of requests, the Contributions Committee initially will use the attached check sheet of questions. This will doubtless be modified as the committee begins to function.

Contributions Committee Check Sheet

1. Is the cause a worthy one?

2. Will the contribution benefit C.I.T. directly or indirectly?

3. Is the request likely to lead to other similar requests in the future? Is this objectionable?

4. Does the organization have widespread acceptance and support?

5. Is it efficiently and honestly managed?

6. Is the immediate need significant or does the organization have substantial reserve funds?

7. Does it aid all kinds of people, or is it restricted in its operations?

8. Is the request consistent with our place in the community?

9. Will there be a public reaction if we give or do not give?

10. Will the contribution advance the community and public relations of the Company?

11. Are important customers, dealers or other business contacts interested in the solicitations?

12. Are other organizations in the community similar to ours supporting the soliciting organization, and if so, in what amounts?

If the committee decides the contribution should be made, it takes these factors into account, among others, in deciding what amount should be given:

1. Does the amount available in the Contribution Reserve justify a gift?

2. What is the best measurable extent of the Company's benefit? Is it great or small?

3. What is the total amount being asked for in the campaign? What seems to be a reasonable share for us to assume?

4. What amounts are other businesses in the community giving? What are other businesses most similar to our operation giving?

5. What is the size of the community from which the request came?

6. What is the size of the Company's operation in the community?

7. How profitable are our operations centering in the community?

8. How many employees do we have in the community? Should there be a relationship between employees and the amount we should give?

9. We cannot accept suggested formulas prepared by some organizations as a means of determining how much we should give. We do not believe any such formulas are fair for all types of business in the community. We will consider suggested formulas, but all contribution solicitors will be frankly told that we cannot give them significant weight.

APPENDIX G

TABLE 41. CORPORATION CONTRIBUTIONS SHOWN BY FEDERAL
INCOME-TAX RETURNS: AMOUNT AND PER CENT OF
NET PROFIT, BY MAJOR INDUSTRIAL GROUPS, BY YEAR,
1936 TO 1948

Dollar figures in thousands

Industrial group	Corpora-tions	Net profit	Contributions		
			Amount	Per cent of total	Per cent of net profit
1936					
Mining and quarrying	13,788	$ 178,995	$ 749	2.5	0.42
Manufacturing	92,030	3,724,047	12,903	43.0	0.35
Public utilities[a]	24,853	1,033,012	2,894	9.7	0.28
Trade	145,520	929,582	6,416	21.4	0.69
Service[a]	59,703	9,978[b]	1,994	6.6	—
Finance, insurance, real estate, lessors of real property[a]	115,694	1,848,237	4,286	14.3	0.23
Construction	16,645	38,015	372	1.3	0.98
Agriculture, forestry, and fishery[a]	8,945	33,524	353	1.2	1.05
Not allocable[a]	1,679	4,549[b]	1	0.0	—
Total	478,857	$7,770,887	$29,968	100.0	0.39
1937					
Mining and quarrying	13,567	$ 302,392	$ 882	2.7	0.29
Manufacturing	91,979	3,720,951	14,440	44.1	0.39
Public utilities[a]	24,672	1,101,684	3,542	10.8	0.32
Trade	143,084	837,248	7,289	22.3	0.87
Service[a]	60,208	16,831	1,764	5.4	10.48
Finance, insurance, real estate, lessors of real property[a]	117,079	1,782,021	4,136	12.6	0.23
Construction	16,864	48,535	383	1.2	0.79
Agriculture, forestry, and fishery[a]	8,703	24,110	290	0.9	1.20
Not allocable[a]	1,682	3,479[b]	2	0.0	—
Total	477,838	$7,830,293	$32,727	100.0	0.42

[a] Title of group used after 1937 is substituted here for that used in the report of this year.

[b] Net loss.

SOURCE: *Statistics of Income*, 1936–1945; Treasury Press Releases, 1946–1948.

TABLE 41. CORPORATION CONTRIBUTIONS SHOWN BY FEDERAL INCOME-TAX RETURNS: AMOUNT AND PER CENT OF NET PROFIT, BY MAJOR INDUSTRIAL GROUPS, BY YEAR, 1936 TO 1948—(*Continued*)

Dollar figures in thousands

Industrial group	Corpora-tions	Net profit	Contributions		
			Amount	Per cent of total	Per cent of net profit
1938					
Mining and quarrying	10,942	$ 49,636	$ 447	1.6	0.90
Manufacturing	88,067	1,604,560	10,464	38.4	0.65
Public utilities	21,961	674,111	3,230	11.9	0.48
Trade	139,192	417,942	6,503	23.9	1.55
Service	40,973	50,423	1,216	4.4	2.41
Finance, insurance, real es-tate, lessors of real prop-erty	140,437	1,320,842	4,629	17.0	0.35
Construction	16,341	25,803	405	1.5	1.57
Agriculture, forestry, and fishery	8,993	2,921[b]	211	0.8	—
Not allocable	4,126	9,411[b]	128	0.5	—
Total	471,032	$4,130,986	$27,233	100.0	0.66
1939					
Mining and quarrying	10,820	$ 132,386	$ 441	1.4	0.33
Manufacturing	86,183	3,580,102	14,035	45.7	0.39
Public utilities	22,064	1,171,386	3,167	10.3	0.27
Trade	138,207	814,663	7,201	23.4	0.89
Service	41,030	80,428	1,174	3.8	1.46
Finance, insurance, real es-tate, lessors of real prop-erty	142,332	1,359,612	4,251	13.8	0.31
Construction	16,061	33,055	333	1.1	1.01
Agriculture, forestry, and fishery	8,636	12,884	108	0.4	0.84
Not allocable	4,284	6,700[b]	20	0.1	—
Total	469,617	$7,177,815	$30,730	100.0	0.43
1940					
Mining and quarrying	10,383	$ 206,537	$ 577	1.5	0.28
Manufacturing	85,588	5,317,005	18,530	48.6	0.35
Public utilities	22,053	1,315,409	3,693	9.7	0.28
Trade	139,849	1,084,072	8,523	22.4	0.78
Service	41,385	108,595	1,415	3.7	1.30
Finance, insurance, real es-tate, lessors of real prop-erty	142,602	1,280,132	4,856	12.8	0.38
Construction	15,749	68,265	396	1.0	0.58
Agriculture, forestry, and fishery	8,400	17,070	85	0.2	0.50
Not allocable	7,033	48,865[b]	50	0.1	—
Total	473,042	$9,348,221	$38,124	100.0	0.41

[b] Net loss.

343

Dollar figures in thousands

Industrial group	Corpora- tions	Net profit	Contributions		
			Amount	Per cent of total	Per cent of net profit
1941					
Mining and quarrying	9,667	$ 380,318	$ 880	1.5	0.23
Manufacturing	84,431	10,439,272	28,919	49.4	0.28
Public utilities	21,921	1,928,911	4,988	8.5	0.26
Trade	138,703	2,082,190	13,964	23.9	0.67
Service	40,494	183,757	1,707	2.9	0.93
Finance, insurance, real es- tate, lessors of real prop- erty	143,494	1,438,142	6,904	11.8	0.48
Construction	14,996	178,352	899	1.6	0.50
Agriculture, forestry, and fishery	7,901	63,328	153	0.3	0.24
Not allocable	7,299	*19,548*[b]	84	0.1	—
Total	468,906	$16,674,722	$58,498	100.0	0.35
1942					
Mining and quarrying	8,915	$ 390,650	$ 1,281	1.3	0.33
Manufacturing	82,174	13,659,564	54,881	55.8	0.40
Public utilities	20,237	3,630,747	7,392	7.5	0.20
Trade	128,969	2,570,867	21,272	21.7	0.83
Service	38,449	357,122	2,687	2.7	0.75
Finance, insurance, real es- tate, lessors of real prop- erty	136,882	2,364,881	8,410	8.6	0.35
Construction	13,697	340,023	1,964	2.0	0.58
Agriculture, forestry, and fishery	7,318	80,638	291	0.3	0.36
Not allocable	6,024	*5,838*[b]	117	0.1	—
Total	442,665	$23,388,656	$98,296	100.0	0.42
1943					
Mining and quarrying	8,133	$ 338,972	$ 2,309	1.4	0.68
Manufacturing	78,716	16,593,679	92,623	58.1	0.56
Public utilities	19,279	4,499,056	11,589	7.3	0.26
Trade	120,880	3,093,949	33,430	21.1	1.08
Service	35,594	546,689	4,248	2.7	0.78
Finance, insurance, real es- tate, lessors of real prop- erty	133,655	2,664,510	11,595	7.3	0.43
Construction	12,128	267,762	2,540	1.6	0.95
Agriculture, forestry, and fishery	6,884	114,058	669	0.4	0.58
Not allocable	5,252	7,776	218	0.1	2.80
Total	420,521	$28,126,451	$159,221	100.0	0.57

[b] Net loss.

344

Dollar figures in thousands

Industrial group	Corpora-tions	Net profit	Contributions		
			Amount	Per cent of total	Per cent of net profit
1944					
Mining and quarrying	7,620	$ 317,854	$ 3,394	1.4	1.07
Manufacturing	76,619	14,864,313	142,065	60.7	0.96
Public utilities	19,242	4,147,831	18,213	7.8	0.44
Trade	117,363	3,254,679	44,900	19.2	1.37
Service	34,712	578,931	6,090	2.6	1.05
Finance, insurance, real estate, lessors of real property	133,879	3,114,654	16,267	6.9	0.52
Construction	11,514	139,448	2,166	0.9	1.55
Agriculture, forestry, and fishery	6,417	120,104	908	0.4	0.75
Not allocable	5,101	8,787	190	0.1	2.16
Total	412,467	$26,546,602	$234,194	100.0	0.88
1945					
Mining and quarrying	7,296	$ 242,669	$ 3,126	1.2	1.29
Manufacturing	79,112	10,256,776	149,728	56.3	1.46
Public utilities	19,736	2,939,918	23,596	8.8	0.80
Trade	120,948	3,364,059	55,634	20.9	1.65
Service	35,107	601,864	8,097	3.3	1.34
Finance, insurance, real estate, lessors of real property	135,573	3,688,869	22,046	8.2	0.60
Construction	11,834	112,913	1,899	0.7	1.68
Agriculture, forestry, and fishery	6,152	133,967	1,375	0.5	1.03
Not allocable	5,367	4,456	177	0.1	3.97
Total	421,125	$21,345,491	$265,679	100.0	1.24
1946					
Mining and quarrying	7,675	$ 334,943	$ 2,085	1.0	0.62
Manufacturing	98,131	11,701,079	111,513	52.1	0.95
Public utilities	21,823	2,345,798	11,780	5.5	0.50
Trade	151,511	5,583,037	58,148	27.2	1.04
Service	39,648	802,775	8,120	3.8	1.01
Finance, insurance, real estate, lessors of real property	144,373	4,198,183	18,642	8.7	0.44
Construction	15,849	232,453	2,361	1.1	1.02
Agriculture, forestry, and fishery	6,663	183,816	963	0.4	0.52
Not allocable	5,479	16,835	262	0.1	1.55
Total	491,152	$25,398,919	$213,872	100.0	0.84

345

TABLE 41. CORPORATION CONTRIBUTIONS SHOWN BY FEDERAL INCOME-TAX RETURNS: AMOUNT AND PER CENT OF NET PROFIT, BY MAJOR INDUSTRIAL GROUPS, BY YEAR, 1936 TO 1948—(*Continued*)

Dollar figures in thousands

Industrial group	Corporations	Net profit	Contributions		
			Amount	Per cent of total	Per cent of net profit
1947					
Mining and quarrying	8,294	$ 786,179	$ 3,031	1.2	0.39
Manufacturing	112,184	16,655,616	129,080	53.5	0.78
Public utilities	23,729	2,717,738	12,664	5.3	0.46
Trade	177,297	6,081,776	64,465	26.7	1.06
Service	45,975	723,685	8,272	3.4	1.14
Finance, insurance, real estate, lessors of real property	151,043	4,027,030	18,960	7.9	0.47
Construction	20,287	391,961	3,512	1.5	0.90
Agriculture, forestry, and fishery	7,329	215,522	1,002	0.4	0.46
Not allocable	5,669	15,612	242	0.1	1.55
Total	551,807	$31,615,119	$241,228	100.0	0.76
1948					
Mining and quarrying	9,085	$ 1,153,169	$ 3,447	1.5	0.30
Manufacturing	116,746	18,117,383	119,450	49.9	0.66
Public utilities	25,225	3,448,727	16,025	6.7	0.46
Trade	196,748	5,759,055	66,088	27.6	1.15
Service	50,456	630,465	8,164	3.4	1.29
Finance, insurance, real estate, lessors of real property	160,643	4,682,631	20,170	8.4	0.43
Construction	23,480	577,323	4,849	2.0	0.84
Agriculture, forestry, and fishery	7,694	219,656	1,038	0.5	0.47
Not allocable	4,166	413[b]	106	0.0	—
Total	594,243	$34,587,996	$239,337	100.0	0.69

[b] Net loss.

SOURCE: *Statistics of Income*, 1936–1945; Treasury Press Releases, 1946–1948.

TABLE 42. CORPORATION CONTRIBUTIONS SHOWN BY FEDERAL INCOME-TAX RETURNS FOR CORPORATIONS HAVING NET INCOME AND FOR THOSE NOT HAVING NET INCOME: AMOUNT AND PER CENT OF NET PROFIT, BY AMOUNT OF CORPORATION ASSETS, 1945

Dollar figures in thousands

Asset class	All corporations reporting balance sheets				Corporations reporting balance sheets, having net income				Corporations reporting balance sheets, not having net income		
	Corporations	Net profit	Contributions Amount	Per cent of net profit	Corporations	Net profit	Contributions Amount	Per cent of net profit	Corporations	Net loss	Contributions
Under $50	177,788	$ 267,783	$ 4,194	1.57	114,813	$ 402,593	$ 3,731	0.93	62,975	$134,809	$ 462
50 under 100	61,431	376,597	5,386	1.43	49,254	440,252	5,218	1.18	12,177	63,656	168
100 under 250	60,308	837,872	13,294	1.59	50,370	933,543	13,017	1.39	9,938	95,672	277
250 under 500	27,583	914,465	15,459	1.69	23,608	995,605	15,152	1.52	3,975	81,140	307
500 under 1,000	17,669	1,196,416	19,637	1.64	15,490	1,268,395	19,478	1.54	2,179	71,980	158
1,000 under 5,000	22,057	3,450,003	53,314	1.54	20,108	3,613,510	52,984	1.47	1,949	163,507	330
5,000 under 10,000	3,948	1,719,313	24,896	1.45	3,684	1,775,978	24,843	1.40	264	56,664	53
10,000 under 50,000	3,197	3,900,112	48,169	1.23	3,002	3,980,508	47,948	1.20	195	80,396	222
50,000 under 100,000	427	1,521,776	16,825	1.11	403	1,553,410	16,805	1.08	24	31,634	20
100,000 and over	542	7,935,344	62,409	0.89	512	7,182,108	62,311	0.87	30	146,763	98
Total	374,950	$21,219,681	$263,583	1.24	281,244	$22,145,902	$261,487	1.18	93,706	$926,221	$2,095

SOURCE: U. S. Treasury Department, *Statistics of Income*, 1945, Part 2, pp. 218–223. Percentages calculated.

INDEX

Index

351